REAL PRESENCE

REAL PRESENCE

Worship, Sacraments, and Commitment

❆

Regis A. Duffy, O.F.M.

1817

HARPER & ROW, PUBLISHERS, SAN FRANCISCO

Cambridge, Hagerstown, New York, Philadelphia
London, Mexico City, São Paulo, Sydney

FIRST EDITION

Designer: Jim Mennick

Library of Congress Cataloging in Publication Data

Duffy, Regis A.
  REAL PRESENCE.

  Includes index.
  1. Worship. 2. Sacraments—Catholic Church. 3. Christian life—Catholic
authors. I. Title
BX1969.D77   234′.16   81-47877
ISBN 0-06-062105-2   AACR2

---

82 83 84 85 86 10 9 8 7 6 5 4 3 2 1

For my mother, a model of commitment

Contents

Acknowledgments

This book is the result of ten years of reflection on the question of how the Christian symbolizes commitment. It is a pleasure for me to acknowledge a debt of gratitude to the many people who have facilitated this work in one way or another during that decade.

The Washington Theological Union afforded me a year's sabbatical, during which a good deal of the life-cycle research was done. The Franciscan friars and sisters of St. Francis Parish Community, Long Beach Island, New Jersey, provided me with both the quiet necessary for research and an example of shared Christian commitment that I carry with me. The Augustinian friars in Würzburg, West Germany, graciously hosted me during my work at the university, and Dr. A. Ganoczy and Dr. R. Zerfass of the Faculty of Theology graciously took time to discuss my work and make suggestions.

Dr. Kenan Osborn, O.F.M., as President of the Catholic Theological Society of America, invited me to deliver the opening major address at the society's convention in Atlanta, Georgia, in 1979 and thus provided me with an opportunity to benefit from the reactions of my colleagues to the work in progress. I would especially like to thank Drs. J. Coriden, E. Dobbin, and M. Scanlon of the Washington Theological Union, Dr. E. Kilmartin of the University of Notre Dame, Dr. D. Browning of the University of Chicago, and Dr. P. Philibert of the Catholic University of America for their critiques and encouragement.

Some of the ideas developed in this book originally appeared in articles in various theological journals. In addition to the citations given in the footnotes, I should like to thank the editors of *Worship, The Heythrop Journal,* and Dr. F. Eigo, O.S.A., editor of the collection *The Sacraments: God's Love and Mercy Actualized* (Villanova, Penn.: Villanova Press, 1978).

Finally, I have been particularly fortunate in having John Loudon, of Harper & Row, Publishers, as my editor. He not only initiated this project but by his perceptive critiques and patient editing evoked some clarity in thought and style. May all writers be as fortunate as I in having such an editor.

REGIS A. DUFFY, O.F.M.

Washington Theological Union
July 30, 1981

Introduction

John Gardner has given us something of a minor classic in his *Grendel*, a retelling of the Beowulf epic from the viewpoint of the monster. In one scene, Grendel is secretly watching the priests of the tribe ritualizing before their pantheon. He remarks:

There is no conviction in the old priests' songs; there is only showmanship. No one in the Kingdom is convinced that the gods have life in them. The weak observe the rituals—take their hats off, put them on again, raise their arms, moan, intone, press their palms together—*but no one harbors unreasonable expectations.*[1]

That cynical summary—"but no one harbors unreasonable expectations"—refers to the rituals of the uncommitted. Meanings, new or old, do not trouble the lives of these people. Their rituals perpetuate the vacuum they willingly tolerate. Because new meanings do not challenge or clarify their shared and individual experience, new commitments are not possible. Gardner has Grendel lay much of the blame on theology:

Theology does not thrive in the world of action and reaction, change: it grows on calm, like the scum on a stagnant pool. And it flourishes, it prospers on decline. Only in a world where everything is patently being lost can a priest stir men's hearts as a poet would by maintaining that nothing is in vain.[2]

Before the Christian bridles at Gardner's cavalier generalization, the merits of his argument should be acknowledged. When, in fact, there has been a cleavage between theory and praxis in Christianity, has it not been, in part, because "the world of action and reaction, change" had somehow been ignored?

Questions, if not examples, can be drawn from any period in the Church's history. Did the sophisticated medieval theories of sacramental causality and matter and form affect the real practice of the Church? Did they facilitate or obstruct ecclesial commitment? Should one have expected a more credible ecclesial witness in the German Christian churches of the thirties and forties or even now in other countries where radical injustice gives lie to the Gospel? When do Christian expectations, in other words, become too reasonable? When do both liturgy and theology collude and offer rituals and reasons not to recommit oneself, communally and individually, to Gospel demands, but to escape them?

Paraphrasing an insight of Michael Polanyi, we know more than we care to tell.[3] Our reluctant experience, shaped and pulled by the struggles of each life-stage, is the stuff out of which commitments are fashioned. But to gain such new commitment in our lives we must be able to discern our old experience with new eyes. This is the function of images and symbols: to help us see the elusive shapes, the muted colors of our stories that we miss the first time around.

Worship and sacrament have always formed an important part of the Christian heritage. The disturbing question, however, persists: why is there so much worship and so little commitment? For the Christian, the answer does not lie in God's absence but, perhaps, in our own. Worship and sacrament as symbols are filled with God's presence. But we can only symbolize out of our experience. There's the rub. Do we use the signs of God's presence in worship and sacrament to avoid his presence?

This subjective dimension of faith/sacrament has never been adequately developed in the history of theology for two reasons. The first reason is related to a continuing historical problem:

how do you respect the graced and unearned nature of God's salvation at the same time that you spell out the response it demands? The second reason is methodological: any discussion of the subjective dimension of symbol must involve the human sciences which have only fully developed in this century.

This book presumes God's presence and commitment in worship and sacrament but is concerned about ours. In Chapter 1, faith and commitment will be closely linked with what we do (praxis) and how we communicate in symbol and sacrament. This discussion leads us, in Chapter 2, to a rediscovery of the Pauline insight: God goes before us in our story (justification). This gift precedes the challenge of each stage of our shared lives. Here is the root of all commitment that removes our excuses. Having stated the ideal, Chapter 3 deals with the conflicts of each life-stage as a source of new commitment in our lives to building a peaceable Kingdom. The concerns of these first three chapters converge in Chapter 4 as the question of presence, the heart of all symbol, is discussed.

Chapters 5, 6, and 7 take three traditional sacraments (Initiation, Eucharist, and Penance) and question the cost and purpose of the commitment they symbolize. Finally, Chapter 8 sums up some of the implications for a Christian community that wants honest sacraments and not simply "relevant" ritualizing.

Commitment entails some hard questions for the Christian community. Does our faith "rest on the wisdom of men or on the power of God" (1 Cor. 2:5)?* Do our current moral theologies systematically and sufficiently reflect the "unreasonable expectations" of the Gospel within the context of our specific life-cycles? Do our current ecclesiologies talk of discipleship but, in reality, demand only membership? Do our sacraments, as Pascal once remarked, excuse us from the cost of loving?

In other words, this book suggests that the final test of our theological theories and religious praxis will be the committed

---

* Unless otherwise indicated, Bible quotations are taken from the New American Bible.

people who witness to the impact our lives have had on theirs. Otherwise, why would we bridle at John Gardner's searing comments on theology if we ourselves are Grendels commenting on a praxis that, in effect, tolerates no unreasonable expectations?

NOTES

1. J. Gardner, *Grendel* (New York: Ballantine, 1972), p. 111. Italics mine.
2. Ibid., pp. 139–40.
3. M. Polanyi, *The Tacit Dimension* (Garden City, N.Y.: Doubleday, 1966), p. 4.

CHAPTER 1

The Cutting Edge of Faith: Commitment

For many people today, Dorothy Day and Mother Teresa of Calcutta are outstanding examples of Gospel commitment to the poor of the world. A century ago, Robert Louis Stevenson praised Damien of Molokai for his selfless commitment to the lepers. In our own lives, we, too, can recall the names of people who strike us as models of commitment: a parent, a friend, a doctor, or a priest. Although we may never have tried to define commitment, we can usually recognize a committed person.

Dorothy Day, Teresa, and Damien were motivated by religious commitment. Yet many contemporaries who have no interest in religion find these people challenging because their convictions and practical service spilled over into the so-called "secular" areas of life. We are sometimes willing to reconsider questions of religion, long ago put aside, because the impressive work and personal maturity of committed religious individuals like Teresa or Damien make sense to us. Faith becomes a challenging possibility once we have seen a committed man or woman motivated by faith.

This book is about the ways in which people choose either to become increasingly committed in their lives or to stand still. Our subject is religious commitment, which cannot be divorced from the stages of our lives, the work that we do, and the friends that we cherish. When speaking of religious commitment, there are no "secular" areas of life. For it is the practical contexts of our lives that we discern our real understandings of faith and sacrament, of service and of church. In other words, theories about religious commitment must reflect what is actually happening in our lives.

Erik Erikson, in his definition of "true change," provides us with an excellent working definition of commitment: "a matter of worthwhile conflict, for it leads through the painful consciousness of one's position to a new conscience in that position."[1] Erikson is describing a process of awareness and decision that has important consequences for living.

Dorothy Day, Mother Teresa, and Damien are examples of this process. As they became aware of the terrible need of workers, of slum dwellers, and of the lepers, questions about what they were doing with their lives emerged. Having honestly answered those questions, Day devoted her life to the needs of the working class, Mother Teresa went into the slums of Calcutta, and Damien lived among the lepers. Religious commitment for these people involved a reawakening to the reality of their world and decisions about what tasks they would undertake at a turning point of their lives.

I have chosen dramatic examples to illustrate a simple experience of everyday living: the quality of our commitments reveals the values we live by and determines the meaningfulness of the tasks we perform. In each phase of our lives, new questions about our old commitments arise. Does our continued attendance at Sunday worship, for example, indicate a deeper commitment to Gospel values or only the security of familiar rituals? Does a wedding anniversary celebrate past or renewed commitments to another person? Do we still find the challenge and satisfaction in our work or family lives that we found in the past? To answer such questions with some degree of honesty is to be painfully aware of one's current stage of life and, perhaps, the beginning of a new conscience in that stage. Such answers are a necessary part of any religious commitment.

A puzzling contradiction for both the theologian and the sociologist is the fact that widespread Christianity does not necessarily indicate deep religious commitment. Churches can be crowded on Sunday in countries where torture and injustice are a standard part of life. The religious symbols of worship and sacrament in these countries do not seem to call out a deeper sense of commitment to Gospel justice and peace from the majority of participants. In affluent countries of the Western world where Christianity has been part of the social fabric for centuries, Christians are seldom distinguishable from their nonpracticing neighbors by the appearance of any reconsidered commitment to the poor and the underprivileged. In fact, it is sometimes the non-Christian who is the paradigm for concern and commitment. In other words, why is there so much participation in sacrament and worship with so little commitment?

If we are to answer such a question, an important and traditional distinction must be made at this point between religious rituals and symbols. Religious rituals are external signs of response and commitment to God. They may or may not reflect our inner attitudes. Someone enthusiastically singing "Come, Lord Jesus" on a Sunday morning, for example, may not really want that event to happen here and now. We can listen to the Scriptures being proclaimed in such a way that they do not disturb the complacency or selfishness of our lives. Each of us can, no doubt, add his or her own examples of ritual being mistaken for symbol.

A symbol in Christian experience and theology is the presence of God calling us to presence. Presence is, of course, more than attention. It is self-gift and enabling love. God's presence as described in the Scriptures is not to be idly noticed but to be responded to. When God speaks to Moses or David, when the risen Christ encounters doubting Thomas or the two disappointed disciples on their way to Emmaus, there is always a question of response and responsibility, of change and commitment.

Christian sacraments and worship have always been regarded as symbols, that is, rituals which are filled with the presence of God and which enable us to be his convenant people. Such religious symbols initiate a process of conflict and change because God calls us to re-examine the purpose of our lives and the use of our time. Religious symbols are God's practical way of inviting us to assess the current position of our lives and the new commitments that may be needed.

It is easy to understand the connection between Mother Teresa's Eucharist and her daily self-gift to the poor of the world's slums. It makes sense when we hear that Father Damien's prayer life and Mass were sources of continuing strength in overcoming the tremendous opposition to his work among outcasts and lepers. Yet our own Sunday Mass may have little or nothing to do with Monday in the office or at home. The impact of religious symbol on the committed lives of a Teresa or a Damien is fairly obvious, but its impact on our own lives may be far less apparant.

Dorothy Day, Mother Teresa of Calcutta, and Father Damien received sacraments and worshipped in much the same way as their fellow Christians. But there was something different about the impact of these familiar rituals on their lives. Their worship was an honest expression of and a constant challenge to their commitment. The manner in which they celebrated their faith in sacrament and in service called out commitment from others. The people who gathered around Damien or who followed Mother Teresa into the slums to serve the poor were inspired to live a community life in Gospel service and prayer. Where there is commitment, there is usually community, whether it be that of a family, a religious order, or a parish.

The question of symbols and rituals does not stop with the individual. We celebrate God's presence among us as a community. In worship and sacrament, God calls Christian communities to be a credible witness to his presence and teaching. In the history of Christianity, however, there have always been cases of communities using ritual to escape the cost of commitment. The first-century Corinthians are a case in point.

A TEST CASE: THE CORINTHIANS

To be a Christian at Corinth in the middle of the first century was not an easy task. In effect, Corinthian Christians cut themselves off from that part of the public and social life which contradicted the Gospel values they had accepted. Part of the attraction of Christianity, however, was the strong sense of community that brought together a cross section of the city's population: dockworkers and magistrates, soldiers and slaves. Corinthian Christians had given up one type of community to be welcomed into another, more closely knit community.

That was the theory, at least. As we begin to read 1 Corinthians, we find that the actual situation was quite different. "I have been informed, my brothers, by certain members of Chloe's household that you are quarreling among yourselves" (1 Cor. 1:11). This accusation is all the more startling since an outsider would probably have seen an impressive unity in the Corinthians' common doctrine and shared rituals.

Another distinction must be introduced at this point if we are to understand the Corinthian situation. Theory tries to pin down and express the complexities of reality. The Corinthians, for example, believed the theological doctrine that "Jesus is Lord." This theoretical statement is an attempt to capture the complex process of salvation. Praxis (Greek *praxis:* "activity, deeds") sums up the way individuals and communities actually deal with reality, for better or worse. Praxis reflects our experience and its unresolved contradictions and questions. The quarreling that Paul mentions is a praxis situation that seems to contradict the theological theory of the Corinthian community. "Brothers, you are among those called. Consider your situation" (1 Cor. 1:26). Paul restates the theory and then calls for a re-evaluation of the Corinthian praxis.

Just because a Christian community has a unified theological theory ("Christ died for us and was raised by the Father") does not necessarily mean that its praxis corresponds to that theory. In fact, the most devious way to divide a community and to undermine its theology is to allow its wayward praxis to be clothed in apparently unifying liturgical trappings.

To understand this, we have only to see a typical Corinthian Eucharist through Paul's eyes. Both rich and poor Christians arrive for the love-feast and Eucharist, bringing their own provisions. The rich embarrass the poor by the quality and quantity of their food and drink: "When you assemble it is not to eat the Lord's Supper, for everyone is in haste to eat his own supper. One person goes hungry while another gets drunk. Do you not have homes where you can eat and drink? Would you show contempt for the church of God and embarrass those who have nothing?" (1 Cor. 11:20–22).

And yet, the "relevance" of the Corinthian Eucharist, with its intimate and charismatic dimensions, would be the envy of any liturgist. An outsider, dropping in on such a liturgy, might be impressed by the spontaneity of a ritual that could bring together such diverse social groups.

But Paul was not impressed. He saw a practical situation, which was directly opposed to the Gospel teaching: the insensitivity of the rich continued to oppress the poor even in the very rituals that, theoretically, were to make all one because Christ had died for all. Nowhere in his analysis of the Corinthian problem did Paul suggest that God was absent from the Corinthians' celebrations. *Rather, Paul accused these Christians of using the signs of God's presence (liturgy) to avoid his presence.* It was the Corinthians, in fact, who were absent in spirit from the celebration of God's presence.

The Corinthians' situation offers some pointed lessons. Paul knew something was wrong with the theological theory of these Christians, not from doctrinal testing, but from the praxis of the community that was disclosed in its religious symbols of assembly and celebration. The Corinthians' theory of sacrament reinforced their working definition of faith: enjoying only the glory and enlightenment of the resurrected Lord. The Cross had become a safe historical event for these people, because they no longer recognized their redemptive need or their lack of Gospel service.

Paul's response to the bad praxis and the incorrect theory of the Corinthians is the paradox of the Cross: "The message of the Cross is complete absurdity to those who are headed for ruin, *but to us who are experiencing salvation it is the power of God*" (1 Cor. 1:18, italics added). In Paul's argument, the experience of salvation is the source of honest praxis and correct theory. Theory includes meanings we share and commitments we live by. But dialogue with our experience reveals the misread and, perhaps, self-serving meanings of our commitments. To hold a dialogue with our praxis is to discover the real commitments of our lives.

The Corinthians had misread their own experience of salvation. In doing so, they had coveniently left out the Cross of Christ, the ultimate Christian symbol of service as well as salvation. As a result, their Baptism and Eucharist did not incorporate them into the "Body of Christ" for the service of the Gospel but into an elitist group of "saved" individuals. In all this, there was only "private" commitment, which, as we shall see, is no commitment at all.

We learn our first lesson in commitment by comparing the Corinthians and our first models. Dorothy Day, Mother Teresa, and Father Damien arrived at the rich integrity and selfless service of their lives through awareness of their experience and honesty in their religious symbols. Their commitment called out that of others. The result was communities of Gospel service and praise. By contrast, the Corinthians had a semblance of unity and relevant rituals. But their praxis revealed a misreading of their Christian experience. Paul's assessment of the community was accurate: "For as long as there are jealousy and quarrels among you, are you not of the flesh? And is not your behavior that of ordinary men?" (1 Cor. 3:3).

THE PAULINE RESPONSE

The Corinthians were not an ecclesial community, but several rival splinter groups: "One of you will say, 'I belong to Paul,' another, 'I belong to Apollos,' still another, 'Cephas has my allegiance,' and the fourth, 'I belong to Christ.' Has Christ, then, been divided into parts? Was it Paul who was crucified?" (1 Cor. 1:12–13).

Paul, in response, offered a theology of Church in praxis, one founded on the larger purposes of unique personal giftedness (1 Cor. 12:1–31).[2] The Corinthians believed in a self-serving eschatology or theology of the Kingdom which allowed them to be irresponsible and knowingly unsurprised at God's end-time mystery in the future. Paul, in contrast, did not concern himself with the glory of private redemptions. He was too caught up in the mystery of Christ's work becoming our task to separate it from God's Kingdom (1 Cor. 15:50–58).[3]

Paul, in effect, believed in a dialogue between honest praxis (orthopraxis) and accurate doctrine (orthodoxy) within the Christian community. He knew that the Kingdom of God remains a vague teaching until people can see in a reconciled and serving community of Christians the attitudes of faith, hope, and love that challenge a careless world. Until God ends time, the Gospel involves the continuing effort of living with integrity and a deepening sense of purpose. "Be steadfast and persevere, my beloved brothers, fully engaged in the work of the Lord. You know that your toil is not in vain when it is done in the Lord" (1 Cor. 15:58). One wonders, though, if the Corinthians really knew this. Hans Conzelmann pointedly summarizes Paul's teaching to this troubled group: "The Spirit is the guarantee of the coming salvation, not yet the transformation into a celestial mode of existence. We still find ourselves this side of resurrection."[4]

As a good teacher, Paul spoke out of his own experience of salvation so that the Corinthians might learn to speak out of theirs. He did not hesitate to say, "Imitate me as I imitate Christ" (1 Cor. 11:1). In Paul's own life this commitment was visible, both in his ministry (2 Cor. 11:16–33) and in a reframing of his own experience (2 Cor. 12:1–10). Yet even as he wrote, Paul was painfully growing into a new stage of his life and its meaning for others.[5] Paul's hope-filled ministry is realistic because it was worked out in this painful setting (2 Cor. 3:4–6; 3:12–18; 4:1–18). His ministry was the result of a dialogue with his experience that allowed for new vision.

For Paul, the Spirit is always at the core of such dialogue with our experience.[6] Such a Spirit-framed theology explains why Paul could be so demanding in terms of commitment (2 Cor. 5:1–10). He invited the Corinthians to re-examine the reality of their lives and, in doing so, draw out corollaries for their praxis of commitment. If their past praxis revealed them to be self-centered Christians, then their present and future praxis must be shaped by the symbol of announcing "the death of the Lord until . . ." (1 Cor. 11:26). As they struggled to understand the meaning of that symbol in the context of their shared lives, their sacraments would reveal the commitment demanded of them at each stage of their journey.

Praxis is not an infallible guide to the quality and extent of commitment that may be demanded of the community or its individual members. Only the Spirit is such a guide. Listening to the Spirit, speaking in a complex situation, is never easy. That is why we should not be too eager to condemn the original Corinthians or their counterparts in any age. Our own praxis may show us to be even less adept at listening and responding.

The Corinthian exercise in self-deception is the most dangerous game that Christians can play. Only God's active presence can contest our smug self-sufficiency and reveal our deep need. Only God's healing presence strengthens us to accept the gift of life, time and again, "for the sake of others." When Christians, individually or communally, hide behind the liturgies of God's presence without entering into their meaning, they, like Adam, try unsuccessfully to evade the living God, content with their memories of him. Such situations arise when Christian communities and individuals refuse to re-examine the direction and choices of their lives. Unexamined lives result in mindless sacramental participation without any real presence on our part.

LEX ORANDI

Although Paul did not know this axiom, he would have approved of it: "the law of worship is the law of belief" (*lex orandi lex credendi*).[7] "Worship," in the most profound sense of this axiom, does not refer to rituals but to the symbolized experience of God's presence, contesting our lack of presence.[8] From such experience true doctrine and reliable theory may be derived and current praxis reformed. Liturgy (*lex orandi*) is a privileged expression of God's presence and our prayerful response. It is also an accurate source for good theology and the criterion that Paul used to criticize the praxis-situation of the Corinthians.

For that community, worship and sacraments were the luxury of the saved. For Paul, they could be nothing less than the further acceptance of the saving death of Jesus and its deepened meaning for our shared lives. In other words, Paul believed in the pedagogical strength of true liturgy. In daily situations, this liturgy reveals our sinful praxis in its true light and, at the same time, offers the unearned strength to change. If the Corinthians misunderstood the theory of salvation (*lex docendi*), it is because their worship had not taught them the price of Gospel commitment on such salvation: "offer yourselves to God as men who have come back from the dead to life, and your bodies to God as weapons for justice" (Rom. 6:13).[9] The Pauline resonance in a later New Testament writing again clarified the cost of such commitment: "Bear your share of the hardship which the Gospel entails" (2 Tim. 1:8–10).

What are the consequences of naive or even dishonest use of religious symbols? Paul's teaching is summed up in his famous judgment theme: "Whoever eats the bread and drinks the cup of the Lord unworthily sins against the body and blood of the Lord" (1 Cor. 11:27). We can restate Paul's warning this way: our sacraments and worship cannot be divorced from our lives. If the religious symbols we participate in express commitment to the Gospel vision of love and service but our lives remain unchanged, then something is radically wrong. In effect, Paul asked the Corinthians where they could find the necessary vision for their lives when they would not discover it in the powerful symbols of God's presence in worship and sacrament. Two thousand years later, the Pauline question still troubles honest Christians.

RECURRING CORINTHIAN SITUATIONS

The Corinthian problem, then, is that of good people who are not good enough. The unique aspect of the problem is the deceptive use of Christian symbols of worship to avoid their implications: renewed commitment and deepened responsibility. This deceptive use of symbol is not, as a rule, a conscious and intentional action of good people. It is rather the quiet collusion of people who prefer old memories to new commitment and tranquilizing rituals to revelatory sacraments.

This perhaps explains why the Corinthian problem keeps reappearing as the temptation of each new generation of celebrating Christians. Examples from any historical period are easy to find. One has only to read Joseph Jungmann's classic two-volume history of the Mass of the Roman rite, for example, to see the gradual medieval reification (literally, "making a thing of") and distancing of the biblical notions of God's pervading presence and the meaning of Jesus' death for his community of believers.

The lesson is clear: to the extent that a Christian people loses sight of the Gospel teaching on faith and sacrament, superstition and ritualism replace symbol. Jungmann documents many instances of this deterioration. In the Middle Ages, for example, when regular reception of the Eucharist at Mass had become infrequent, looking at the host was considered salvific.

See the Body of Christ at the consecration and be satisfied! In the cities people ran from church to church, to see the elevated Host as often as possible, since rich rewards could be expected from such a practice. People even started lawsuits to ensure their getting a favorable view of the altar. There are examples of congregations where the majority of faithful waited for the sance-bell signalling the approach of the consecration before they entered the church and then after the elevation they rushed out as quickly as they had come in.[10]

This almost comical example of superstition would not have amused Paul. Even the first-century Corinthians might have been scandalized. If our axiom ("the law of worship is the law of belief") is applied to this example, the teaching it offers is apparent. Eucharist, in this praxis, was no longer seen as a responsible proclamation of the death of the Lord until he comes but as an insurance policy for present and future bliss. At the very time of this particular praxis, sophisticated sacramental theories were being taught in the great universities of Paris and Bologna. Yet these brilliant theoretical statements had little or no effect on the praxis of Eucharist or other religious symbols in the Middle Ages. There was a dangerous split between theory and praxis. The results were devastating. Devotional piety with its privatized interests became a substitute for an ecclesial and responsible sacramental life.

An example in our day might be the German Christian churches of the thirties, a case mentioned earlier. Without wishing either to oversimplify a complex situation or to denigrate the heroic witness of many individual Christians, one can argue that the ecclesial witness of the German church against the radical evil of genocide was neither impressive nor adequate. During those years when a godless theory and praxis allowed hundreds of thousands of Jews and others to be killed in an at least nominally Christian country, what were the symbols of Jesus' death and resurrection teaching the German church of the thirties? If the Corinthians received more than one letter from Paul for their poor praxis, is it rigoristic to ask what kind of letter the German Christian church would have received from him?

Another example of disparity between theory and praxis can easily be found in the social climate of the past two decades. It was not unknown in the United States of the sixties to see those who marched for the basic Gospel rights of blacks and chicanos harassed in ethnically Catholic neighborhoods where sacraments were being regularly dispensed. With some notable exceptions, the position of the American Christian churches on the morality of the Vietnam War was, at best, diplomatic and largely unprophetic.

The Church in the Third World countries where torture and denial of basic human rights are a way of life finds itself in a position similar to the German church of the thirties.[11] Yet where there were and are so much sacrament and worship the accompanying Pauline question is always there: Do we eat and drink judgment to ourselves? Has the Corinthian problem now become the American or Bolivian or South African problem? Who will receive the next Pauline letter?

A rigorist, in the face of such historical examples, would measure out the commitment that Christian sacraments and symbols should demand in such situations. A realist would caution against imposing impossible demands on good but, after all, limited people. A Christian will begin with what God can do in these impossible situations and, as a result, with what we should do. For among the many challenging insights of the Pauline heritage, one is particularly germane here: God's saving presence, symbolized in worship and sacrament, frees us for the adequate service of others. This hope and belief alone transform the unjust situations of our day and keep our worship honest.

PRAXIS

In brief, all Corinthian problems in Christian communities are ultimately praxis problems. A very general description of praxis was suggested above: the way individuals and communities deal with reality for better or worse. Corinthian Christians of any epoch who use transforming symbols perversely to remain untransformed in their praxis are in trouble. They block a major source of change in their lives, for those symbols should be a crossroads where praxis and theory meet.

We see praxis in the lives of people we know well. Their lives are played out on many levels: personal, social, economic, cultural, historical, religious. Our autobiographies, for example, would have to include, among other things, some details of our day-to-day living, family life, important friends, the pertinent political events of our time, as well as the tasks and accomplishments of our work lives. If theology is to be helpful in clarifying the meaning of what is going on in our lives and thus aiding us to be more responsible, there must be dialogue with the human sciences (psychology, sociology, etc.).[12] With the help of these sciences, we gain a more profound insight into the commitments and responsibilities of people and the psychosocial dimension of their religious symbols. In both theology and the human sciences, after all, we struggle with the same question: why do religious symbols so easily become clichés in the day-to-day lives of people?

We cannot talk about the faith of individuals and communities without discussing their praxis in its many dimensions. For faith is always the response that God makes possible for a specific person or community at a specific moment in history. This is not to relativize faith but to specify it. Faith is always a response to God's offer of salvation.

But "salvation" remains a theological abstraction until actual people and situations come into play. Paul's descriptions of salvation were the result of his personal experience of God's call at successive stages of his life, each stage having its own temptations and challenges. As Paul continued to deal with the crises of his life and ministry, his definitions of "salvation" and "faith" were refined in the crucible of living. When he said, "We do not lose heart, because our inner being is renewed each day even though our body is being destroyed at the same time" (2 Cor. 4:16), he captured the complex process of dealing with God's ongoing call to salvation at a precise time in one's own life.

Faith, then, is not a static creed but a matter of praxis, rooted in the transforming demands that God never ceases to make until our death.[13] To speak of Mother Teresa's faith, for example, is to describe a series of lived events and choices in which God's presence has been acknowledged by her continuing self-gift. It is in this sense that Vatican II's biblical definition of the "obedience of faith" should be understood: the gift of our whole self given freely to God.[14] This is a definition we will return to many times.

Such a definition assumes that faith is always an unearned gift but underlines God's decision to have those who believe share in the work of salvation. "God, in Christ, was reconciling the world to himself, not counting men's transgressions against them, and . . . he has entrusted the message of reconciliation to us. This makes us ambassadors for Christ, God as it were appealing through us. We implore you, in Christ's name: be reconciled to God" (2 Cor. 5:19–20). To give our whole self freely to God will inevitably affect the lives of others. Mother Teresa's faith is but one dramatic example of this basic truth.

Christian praxis, then, is the result of God's action in our interlocking lives. We need to constantly reform and alter what we believe as we attempt to live out a Gospel life within the changing complexities of our world and become the beloved community of Christ in this world. Through such a community God makes known his revelation for the sake of others. It is in the praxis of such a community that we see the first inklings of God's future Kingdom already begun among us. Finally, in such praxis we begin to discern God's loving action everywhere.

PRAXIS AND COMMUNICATION

"What you are so thunders at me that I cannot hear what you are saying" is the perennial wisdom that has been expressed in many different ways over the centuries. In other words, communication on the deeper levels of our lives is shaped by our experience, not our words. In an age when manipulative communication (for example, some forms of advertising) has become a science, we can easily forget the connection between what we live and what we say to others. This is true of both individuals and communities.

The Latin root of *communication* denotes "something in common." Communication is possible because of shared language, shared ideas, and, most importantly, shared experience. We can say "I love you" because our experience preceded any knowledge of words or ideas about love. Honest communication, then, is intimately tied to the praxis of our lives and the experience from which it derives.

Communication uses both signs and symbols. The distinction between the two has been explained in a number of ways. For our purposes, we can begin by saying that a sign gives directions or information but does not enable us to take advantage of these. A highway sign, for example, may tell us that New York is sixty miles east of our present location, but that sign will not get us there. In addition, signs, as Paul Ricoeur has pointed out, do not carry us beyond their first and obvious meaning. As a sign, a stain on a white pair of pants communicates merely a simple physical fact to us: the pants are soiled.

A symbol is a sign and much more. To use Ricoeur's famous phrase, "The symbol gives rise to thought."[15] A symbol has a deeper meaning than we might first expect. Our example of the stain on a white pair of pants can also be a symbol of defilement, as Ricoeur has brilliantly shown. This symbol then becomes a doorway into the deeper complexity of our experience because it allows us to move past the first meaning of the stain to a second, more complex meaning. Theology adds something more to this discussion of symbol. A religious symbol enables us to appropriate the meanings it proposes. An obvious example for Christians is a sacrament that is defined as effecting what it signifies. For Paul, Eucharist is a symbol through which we proclaim the death of the Lord (1 Cor. 11:26). We could not do that proclaiming without symbol.

In the archives of our experience and in the current praxis of our lives, symbols have an important place. *Signs do not demand commitment; religious symbols do.* We can stare at a sign, but symbols are an invitation to move and grow in our lives because of the new meaning and strength they offer. A tourist can stare at Michelangelo's painting of *Creation* on the ceiling of the Sistine Chapel. In that case, the painting is a sign that depicts nothing more than the physical actions of creation. But someone who makes the effort to understand this painting as a great symbol is richly rewarded by its new and power-filled meaning that can effect change in the viewer.

Augustine has provided us with a magnificent example of the dynamic character of religious symbol. In homily 272, he comments on how the priest presents the Eucharist with the words "The Body of Christ," to which the Christian responds "Amen." Augustine then reveals the complex meaning of the Eucharist as symbol, the Body of Christ. He says, in effect: "Be what you see. Receive what you are." If we were dealing with mere ritual or signs, we could stretch out our hands for the host and give the proper response. But Augustine's explanation includes both the committed self-gift of the Christian ("Be what you see," that is, the Eucharist as Body) and the Christian's relation with Christ and the Church ("Receive what you are," that is, the Body of Christ as Church). In Augustine's mind, our symbols and the praxis of our lives cannot be separated.

To clarify the commitments implicit in what we are doing, we must critically examine our praxis. The "we" of praxis is crucial. Our lives are not solitary monuments to the way we spend our time, but stories of shared experiences and interacting decisions and expectations. We spend a good part of our waking hours not only communicating with ourselves but with others. In fact, the quality of our self-communication is inseparably linked to the quality of our communications with others.

With each day's experience there are implicit questions about meanings we would rather take for granted than re-examine. (Does proclaiming the death of the Lord, for example, involve anything more than "keeping the commandments" and writing out an annual check for Catholic Charities or the United Appeal?) Meaning in this process no longer remains an abstraction. Nor can it be reduced to what "gets us through another day." Meaning pinpoints the "what and who" we value in a given space and time. Meaning also bears the traces of others' values and their influence in our lives.

To return to the example of the German Christian churches of the thirties, wasn't there obviously a separation of symbols of worship, with their prophetic meaning, from the public sphere of praxis and values? With the help of symbols, we can once more question the meaning and values, both those presumed and those actually lived, of our praxis. If we go through the external motions of symbols but do not appropriate their challenging meaning, then our symbols are reduced to signs and our communication becomes distorted.

Distorted communication, as we employ the term here, is the result of partial and inadequate contact with our experience and, therefore, of blithe assumptions about our meanings and values.[16] Put more simply, we have an inadequate and sometimes unreliable awareness of what we actually value in our lives. Only appropriated values can be the basis of healthy commitment. To be deceived about our values is to become a prisoner to false commitments.

In the case of the Christian who would never "miss Mass" on Sunday, what are the real values in this stage of the person's life that prompt such consistency? Does he or she need religious discipline or fear being punished by God or desire to live the Gospel life, or is a combination of these and other values at work? No answers will be forthcoming if we have not learned to read and tell our own story with the courage of real objectivity.

Inadequate reading of our experience will inevitably affect the way we use our symbols, religious and otherwise. When there is a question of systematic distortion of our experience, the very possibility of honest response in faith and its expression in symbol is called into question. The reason has already been suggested.

God speaks and awaits our response in the context of our lives together. Our faith response is fashioned in a specific life situation. Our ability to perceive God's meaning and our needed response in that context rests, in good part, on our communication skills: our willingness not only to understand but to enter into a dialogue with the God who invites us to move on in our lives.

THE CORINTHIANS AND MISREAD SYMBOLS

The Corinthians continue to provide us with examples of misread symbols. The meaning of what was happening in that community and its celebrations was being misunderstood. But, in saying that, we have not touched the underlying problem. Borrowing a useful distinction from social theory, the Corinthians believed that because they shared common ritual *actions,* they could presume that they shared a consensus on the meaning of those actions. As Paul revealed, their presumptions were false. In a real dialogue, the participants are in a process of communication that respects the complexity of their lives and challenges them with new expectations and risks.

The Corinthians seem to have incorrectly believed that their initiation into the community had already placed them among the saved. Their Eucharistic rituals celebrated what had happened to them once and for all time. Depending on the point of emphasis, these naive aberrations can be termed heretical "enthusiasm" or "sacramentalism." In any case, the Corinthians' behavior illustrates the static ritualism that had replaced the dynamic Pauline "participation" and "announcing the death of the Lord until . . ." (1 Cor. 11:36).

Paul, in effect, teaches us that if Christians do not enter into a learning process in which Christ's death on the Cross can contradict our "wisdom" with its "foolishness," then we do not truly take part in the work of God. We remain unenlightened. Our rituals do not teach us what we must believe.

In brief, distorted sacramental praxis is usually the result of distorted, or at least naive, communication with our reality and God's action there. As we shall see, healing communication is premised on the possibility of a dialectical dialogue with our retrieved experience. In such a dialogue, we more adequately symbolize the meanings and challenges of our stage of life. Without such meanings our experience of community, of celebration, and of renewed commitment will be dangerously limited.[17]

At this point, someone might well ask, "Where have all the sinners gone?" Can we not simply attribute the Corinthian problem and its distorted praxis to sinful Christians? Yes, of course, but in the way that Paul does. In describing the Corinthian Christians as good people who were not good enough, we have been faithful to Paul's attitude. These are people for whom he could bless God: "I continually thank my God for you because of the favor he has bestowed on you in Christ Jesus, in whom you have been richly endowed with every gift of speech and knowledge" (1 Cor. 1:4–5).[18] At the same time, Paul could excoriate their misuse of sacrament and misunderstanding of faith. Their static awareness of their own experience, out of which God would redeem them, was coupled with their fixed views on what service to the world God asked of them. This is the sin of good people who will not allow God to demand new commitment and better service.

In speaking of distorted communication, then, we touch the core problem of how we welcome God's free gift (justification). Distorted communication permits the naive to become indifferent and the selfish insensitive. In the hands of such ordinary sinners, sacraments can become convenient escapes from commitment.

This brief discussion has led us to a core intuition: *praxis bears watching.* To miss the ongoing significance of our self-investments in our lives is to be blind to that praxis. When praxis and symbol are in healthy dialogue, then celebrating Christians can repeat the experience of a Moses who leads his people (despite his initial reluctance before the message of the burning bush) and a Paul who preaches the Gospel (after reeling before the unwanted vision of Christ). Such attention to our praxis in no way detracts from God's action in sacrament and life but, rather, takes it seriously.

COMMITMENT AND SYMBOL

In the opening lines of this chapter, commitment was described in terms of worthwhile conflict, painful consciousness, and a new conscience. At each stage of our lives, these terms retain something of the familiar and yet involve something new.

This combination of the familiar and the new gives each period of our lives a specific shape or profile.

The great Swedish film director, Ingmar Bergman, juxtaposes the familiar and the new of a man's life in his classic, *Wild Strawberries*.[19] An old man, Dr. Borg, makes a trip back to his alma mater to receive an honorary degree. The trip occasions a number of symbolic references to past chapters of his life. The title of the film is, in fact, a major symbol, distilling an important experience in his young life. As these symbols unfold before Borg's eyes, he begins to perceive the meanings and commitments he had chosen but only vaguely, if at all, understood.[20]

To arrive at this point of revelation, Borg must be willing to deal with his own crises, past and present, and the interlocking lives of his son and daughter-in-law.[21] As Bergman presents a series of flashbacks, we glimpse some of the trade-offs made in Borg's life. The doctor's journey through the Swedish countryside becomes a symbol of the inner journey of a man seeking and yet fearing intimacy.[22] It is the genius of a great artist like Bergman to know how to symbolize these intangibles of human life: the quest for and the fear of intimacy and new commitment in our life. With the help of such symbols, the moment of insight and revelation is always lurking nearby. We see beyond the symbol meanings and visions, unsuspected until now. Even more important, we find that the necessary strength comes with such vision.

Each of us, in a sense, is a Borg in search of a Bergman. We need symbol to understand the complexities of our story and to have the courage to move on in our lives. We have no choice but to become symbol-makers, drawing from the stuff of our own existence. Like Bergman, we see more than the faded memories of our burnt-out lives because we refocus our life events and find we are no longer a prisoner to them. We have the examples of great Christians like Paul, Augustine, Francis of Assisi, and Thomas Merton, who learned to read the symbols of their lives with great courage and perception so as to deepen the commitments they had made.

Such symbols are deeply religious. Augustine in his *Confessions* tells us why: "But whoever recounts his actual and true merits to thee, what is he doing but recounting to thee thy own gifts? Oh, if only men would know themselves as men, then he that glories would 'glory in the Lord.' "[23] Stated another way, if we are willing to own our experience in more responsible ways, like a Paul or an Augustine, we will see the unsuspected work of God in our lives and its implications for our future. To anticipate the theme of Chapter 4: with the help of such symbols, God questions our presence so as to invite our commitment.

All Christian symbols are expressions of and invitations to faith. In biblical accounts, faith is never reduced to intellectual affirmation and assent. Rather, it is a response to the living God. Empowered and liberated by this presence, we begin to be more "present" in the deepest sense of the word. Samuel Terrien has aptly termed this presence "commission."[24] (Interestingly enough, both *commitment* and *commission* come from the same Latin root meaning "to send with, to go with"—COM + MITTERE.) Christian symbols help us to deal more realistically and honestly with our experience. Because Eucharist, for example, juxtaposes our dying and the proclamation of Christ's death, we can clarify the unappropriated events and meanings of our lives. If that insight is accepted, then deepened commitment cannot be far behind.

Because our lives are a combination of the social and the personal, of the public and the private, Christian symbols must encompass to some degree the public and so-called secular symbols of our world. When our Christian symbols are cut off from the world, their impact is necessarily lessened because part of our experience has been bypassed. God's power and presence must confront our total experience, not simply selected portions of that experience.[25]

The Corinthians did not see the connection between their Eucharists and their insensitive and immoral conduct with others. Many Christians today do not see the relation between their Christian Initiation (Baptism/Confirmation) and the social and economic injustice that they quietly tolerate in their own countries and communities. Personal blindness may, in part, account for these situations. Usually, however, these symbols have been rendered innocuous by being removed from the public world.

This seems to be the point of Raimundo Panikkar's dictum: "Only worship can prevent secularization from becoming inhuman, and only secularization can save worship from becoming meaningless."[26] There is a necessary interplay between the situation of our personal and social world (which, after all, is also God's world, *saeculum*) and the praise we give God. Our praise is not offered in a vacuum. Paul argues with particular force that all creation proclaims God: "Whatever can be known about God is clear to them; he himself made it so. Since the creation of the world, invisible realities, God's eternal power and divinity, have become visible, recognized through the things he has made. Therefore, these men are inexcusable" (Rom. 1:19–20). If creation does not evoke our praise of him, we are at fault. Ernst Käsemann's commentary on these verses is equally strong: "A person's reality is decided by what Lord he has. . . . He who evades the Creator runs into his Judge."[27]

Naive worshippers like the Corinthians separate whole areas of their lived experience and its social context from God's continuing action in this world. This kind of praise is both abstract and safe: abstract because our own story has been factored out; safe because such praise involves no new commitment. Corinthians of any epoch can thus chant solemn songs of praise in their Eucharists and not notice the need around them. They can be mildly shocked at the Gospel narratives of the Pharisees' blindness and yet be equally blind to the truth of their own stories.

The test of whether we exclude the secular from the sacred is whether our worship clarifies our experience to the point of new commitment. For both worship and secularization are concretized in the stories of individuals and their communities. Those stories become revelatory, in every sense, when our praise of God leads us to a responsible future, shaped from our past and present.[28]

THE TWO SIDES OF SYMBOL AND SACRAMENT

How do good people reduce symbols to mere tokens? Familiar Gospel scenes of Jesus' encounters with people like ourselves should help us answer that question. There we see many people who stood before Jesus as spectators. They refused to be challenged by his prophetic action-words and parables. They hid behind their own rites and reasons, insisting that God should already love them, and thus did not acknowledge the free gift that is God's salvation. ("I give thanks, O God, that I am not like the rest of men—grasping, crooked, adulterous—or even like this tax collector. I fast twice a week. I pay tithes on all I possess"—Luke 18:11–12.) For such people, signs are enough.

Real presence, the root of all symbol, invites not spectators, but participants: *real presence is a question of commitment.* Conversion in Scripture is always the result of God's presence enabling us to respond in presence. This presence includes participation in God's work which heals others, too. Prescinding from a more precise definition for the moment, we can say that sacramental symbols are expressions of Christ's healing presence among us. The only adequate response to such symbols is participation in Christ's work for others.[29] If, however, we Christians use these symbols as if we were participants but, in effect, remain spectators, then indeed symbol becomes one-sided. This situation does not deny Christ's continuing power in sacrament but rather our refusal of it.

Medieval theology had very succinct technical language to describe the objective and subjective sides of symbol/sacrament. The objective and gratuitous work of Christ in each sacrament (*ex opere operato*) was to be balanced by the attitudes of the one receiving the sacrament (*ex opere operantis*). There are a number of reasons why the subjective dimension of sacrament was never developed.

The original context of this discussion was the question of the worthiness of the minister of a sacrament. In attempting to safeguard the doctrine that Christ is sacramentally present even when the minister is unworthy, the question of the subjective attitudes of the minister or recipient of a sacrament was muted. Rather, there is an emphasis, in Augustine's solution to the Donatist heresy of fifth century, on the rite of a sacrament as the carrier of Christ's action and the permanency of certain sacramental actions ("character"). This allowed later theologians to discuss the "fruitfulness" of subjective responsibility in a sac-

ramental action only as a corollary.[30] The result of this historical
debate is still with us: an undeveloped and uncontextualized notion of participation in symbolic actions. Eventually, some general conditions for the "worthy reception" of a sacrament were
developed. Whether these conditions adequately defined the personal response of a recipient of a sacrament will be discussed
later.[31]

There were other contributing factors. As infant Baptism became more frequent (and adult Baptism more rare), it seemed
unnecessary to discuss the subjective dimension of response in
Baptism. Since the infant is not capable of a faith response,
there has been a consequent development of a theology that underlines the objective faith of the Church.[32] The growing control
of Canon Law (with its interest in objective statements) over
sacramental theology and the tendency of ecclesiology increasingly to express itself in legal concepts combined to reify the
symbolic action of the sacraments.[33] Law and institutionalization
do not easily tolerate the complexity of symbolic action.

When the sixteenth-century Reformers emphasized the subjective dispositions necessary for honest sacrament, their attitude
was interpreted by the Council of Trent as a denial of the objective presence and power of Christ in the sacraments. On the
other hand, Luther and Calvin saw in much of the sacramental
praxis of the Roman church of their day an implicit Pelagian
tendency to deny the gratuitous nature of God's salvation and to
"earn heaven" with the mechanical reception of sacrament.

Both Trent and the Reformers had inherited medieval theories of sacrament which, in borrowing from the philosophy of
Aristotle, canonized this objective emphasis by applying causality and matter/form theories to sacramental theology. Propo-
nents of these theories, such as St. Thomas Aquinas, did not
deny the need for honest personal attitudes in receiving a sacrament. But their philosophical categories and terminology were
not suited to the development of personalist concerns.[34] The
post-Tridentine reaction was to attach even greater importance
to the objective, *ex opere operato* dimension of sacrament.[35]

Even this cursory historical overview should suggest some of
the reasons for the undeveloped character of the subjective dimension of sacrament and worship. Only with the rise of the

human sciences (psychology, sociology, anthropology, etc.) could the intersubjective and developmental nature of symbol be adequately discussed. In response to Vatican II's call for a knowing, active, and fruitful participation in sacrament and worship, use of these sciences helps us to spell out the characteristics and process implicit in such participation.

The one-sided development of sacrament provides a partial answer to why there can be so much sacrament and so little ecclesial and eschatological commitment. At critical moments when a credibility gap exists between sacramental symbol and praxis, the objective sacramental presence of Christ can unwittingly be used to excuse the subjective lack of presence in communities and individuals. We can stress the "real presence" of Christ in the Eucharist, for example, to avoid dealing with the lack of real presence in a crowded church on Sunday morning.

OUR REDEMPTIVE EXPERIENCE

It is God's enabling presence which makes the impossible not only possible but credible in our experience.[36] But a new awareness is required, not only of what God does in our experience, but of what he has already done. Thus, the songs and canticles of God's Word, though often enough a literary borrowing, are impressive redemptive cries because they rediscover both the new and the old of God's presence in the experience of their authors.

Mary, for example, sang a song of praise (Luke 1:46–55) which, at first glance, seems to be a magnificent but general summary of God's action in the lives of his people.[37] In context, however, Mary's song was prompted by God's action in her own life: the Savior will be born of her. What was true for all Israel became new again in Mary's experience: "God who is mighty has done great things for me" (Luke 1:49). Mary's new commitment was the result of her experience and her response to it ("I am the servant of the Lord. Let it be done to me as you say"—Luke 1:38).

By contrast, to define presence in exclusively metaphysical terms is to be reduced to celebrating it in those terms. Expressions such as the "state of grace" and a Christian's "proper dispositions" in the reception of a sacrament refer to ways we can be honestly present, but in abstract language. Such "objective" descriptions of Christian presence can allow us to ignore the perspectives proper to our experience. This is a dangerously false objectivity.[38] Unlike Mary, who perceived her experience as a crossroads of commitment, our own praise of God's action may be a way of escaping from its implications in our lives.

Yet we must find, as Mary did, that our experience is the key to celebrating our religious symbols in authentic and prophetic ways. Experience, we have more than once proposed, involves not only what has "happened" to us but the meaning that we give those happenings. Sacrament as symbol can help us to frame our experience in such a way as to call out from us more committed service to the Gospel. Our poorly examined experience, on the other hand, can continually provide us with excuses for avoiding new commitments.

At this juncture, some theologians might immediately feel a certain uneasiness. Experience in much philosophical and theological thinking has been treated as a purely subjective phenomenon. Hence, to refer constantly to our experience as a touchstone for redemptive presence can seem to derogate from the gratuity of God's action. This approach can even smack of a certain Pelagian notion of faith, celebrated in sacrament. A healthy reaction has set in, however, to such one-sided fears.

Experience is not the opposite of "objective" reality. Mary's experience was quite objective because it involved her reality interacting with that of God and others. Her "I am the servant of the Lord" summed up a whole process in her story and spoke of deepened commitment in her life.[39] Experience is the result of our encounter with reality. Clarification of that experience will be invariably balanced against the wider experience of others.[40] Commitment is the proof that we have learned to read our shared story more honestly and objectively.

John E. Smith contends that an analogy of experience which benefits from the individual's religious experience can clarify religious meaning.

Experience is a unique level in reality and it serves as a vantage point for the interpretation of the whole of existence. . . . Should it be objected that, since God is "wholly other," human experience is worthless as a medium of understanding, the reply is that for the Judeo-Christian tradition God can never be understood in a sense that makes impossible his ingredience in man's historical experience or, more crucially, in a human life.[41]

Dishonest religious autobiography and deceptive ritualism are the result of superficial treatment of our experience. Our theological theory may be sophisticated, but does it change the praxis of our lives? Thomas à Kempis, in his classic *Imitation of Christ*, stresses a similar point: "I would rather be able to experience compunction than to define it." There need not be a split between the religious praxis of our lives (*lex orandi*) and the good theology it teaches us (*lex docendi*). As in Mary's case, we return to our old stories of God's action in our lives and find there new songs of praise and more accurate theology of God's saving work among us.

SUMMARY

Because the subjective awareness of our experience is so crucial to symbol, we will continue to develop this dimension in succeeding chapters. Our present concern has been the connection of praxis with our symbols. The ways in which we encounter reality (praxis) are directly affected by the manner in which we perceive our experience. Symbol clarifies our experience and thus allows for insight and change.

Symbol is more than the creation of the sum total of our resources. Symbol also proclaims the power-filled presence of God. This presence continues to question our self-understanding and the ritual posturing that can pass for worship of God. Within this context, conversion is once more an experience, gratuitously given and joyously sacramentalized time and again.[42]

The response of faith is committed service. Such a response is always given within the complex and changing contexts of our own experience and of the world we inhabit. We need the symbols of worship and sacrament to deal with this complexity so that new meaning can accompany us at each stage of our lives. This is not the closed world of privatized meaning but rather the insight that strengthens our hands for Gospel service.

The first answer, then, to why there is so much sacrament

and so little commitment lies in the Corinthian situation: worship and sacrament that cost the user little. Corinthians of any generation usually arrive at this irresponsible state of affairs by misreading their experience and ignoring their praxis. Theory substitutes for reality. The comfort of ritual quietly replaces the cost of genuine faith and sacrament. Mary and Paul are invoked, but the meaning of her example and his admonitions rarely hit home.

The Corinthian problem reasserts itself in the lives of Christian people and communities who are irresponsible with their experience and, therefore, naive in their rituals. For God's salvation and our response in faith are seen in the layered experience of our lives. God gives us sacramental symbols so that we can be honest about that experience and about the new directions and tasks it demands of us.

This chapter has sketched the contours of commitment. To hope, however, that Corinthians of any epoch would change would be utopian if it were not for the continuing reality of God's justification. Paul spoke of it in experiential terms. The Christian church has repeatedly asserted that there is no faith or sacrament that is not rooted in justification. When we look at committed people like Dorothy Day, Mother Teresa, and Father Damien, we begin to understand why justification is important: "The love of Christ impels us who have reached the conviction that since one died for all, all died. He died for all so that those who live might live no longer for themselves, but for him who for their sakes died and was raised up" (2 Cor. 5:14–15).

NOTES

1. E. Erikson, *Insight and Responsibility* (New York: W. W. Norton, 1964), p. 30.
2. For the ecclesial dimension of justification, see C. Müller, *Gottes Gerechtigkeit und Gottes Volk: Eine Untersuchung zu Römer 9–11* (Göttingen: Vandenhoeck und Ruprecht, 1964). For the related question of charism and office within the community, see G. Hasenhüttl, *Charisma: Ordnungsprinzip der Kirche* (Freiburg: Herder, 1969).
3. P. Stuhlmacher, *Gerechtigkeit Gottes bei Paulus* (Göttingen: Vandenhoeck und Ruprecht, 1965).

4. Hans Conzelmann, *History of Primitive Christianity* (Nashville, Tenn.: Abingdon, 1973), p. 104.

5. Ibid, p. 105. See also C. K. Barrett, *A Commentary on the Second Epistle to the Corinthians* (New York: Harper & Row, 1973), pp. 32 ff.

6. For a perceptive statement, see E. Käsemann's "Cry for Liberty in the Church's Worship," *Perspectives on Paul* (Philadelphia: Fortress, 1971), pp. 127–37.

7. The axiom is usually ascribed to Prosper of Aquitaine. For its larger context, see R. Federer, *Liturgie und Glaube: Eine theologiegeschichtliche Untersuchung* (Freiburg: Paulus Verlag, 1950); H. Dalmais, "Liturgie et le dépôt de la foi," *L'Eglise en prière: Introduction à la liturgie,* ed. A. G. Martimort (Paris: Desclée, 1965), pp. 231–34. The axiom has different extensions among different writers: see, for example, A. Houssiau, "La liturgie, lieu privilégié de la théologie sacramentaire," *Questions Liturgiques* 54 (1973): 7–12; G. Lukken, "La liturgie comme lieu théologique irremplacable," *Questions Liturgiques* 56 (1975): 97–112.

8. G. Wainwright has devoted considerable attention to the *lex orandi* issue in *Doxology: The Praise of God in Worship, Doctrine and Life* (New York: Oxford, 1980), pp. 218–83. While generally agreeing with his treatment, I would maintain that a praxis theology must deal with the experience of *lex orandi,* which is a question of mutual presence of God and others.

9. E. Käsemann, *Commentary on Romans,* trans. G. W. Bromley (Grand Rapids, Mich.: W. B. Eerdmans, 1980), pp. 176–77.

10. J. Jungmann, *The Mass of the Roman Rite: Its Origins and Development,* 2 vols. (New York: Benziger, 1950), vol. 1, pp. 120–21. See also, vol. 1, pp. 127–33; and P. Browe, *Die Verehrung der Eucharistie im Mittelalter* (Munich: M. Hueber, 1933; reprinted, Rome: Herder, 1967).

11. W. Bühlmann, *The Coming of the Third Church* (New York: Orbis, 1977), esp. pp. 88–98.

12. F. Houtart et al., *Recherche interdisciplinaire et Théologie* (Paris: Cerf, 1970); W. Everett and T. Bachmeyer, *Disciplines in Transformation* (Washington, D.C.: University Press in America, 1979).

13. I am following what M. Lamb describes on the fifth model in "The Theory-Praxis Relationship," *Proceedings of the Catholic Theology Society of America* 31 (1976): 149–78. "Christian praxis is authentically incarnational and eschatological when its very commitment to a particular praxis critically opens it to all other authentic praxis" (ibid, p. 172, n.75).

14. Dogmatic Constitution, *Dei Verbum, On Divine Revelation* 5 in W. M. Abbott, ed., *The Documents of Vatican II* (New York: Herder and Herder, 1966), p. 113.

15. P. Ricoeur, *The Symbolism of Evil* (Boston: Beacon, 1967), p. 352. Cf. also, D. M. Rasmussen, *Symbol and Interpretation* (The Hague: Martinus Nijhoff, 1974).

16. I am indebted here to the continuing work of J. Habermas, especially *Theory and Praxis* (Boston: Beacon, 1973) and *Communication and Evolution of Society* (Boston: Beacon, 1979). See also, T. A. McCarthy, "A Theory of Communicative Competence," *Philosophy of Social Sciences* 3 (1973): 135–56; A. Wellmer, "Communications and Emancipation: Reflections on the Linguistic Turn in Critical Theory," in J. O'Neill, ed., *On Critical Theory* (New York: Seabury, 1976), pp. 231–63; C. Koreng, *Norm und Interaktion bei Jürgen Habermas* (Düsseldorf: Patmos Verlag,

1979). For the hermeneutical and other theological issues in using Habermas' communication model, see the important work of H. Peukert, *Wissenschaftstheorie—Handlungstheorie—Fundamentale Theologie: Analysen zu Ansatz und Status theologischer Theoriebildung* (Düsseldorf: Patmos Verlag, 1976), esp. pp. 303–23; N. Mette, *Theorie der Praxis* (Düsseldorf: Patmos Verlag, 1978).

17. See C. Taylor, "Interpretation and the Science of Man," *Review of Metaphysics* 25 (1971): 1–32 and 35–45; also excerpted in P. Connerton, ed., *Critical Sociology* (New York: Penguin, 1976), pp. 153–93.

18. As H. Conzelmann points out, the blessing is within the context of the profane epistolary style, but is tranformed by Paul's teaching on the source of that blessing: the unmerited and justifying favor of Christ. See *First Corinthians* (Philadelphia: Fortress, 1975), pp. 25–26. For discussion in the same vein, See C. K. Barrett, *A Commentary on the First Epistle to the Corinthians* (New York: Harper & Row, 1968), pp. 36–37.

19. "Dr. Borg's Life-Cycle," *Adulthood,* ed. E. Erikson (New York: W. W. Norton, 1978).

20. Ibid, p. 17.

21. Ibid, p. 13.

22. Ibid, p. 29.

23. Book 9, Chapter 13 in St. Augustine's *Confessions and Enchiridion,* A. C. Outler, trans. and ed. (Philadelphia: Westminster, 1955), p. 199. (This translation will be used throughout unless otherwise noted.)

24. S. Terrien, in his *The Elusive Presence* (New York: Harper & Row, 1978), has arrived at a similar model from a biblical concern.

25. For a particularly eloquent statement of this attitude, see M. Douglas, *Natural Symbols* (New York: Pantheon, 1970).

26. R. Panikker, *Worship and Secular Man* (New York: Orbis, 1973), p. 1.

27. Käsemann, *Commentary on Romans,* p. 43. For additional discussion of the sacred/secular and worship, see H. Schmidt, ed., *Liturgy in Transition,* Concilium 62 (New York: Herder and Herder, 1971).

28. This is a specific application of what Lamb designates as the "Critical Praxis correlation" in *Proceedings* 31 (1976): 171.

29. *Participation* is being used in the Pauline sense (*metexein*). See S. Aalen, "Das Abendmahl als Opfermahl im Neuen Testament," *Novum Testamentum* 6 (1963): 128–52.

30. L. Villette, in his *Foi et Sacrement,* 2 vols. (Paris: Bloud et Gay, 1959–64), provides the background for some of the earlier teaching on personal faith in relation to sacrament; See vol. I, pp. 40–46, 125–29, 137–40, 191–216, 279–300; vol. II, pp. 40–51, 73–75. For the eventual muting of the *ex opere operantis* of sacrament, cf. ibid. vol. II, pp. 264–78, 368–71. B. Leeming is useful for an historical overview of the use of the terms *ex opere operato/ex opere operantis* in *Principles of Sacramental Theology* (Westminster, Md.: Newman, 1960), pp. 7–27, and for the related question of causality, ibid, pp. 333–39.

31. As A. Ganoczy has pointed out, the eschatological demands of Jesus and the faith demands of the early Christian community gradually modulate into the concerns of validity of sacrament as distinguished from "worthiness" with a certain minimalism as the norm: the habitual or implicit intention to receive what the Church gives (*Einführung in die katholische*

Sakramentenlehre (Darmstadt: Wissenschaftliche Buchgesellschaft, 1979), pp. 47–52.

32. For statements of this, see Leeming, *Sacramental Theology,* pp. 76–93; J. Ratzinger, "Taufe und Formulierung des Glaubens," *Ephemerides Theologicae Lovanienses* 49 (1973): 76–86.

33. This historical development becomes quite complicated beginning in the seventh century. For a discussion, see Y. Congar, "L' 'Ecclesia' ou communauté chrétienne, sujet intégral de l'action liturgique," *La Liturgie après Vatican II* (Paris: Cerf, 1967), pp. 241–82; also, Congar's *L'Ecclésiologie du haut Moyen-Âge* (Paris: Cerf, 1968), pp. 90–127.

34. For a good summary of this period, see J. Martos, *Doors to the Sacred* (New York: Doubleday, 1981), Chapter 3.

35. This emphasis is still true in the earlier classical work of K. Rahner in *The Church and the Sacraments* (New York: Herder and Herder, 1963) and of E. Schillebeeckx in *Christ the Sacrament of Encounter* (New York: Sheed and Ward, 1963).

36. Polanyi would call this "interiorization"; see *The Tacit Dimension* (Garden City, N.Y.: Doubleday, 1966), pp. 17–18. The Johannine "seeing" transposes this process to a redemptive context; cf. R. E. Brown, *The Gospel According to John* (New York: Doubleday, 1966), vol. 1, pp. 503–05.

37. For a detailed analysis, see I. H. Marshall, *The Gospel of Luke: A Commentary on the Greek Text* (Grand Rapids, Mich.: W. B. Eerdmans, 1978), pp. 77–85.

38. R. Poole gives a fine statement of this problem in his *Towards Deep Subjectivity* (New York: Harper & Row, 1972), pp. 115–19.

39. D. Mieth, "What Is Experience?" *Revelation and Experience, Concilium* 113, eds. E. Schillebeeckx and B. van Iersel (New York: Seabury, 1979), pp. 40–53; here, p. 44.

40. For extended arguments in this vein, see, for example, John E. Smith, *Experience and God* (New York: Harper & Row, 1968), pp. 30–31, and *The Analogy of Experience: An Approach to Understanding Religious Truth* (New York: Harper & Row, 1973), pp. 40–41.

41. Smith, *The Analogy of Experience,* pp. 54–55. Smith's concept of the "beloved community" as redemptive and celebrating community results from this shared redemptive experience and meaning; cf. ibid, pp. 58–60, 112–20.

42. See B. Lonergan, *Method in Theology* (New York: Herder and Herder, 1972), pp. 247–271.

CHAPTER 2

Unearned Gifts and Their Symbols

There are editors in the publishing world who are notorious for the extended changes and cuts they make in writers' texts. Autobiographers are also tempted to change or edit particular episodes of their lives. But there is a difference between the two kinds of editing.

Editing can be of great service if it helps us read with more understanding. But when it comes to the stories of our experience inseparably linked with that of others, changes and editing often only help us to misinterpret the meaning of what we have lived.

In the previous chapter, we argued that misreadings of our own experience affect our symbols and our commitments. R. D. Laing, in *The Politics of Experience,* has expressed this quite succinctly: "Our behavior is a function of our experience. We act according to the way we see things. If our experience is destroyed, our behavior will be destructive. If our experience is destroyed, we have lost our own selves."[1]

This chapter will explore the theological basis of honest story and symbol: God's unearned action in our lives and its purposes (justification). This chapter will not present a theological theory. Justification is part of God's praxis and our experience. The persistent question of this chapter is: can there be honest symbols of sacrament and worship without growing awareness of our deeper needs and God's continuing action in our stories?

Too often we cannot tolerate the flawed narratives of our lives or find in them any hopeful meaning that would help us face the future. In Christian terms, we do not find the footprints of God in our story. Augustine in his autobiography admitted to this way of looking at his own life: "You were right before me but I had moved away from myself. I could not find myself. How much less, then, could I find you."[2] Thus, Peter Brown aptly terms the writing of the *Confessions* for Augustine in the middle period of his life an act of therapy.[3] Augustine himself remarked how people marvel at the glories of nature "and yet they leave themselves unnoticed; they do not marvel at themselves."[4]

To misinterpret our experience is ultimately to deny that God has gone before us in that experience. It is the perfect alibi. We can limit our tasks and commitments, because we argue out of our self-serving stories that seek to excuse us from responsibility. By contrast, to be able to marvel at what God has done in us is to recapture the startling insight that prompted Mary's song of praise and that inspired Paul to teach us the doctrine of justification.

PAUL'S EXPERIENCE

The mystery of how God's presence both challenges and heals his people was, for Paul, a profound personal experience, not a sterile doctrine. Paul experienced justification in his life and then wrote about it. That sequence is but one more example of the axiom we discussed in the previous chapter: the law of worship is the law of belief.

If a more honest reading of our own complicated experience teaches us anything, it is this: we have a deep need of healing and strengthening for the sake of others. Need is usually understood in negative terms as the lack of something. There is, however, another, more positive interpretation of the term. As I have defined it elsewhere, need is the space for each one's growth today so that God's tomorrow will not happen without us.[5] We will return to this definition repeatedly throughout this chapter. The immediate question arising from such a definition is: how can our fragmented experience allow us to be aware of this need and God's healing?

Paul's answer is called the doctrine of justification: "The gift of God is eternal life in Christ Jesus our Lord" (Rom. 6:23). But this gift only intensified Paul's intuitions about his complex experience: "My inner self agrees with the law of God, but I see in my body's members another law at war with the law of my mind" (Rom. 7:22–23). Justification, in Paul's mind, dealt with a situation from which we cannot extricate ourselves without God's action. It is a radical impotence in the face of life's flaws and incompleteness. "All men have sinned and are deprived of the glory of God. All men are now undeservedly justified by the gift of God . . ." (Rom. 3:23–24).

There is no more concrete expression of this teaching and its context of worship than in Jesus' parable of the two men praying in the temple (Luke 18:9–14). The pharisee's recounted good works were not denied by Jesus, but implicit in the prayer of such a self-justifying man is the false satiety which needs the gifts of no one, including God. The disturbing conclusion of the parable, as so many exegetes have pointed out, teaches us quite clearly that the personal goodness out of which we might pray will never suffice. The parable astounds us with the depth of God's gratuitous gift: the sinner is enabled to cry to God out of his needy experience and return home justified. And yet there is nothing in the parable to suggest that the sinner would leave the notorious profession of tax collecting.[6]

Justification is the unearned power of God breaking into our lives. It reveals our profound need in such a way that it does not destroy us. It continually heals our wounds so that we might serve the others. As we shall see, it is a process that necessarily stretches over the whole of one's life. It is the source of the ongoing conversion we are called to and the root of all faith, and thus of all worship and sacrament.[7]

JUSTIFICATION IN A NEW LIGHT

Our real understanding of justification is symbolized in worship. But there was much in the sometimes scandalous and deteriorated worship and sacramental praxis of the late medieval church which seemed to contradict Paul's teaching about the unearned gift of salvation. (It seems evident that Luther's retrieval of the Pauline teaching was a deep reaction to some of the Corinthian worship of his day.[8])

The Reformers' analysis of the worship of their time induced them to call for more honest worship (*lex orandi*) which might generate more authentic doctrine (*lex credendi*).[9] The polemical context of the justification debate and general state of biblical scholarship in the sixteenth century did not favor the most productive use of Paul's specific development of this doctrine or its Old Testament precedents.[10] This permitted both Catholic and Protestant theologians to assume positions that were narrower than the biblical sources they were citing.

Even today this problem remains with us on communal and personal levels. Particular Christian churches, looking at one another's worship, can still wonder if there are not implicit denials of justification in certain sacraments or practices. For example, one Christian church might see in the frequent celebration of Eucharist by another denomination a subtle denial of the once-for-all character of Christ's death on the Cross.

Another example that touches both the communal and personal level is the revised and experimental rituals of worship and sacrament not only in the Roman Catholic community but in other Christian communities since Vatican II. That experience has reminded many Christians that the temptation to self-justification does not disappear with more relevant forms of worship.

In recent years, biblical scholarship has thrown new light on the dimensions of justification for the Christian life.[11] In the past, God's action in a person's life was seen as static, a "once-for-all" event. In contrast, Käsemann and other scripture scholars view God's justifying work, described by Paul, *as both gift and power.* The more we attempt at each life-stage to appropriate this gift/power for the service of others, the more we realize how much remains to be done before God's peaceable reign is a completed reality.

Furthermore, in the older view of justification, God seemed to be concerned exclusively with the individual. This interpretation effectively separated Paul's teaching on universal mission and eschatological goals from that on justification. Yet all God's gifts and the power which accompanies them point toward a larger concern: "Through us and in us he [God] reaches out towards the world to which we belong. Paul's doctrine of justification means that under the sign of Christ, God becomes Cosmocrator, not merely the Lord of the believing individual or the god of a cult."[12]

In other words, we are not privately justified and saved. As Käsemann pointed out, the New Testament teaches that we are only saved in serving others.[13] Paul's reaction to the self-justification of the Corinthian community is part of the same teaching. He saw the individual gifts of Christians as receiving their orientation from the mission of the Church. All these gifts continually build up a community whose unity already bespeaks the reign of God breaking in on us. In fact, this unity is a visible sign of God's work among us: "There are different gifts but the same Spirit; there are different ministries but the same Lord; there are different works but the same God who accomplishes all of them in everyone. To each person the manifestation of the Spirit is given for the common good. . . . But it is one and the same Spirit who produces all these gifts, distributing them to each as he wills" (1 Cor. 12:4–7, 11).

David Kelsey takes a similar position in attempting to specify the authority of Scripture for theological reflection: "The activities comprising the common life of a Christian worshipping community should all be ordered to one end, viz., shaping the identities of its members so that their forms of speech and action will publicly enact in the world the mission to which the community is called and by which it is defined."[14]

For Paul, these unifying gifts were hardly a theoretical consideration. He associated such service with disciples such as Aquila and Prisca (1 Cor. 16:19), Tychicus (Eph. 6:21), and Titus (2 Cor. 8:23). In our day, the figures of Mother Teresa of Calcutta and Dorothy Day personify this same Gospel service and its source, God's continuing action in their lives. Their examples gently goad the consciences of both Christians and non-Christians to give the service that makes us community.

Justification results in a "new creation" in Christ, concretized in specific communities of Christians whose shared presence is a challenging premonition of what the Kingdom of God will be like. Paul's "Body of Christ" theology and his ecclesial teaching are expression of this "new creation" which calls Christians, individually and communally, into the service of God's wider concerns and covenant.[15] Justification, then, must be seen within the call to "be sent" for the service of others. It is only in responding to such a call that the ecclesial identity of a Christian community becomes credible.

The final thrust of all mission and the ultimate purpose of the Church in this world is, of course, the reign of God. Paul's Christ is the enfleshment of God's justification, of his world creation and continuing faithfulness to it.[16] In the Kingdom, God's relation to his creation will be verified. Mission and Church will be no more because their purpose will have been realized in God's peaceable reign. In the meantime, justification is the freeing and strengthening call in which we are enabled, through Jesus' Word and Way, to believe even as we are sent into our time as his witnesses.

Although these positions are not shared by all exegetes,[17] they seem to me the most consistent with Paul's overall theology of salvation and Church. The systematic theologian cannot await an exegetical consensus before trying to develop a theological position on this central issue. There are certain principles of interpretation which we must all acknowledge in attempting to understand justification. The first principle has already been mentioned: the general context of Pauline thought is the overriding guide in understanding his particular concerns.[18] Paul's insight into how Jesus' death, proclaimed in mission, makes his peaceable Kingdom possible is at the core of his writing. Justification cannot be understood apart from this.

A second hermeneutical principle was also suggested earlier. Justification in Paul is a symbol for the multivalent mystery he was struggling to express theologically.[19] Everything he wrote of (freedom and unity in Christ, faith, Initiation and Eucharist, Church, mission, Kingdom) was rooted in the experiential knowledge that God makes the impossible possible and believable.

For the average Christian, the ordinary testing ground for the otherwise remote doctrines of justification is worship or a particular form of sacramental expression (the Eucharist, for example). As in Paul's case, we do not learn the doctrine and then have the experience of justification. The way a family celebrates a Baptism or a parish community the Eucharist on Sunday either invites or hinders a more conscious acceptance of God's unearned gifts.

WORSHIP GROUNDED IN JUSTIFICATION

Only those who have failing eyesight or hearing fully appreciate what sights and sounds have been restored to them through the use of eyeglasses or a hearing aid. Ordinary experiences, such as the colors of a sunset or conversations with a valued friend, are once again relished. Symbol also restores sight to the blind and hearing to the deaf for it reveals the reality of our world not perceived until now. It is our turn to learn what justification means as Paul did long ago, not from books but from the sights and sounds of God in our own lives. Religious symbols of worship and sacrament teach us to see and hear God again.

Worship as symbol reveals both our praxis and theory of justification and, thus, of faith and sacrament. Markus Barth, in his *Justification,* provides the appropriate context for our thesis: "There is no acceptance and praise of God's judgment except by a congregation in which different people and groups are united. . . . Therefore the celebration evoked by God's verdict can only be a common celebration."[20]

We have already suggested that the origin of Paul's justification teaching was in his own redemptive experience of Christ's work in him. This mystery was symbolized, and thus clarified, in Paul's worship long before it was partially expressed in his teaching. Theological expressions of the mystery of justification always remain partial and incomplete summaries of that symbolized experience. But how does worship, then, symbolize our experience of justification?

God does not write theoretical statements about his saving

presence. But worship is one of God's strongest praxis statements about that presence. Unlike the distracted schoolchild's cry of "present" in response to roll call, the worshipper's blithe "present" is challenged by the total and attentive presence of God. We can only respond to God in worship because he first loved us and attended to us.

In worship, we continue to learn our need so as to praise God for his justifying care. In worship, we also begin to perceive our gifts so as to do the work of the Gospel. In this sense, the justified Christian is, as the classical axiom states, both sinner and saint at the same time: sinner because what God has freely given has not been fully accepted; saint because the essential first step of salvation, God's justifying love, is already present.

In Christian worship, however, the Sign of the Cross has traditionally been used to emphasize the source and symbol of our justification. In the sacraments of Initiation and Eucharist, the Sign of the Cross became a privileged reminder to potential Corinthians to take up the cross (Luke 9:23) in turn.[21] The theology of the Cross, in fact, pervades all worship as a reminder of what justification entails.[22]

Within such a context, Baptism, for example, symbolizes the gift of justification while warning against a ritualist enthusiasm which would like to forget the Cross and believe that the end-time is already here and that faith can be replaced by one-sided rituals of resurrection. Eucharist does indeed proclaim the death of the Lord "until" (1 Cor. 11:26). For it counters the passive and self-serving response of Corinthians of any epoch with the active self-gift of a crucified, and thus glorified, Christ.

Worship, then, is not only premised on a faith, rooted in God's gracious gift, but is a clarification of how incomplete such faith will always be. Incomplete faith usually betrays itself in our praxis long before it does in our religious statements. When the members of a Christian community think they have done all that the Gospel asks, they can be startled by God's specific demands as imaged in their worship.

Such worship, for example, can occasion some unsettling questions for a middle-class community of American Christians which knows the plight of Cuban or Vietnamese refugees but does nothing as a Christian community to help. If Paul, in collecting money from the Gentile churches for the poor Christians of Jerusalem, could argue, "For if the Gentiles have shared in the spiritual blessings of the Jews, they ought to contribute to their temporal needs in return" (Rom. 15:27), how can the Christians of today, gathered for worship, be so unconcerned? If Christ could offer as a prophetic warning the example of the Jewish priest who, when returning from worship in Jerusalem, callously walks by the need of the mugged traveler (Luke 10:31), can we Christians blithely walk past the "bag-ladies" of our large cities in the same way?

Paul expressed this justifying and yet incomplete faith in a dialectical fashion, as both tempted and hopeful, possessed and yet not fully so: "Now that we have been justified by faith, we are at peace with God through our Lord Jesus Christ. Through him we have gained access by faith to the grace in which we now stand. . . . But not only that—we even boast of our afflictions! We know that affliction makes for endurance, and endurance for tested virtue, and tested virtue for hope" (Rom. 5:1–4). It is such a faith, grounded in the justifying work of a crucified and risen Lord, that finds its communal and individual symbolization in worship.

After Baptism the believer, with the encouragement of justification and in the power of the Spirit, is called to take part in the "new creation." But "new creation" for Paul was no vague theological label. Rather, it summed up the practical ways in which God's mystery of salvation was already made visible in the Roman Empire of his day: core groups of Christians, caring for the poor, visiting the imprisoned, sheltering the homeless. Even the Corinthians, after all, had done such Gospel tasks, if not consistently enough. For us also, the praise of our worship cannot be separated from our response to the work of the Gospel and its demands on us.

WORSHIP AND EXPERIENCE

Worship symbolizes this process of God's presence and our response. It goes beyond the rituals we use to the experience we may not yet have appropriated. Honest worship and sacrament constantly test our awareness of our need for the vivifying presence of God and our acceptance of the demands for commitment. That acceptance must be symbolized to remain both sincere and ongoing.

Matthew gave us a concrete example: "If you bring your gift to the altar and there recall that your brother has anything against you, leave your gift at the altar, go first to be reconciled with your brother, and then come and offer your gift" (Matt. 5:23–24). It is no accident that this moment of personal awareness occurs at worship, as we have already indicated. To accept that awareness, however, means that we interrupt our rituals and pay attention to our symbols. How many churches would be emptied on a Sunday morning if Matthew's example were taken seriously?

Honest worship, then, demands more aware contact with the praxis of our lives. We have come a step further in saying that God's justifying action in our lives is, in revealing ways, either accepted or rejected in that praxis. Even in the first century of Gospel living, James had to remind his community not only to "welcome the word that has taken root in you, with its power to save you," but also to "act on this word" (James 1:21–22). He then went on to give examples of Christians whose worship allowed them to look away from the need surrounding them: "Keep warm and well-fed," says the Christian to the needy from whom he tries to escape (James 2:15–17), a theme reminiscent of the Corinthian problem.

This is indeed a faith (and, therefore, a worship and sacrament) "that does nothing in practice" (James 2:17). Despite Luther's fears on the subject, James was not contradicting Paul when he said that "a person is justified by his works and not by faith alone" (James 2:24). On the contrary, James, like Paul, appreciated the larger purposes of God's power healing us: to serve as Jesus did.[23]

A contemporary illustration of the connections between a justifying faith, worship, and commitment is the problem experienced by many Christian parents who are concerned over their older children's unwillingness to "go to Mass" on Sunday or to receive other sacraments. Some parents insist that as long as their children are under their roof, they must "attend church." Though such parents are obviously well-intentioned, are they themselves clear about the distinction between mere "attendance at Mass" and real commitment to the Gospel, based on responsible faith?

Young adults have to begin to appropriate their Baptism of long ago, which they did not, as a rule, originally seek. Freely choosing Jesus as Savior and gratefully accepting the unearned and justifying love of God involves much more than physical attendance at Mass or "having the baby baptized Catholic." A Gospel faith involves the acceptance of a Jesus who described the radical commitment of the Gospel as "division": "From now on, a household of five will be divided three against two and two against three; father will be split against son and son against father . . ." (Luke 12:52). This Jesus told those who would believe: "Your light must shine before men so that they may see goodness in your acts and give praise to your heavenly Father" (Matt. 5:16).

Further, the worship and sacraments that we insist these young people participate in are privileged symbols of these demands for a shared, ecclesial commitment in the Gospel. We know that God's faithful presence permeates these symbols. But what of the responsibility of the celebrating community? Just as the Corinthians, by their sacramental praxis, could hinder the work of the Gospel and tear down the faith of some, cannot today's Corinthian communities do the same? Without excusing young people from their responsibility to search for the faith, we must also be responsible for the credibility of our celebrations of faith in the eyes of the young. Flawed Christians are not a stumbling block to these young people, but uncommitted Christians are.

Honest worship accurately reflects how we welcome God's larger vision and our participation in it. For worship and God's mystery should never be far apart. Traditional theology has always taught that God's invisible action should become more visible under the light of our symbols for the sake of others as well as for ourselves. Through God's power, we begin to "see" the meaning behind the reality of our lives. The very narrative of our lives that sketches God's free gift of love has the power to help us deal with the complexity and ambiguity that make up our world. Otherwise, how will the salvation history announced in our assemblies of worship ever become the narrative of our experience?[24]

A striking artistic illustration of this honest worship can be seen in the sculptured capitals in the Romanesque cathedral at Vézelay, France. Unlike the beautiful but highly stylized Gothic sculptures of Chartres, Vézelay's figures are a mélange of the ordinary events of life and the symbols of salvation and evil. The mystery of God's justifying action is dramatically underlined and contextualized by the seemingly banal themes of daily life and prayer portrayed so vividly on those columns. They are not out of place in a cathedral that is remarkable as a religious and artistic statement about a transcendant God contesting our lack of transcendance.

Another reason why the Corinthian problem is still with us is our tendency, communally and individually, to justify ourselves. We have already cited Luke's pharisee who cloaked his arrogance with his good works (Luke 18:9–14). Paul dealt with similar attitudes among the Corinthians: "Who confers any distinction on you? Name something you have that you have not received. If, then, you received it, why are you boasting as if it were your own?" (1 Cor. 4:7; also, 1 Cor. 10:1–12). In our own day, François Mauriac has given us a classic delineation of these same self-justifying attitudes in *The Woman of the Pharisees.*

Self-justification is more often the result of self-serving reading of our experience than of uninformed doctrine. We use the real or imagined good in our lives to counter any sense of our limitations, our finitude. As we grow, we learn the limits of our human activities, in the pain and joy of love, in sexual expression, in the fear of new careers and new commitment, and, finally, in the inevitability of death. Inseparable from this deepening awareness is another insight: God has none of these limitations.[25] This reality-testing is part of a responsible believer's presence: the realization that we come before God's presence as limited, needy, and dependant people.

Self-justifying Christians try to escape the recognition of personal limits by vaunting good works and attendance records at worship. Their "Lord, have mercy" is polite but does not ring true. Their "righteous" anger at a disappointing parent or a wayward son or daughter is supported by carefully marshalled arguments that ignore the unearned forgiveness God has given them. They use their orthodoxy to persecute others without questioning the honesty of their own praxis. (Thus, in the current religious debate of complex moral issues, such as abortion and the arms race, self-justifying attitudes on both sides of these questions confuse the real purpose of such discussion: a shared Gospel life!)

Once again, Paul taught us a lesson from his own experience. In 1 Corinthians, he had reminded his converts about the meaning of the Eucharist as a proclamation of the death of the Lord (1 Cor. 11:26). In the interim between this letter and 2 Corinthians, Paul suffered a great deal. These experiences demanded that he re-evaluate his ministry and gain a deeper acceptance of his own limitations as well as his gifts. When Paul once again spoke about the central doctrine of the death of Christ, he brought new awareness to a familiar theme: "He died for all so that those who live might live no longer for themselves" (2 Cor. 5:15). In other words, Paul learned from this difficult period of his life to measure self-gift and service in God's terms rather than his own. For God sometimes asks for service that we would never have thought of giving.

PRIVATIZED SYMBOLS?

In the last part of Chapter 1, the historical problem of how we appropriate the meaning and responsibility of sacrament was broached. It should be apparent after this initial exploration of justification as symbol that there can be no integral and responsible appropriation of these sacraments, unless the privatizing tendencies of our rituals are regularly challenged by God's justifying action in our lives. Such private uses are inseparable from the temptation to self-justification. Notions of "state of grace" and "the worthy reception of a sacrament," statically under-

stood, become an evasion of the Gospel's ecclesial and eschatological demands.

When we do not bring our experience to sacraments and worship, we tend to forget why we even need God's justifying action. This approach impoverishes our awareness of the mystery
of God in these sacraments. When we insist on the importance
of this subjective pole, we reaffirm the gratuity of God's gift of
salvation in the way we first knew it: not doctrinally but experientially.

There is another reason why worship and sacrament are so
easily privatized. We forget that our symbols must include others. Significant others are woven into the fabric of our lives.
Their needs are often the meaning of our gifts. Their pain is too
often the result of our misdirected self-concern. Our religious
symbols must respect and clarify our roles in each others' lives.
A mother and son, for example, are together at Sunday Mass.
Their concern for one another at that moment cannot be limited
to praying for each other's needs. Their life together and its
symbols have been too deeply influenced by one another for such
narrow remembrance. The way both mother and son praise
God, hear the Gospel proclaimed, and reach out for the Eucharist is influenced by much shared experience and mutual need.
The renewed service and healing, which is the eventual result of
honest worship, must touch the current lives of both people.

Within the Christian perspective, this basic intuition is transposed into a new key: the ecclesial shaping of our gifts for the
service of others. This is, in fact, the Pauline corrective to the
Corinthian community's sacramentalism. How do your gifts
build up the Church? Paul asks (for example, 1 Cor. 14). If
justification, in part, means that God precedes us in our experience and thus radically renews our possibilities as individuals
and as a community, did he not do this so that we might serve
others as Jesus did?

Sacrament, then, is a symbol that enables us to carry God's
abundant gifts to others. Historically, an *ex opere operantis* or
subjective responsibility for sacrament could never develop as
long as this ecclesial and mission aspect of God's symbols was
lacking. Once these larger dimensions are taken seriously, how-

ever, commitment to God's wider purposes is inextricably bound up with the individual and communal response in all sacrament and worship.

COMMITMENT AND SACRAMENT

Our argument up to this point runs this way: The Corinthian problem occurs when commitment is separated from worship and sacrament. Both the strength for and the demand of commitment is rooted in God's justification, as is our response in responsible faith and sacrament. Our lived experience is the field of God's action and our symbolic response. That is why both our praxis (as our response to reality) and worthwhile change reflect the very nature of that experience, as a continuing retrieval of our meaning for the sake of others.

For the sake of discussions in subsequent chapters, a working definition of commitment was given in Chapter 1. Commitment is a process that engages our whole person in responsive mutuality and widening responsibility. The accompanying responsibility is, as the Latin root indicates (*respondere*), a response to our own and others' needs and gifts, born of our gathered resources. As provisionally defined, these definitions would be acceptable to a large segment of humanistic psychologists and anthropologists.

The specificity of Christian commitment derives from the central teaching of Jesus: the Kingdom or reign of God. Jesus challenged his listeners to participate in building this Kingdom. The Pauline view of salvation, morality, Church, and sacrament cannot be properly understood apart from that context. Christian commitment, then, is a question of the fused purpose of many people gifted for mission out of their shared experience.

If worship and sacrament are framed by such a demand, then the question of the subjective dimension of worship and sacrament is indeed opened up. The danger of privatized rituals replacing sacraments is cast in a new light, and from a more positive angle, the dynamic nature of sacrament as mutual and committed presence is disclosed. Biblical symbols for the Kingdom of God attempt to describe the mutual presence of God and his people at the end of time. These people are strengthened by

God in stages of time to bear the pain and the liberation of disclosure symbols and sacraments, which invite them literally "to go with the others" once more.

Christian commitment, as defined in terms of the Kingdom of God, is more than the sum total of our private purposes and collective congruence. Such commitment illustrates concretely how the in-breaking presence of God, in his son Jesus, enables the impossible to be possible. Ordinary people who will always be sinners this side of the Kingdom of God can be effective symbol-carriers of his healing presence. This is the only experienced proof we have of a future Kingdom, described in terms of total presence.

The biblical term for the results of such committed response to God's presence is "participation." The English word, unfortunately, reveals little of the force inherent in the original Greek terms (*metexein/koinonia*). As Paul, Augustine, and Vatican II have used the term, participation is not measured by the gusto of our liturgical songs or responses. Rather, participation is both the test of justification, accepted time and again in our lives, and the ecclesial result of such acceptance—a joyful noise to the Lord and a liberating praxis. Such participation is always associated with a deepening commitment to God's Kingdom. In the last analysis, it is the only safeguard against a liturgical consumerism that cherishes relevant rituals but not the commitments they demand.

JUSTIFICATION AND NEED

How do the members of an average Christian community test the honesty of their efforts to keep accepting God's graciousness in their lives? The answer seems to be this: Christians may know that their worship reflects both God's gift and their response when they begin to see both their deep need and the surprising abundance of God's graciousness, and when they responsibly praise God for that unearned insight and experience. God's caring action, after all, has always gone before us so that we might gradually discover our shared and individual needs.

Psalm 107 offers us a lesson in how to announce our needs and sing our thanks: "Give thanks to the Lord, for he is good, for his kindness endures forever" (Ps. 107:1). The historical inspiration for this psalm was thanksgiving after the Jews' return from exile. To appreciate how current the psalm's staggering list of needs remains, imagine the "boat-people" of Vietnam or Cuba, the oppressed of El Salvador singing these verses: ". . . The way to an inhabited city they did not find. Hungry and thirsty, their life was wasting away within them. . . . They dwelt in darkness and gloom, bondsmen in want and chains . . . and he led them forth from darkness and gloom and broke their bonds asunder. . . . He hushed the storm to a gentle breeze and the billows of the sea were stilled. . . . He changed the desert into pools of water. . . . And there he settled the hungry and they built a city to dwell in" (Ps. 107:4–5, 10, 14, 29, 35).

The setting of the psalm is synagogue worship. The congregation is invited to see others' needs and thus rediscover their own. Paul Minear comments: "So, too, the psalm bespeaks a communal situation where many . . . join in a single song of joy: yet the experienced desolations and restorations are also individualized. By way of vivid language, worship serves to activate the eyes and ears of each worshiper, so that he becomes newly aware of the depths of need in himself and aware of how this need unites him to his fellows."[26]

The oppressed of every generation have found a model in such psalms for naming needs that spiral to praise. The American black spirituals, for example, eloquently take up similar themes in biblical fashion. Such songs as "Nobody knows the trouble I've seen, nobody knows but Jesus," "There is a balm in Gilead," "I couldn't hear nobody pray," and "Walk together, children" continue to astound and move us with their graphic pinpointing of need and their undiminished praise of God.

God's justifying work does not allow us to stare blindly at need or to listen deafly to cries wrung out of fragmented lives. On the contrary, it empowers the poor to be lavish, the deaf to hear, and the lame to be healed. What other meaning would Mary's prophetic cry have: "He has deposed the mighty from their thrones and raised the lowly to high places. The hungry he has given every good thing, while the rich he has sent empty away" (Luke 1:52–53)?

Justification as experienced in our lives and symbolized in

our worship may, however, be blocked by our naive or dishonest reading of our shared experience. Here is the subtle sin: to substitute false abundance for crying need and a quick handout for healing service.

Some men and women, for example, may be so consumed by their professional work and ambitions that they neglect the need of their spouses or teenage children. They perceive themselves as responsible parents because they financially support their dependents. Meanwhile, their sons and daughters are in search of sexual identity, role models, and empathy as they struggle through a difficult period of their own lives. These young people require not only compassionate understanding but parents who play a more active role in their lives. Teenagers have many ways of perceptively questioning the values and life-styles of their parents at the same time that they learn to love them more realistically. Parents have a rich and sometimes untapped experience to bring to such a dialogue with their children. How does such a family begin collectively to write a new version of Psalm 107?

PARABLES OF NEED

What can you give to people who think they have everything? Tell them the parables of need, as Jesus did. Two parables clearly delineate this need for us: "The Rich Fool" (Luke 12:13–21) and "The Rich Man and Lazarus" (Luke 16:19–31).

Luke's rich fool, at first glance, seems rather responsible in preparing for his future as he assesses his good harvest. He decides to build larger grain bins for his bumper crop and looks forward to the security it will give him. His sudden death as God's judgment is puzzling. It poses the question: is there no justified abundance? To underline the tension of the parable, we must remember that the biblical image of God as a banker who collects the good works of the pious for future return.[27] Following this line of reasoning, anyone who gives to the poor lends to God.

Any Jew could also be presumed to know that our riches have the name of the poor written upon them.[28] Jews were to aid the poor out of their total income and not simply from their superfluity.[29] The fool of the parable is obsessed with his own long-range security and not the need to be a beneficiary of God's abundance. As verse 21 thunders, "That is the way it works with the man who grows rich for himself instead of growing rich in the sight of God" (Luke 12:21).

The same Lucan message is announced in the parable of the rich man and Lazarus. The poor man Lazarus (meaning "God helps") starves while the rich man feasts. They both die and the roles are reversed. While the rich man is in torment, he sees Lazarus afar off in bliss with Abraham. The rich man asks Abraham to be allowed to warn his five brothers, "so that they may not end in this place of torment." In response to the rich man's plea that they would listen to someone risen from the dead, Abraham replies: "If they do not listen to Moses and the prophets, they will not be convinced even if one should rise from the dead" (Luke 16:31).

It is easy to misread this parable which is neither a social commentary on the problem of poverty nor a theology of suffering. The parable draws an insightful sketch of six brothers whose blindness to their own and others' need will not permit them to see even the searing truth of a revelation from God:[30] The deeper need for growth and self-gift was never experienced and, thus, the Kingdom of God could offer little to people who believed they had everything already.

With such parables Jesus challenged his listeners to welcome the reign of God. The parables reveal our need. The needy alone cry out lustily for God's gift that we call justification. The satisfied can only nod politely in appreciation for the unneeded thoughtfulness of God.

The promise of these parables is the same as that of Jesus' healing miracles: the Messiah brings sight to the blind, hearing to the deaf, sanity to the crazed. The teaching behind this promise is even more startling: to genuinely experience salvation we must acknowledge our real blindness, our deafness, our deep-seated confusion about who we are and what we were meant to be. The Lord is truly among us when we refuse to say that we are full when we are in fact starving, surfeited when we are in dire need. A theology of Church, worship, and sacrament can only be grounded in such realization of need.

HUNGER AND THIRST: SYMBOLS OF ABUNDANCE

The teaching of these parables is uncomfortably clear. None of us will enjoy God's future feast if we do not learn to hunger and thirst out of our present need. The Scriptures present hunger and thirst as a privileged image that accurately depicts the deeper needs of our lives. Matthew's beatitude of "hungering and thirsting for righteousness" (Matt. 5:6, and its counterpart in Luke 6:21) is a summary of the biblical images of our need for God's compassionate presence.

Isaiah's panoramic tableau of God's future feast of gourmet food and drink on the tops of the mountains also incites us to hunger for God's abundance:

On this mountain the Lord of hosts
  will provide for all peoples
A feast of rich food and choice wines,
  juicy, rich food and pure, choice wines.
              [Isa. 25:6]

The complementary scene is evoked in the transposed key of warning in Isaiah 65:

Lo, my servants shall eat, but you shall go hungry;
My servants shall drink, but you shall be thirsty;
My servants shall rejoice but you shall be put to shame;
My servants shall shout for joy of heart,
But you shall cry out for grief of heart, and howl for anguish of spirit.
              [Isa. 65:13–14]

In Proverbs 5:15 and 9:5, a supporting image of thirsting for wisdom is equally telling. God's covenant is depicted as a cumulative symbol: the food and drink of the satisfied. Isaiah 55 is the song of such a covenant people:

All you who are thirsty,
  come to the water;
You who have no money,
  come, receive grain and eat. . . .
Heed me and you shall eat well,
  You shall delight in rich fare. . . .
I will renew with you the everlasting covenant.
              [Isa. 55:1–3]

Revelation 7:16 gives a new meaning to the familiar thoughts of Isaiah when it sings:

Never again shall they know hunger or thirst,
  nor shall the sun or its heat beat down on them,
  for the Lamb on the throne will shepherd them.
He will lead them to springs of life-giving water,
  and God will wipe every tear from their eyes.[31]

These magnificent insights, however, challenge us with a paradox: the needs of others are the door of insight into our own needs. Like a parent responding to a growing child, we perceive our own needs in new ways as we struggle to respond to others' needs. Commitment to God's work must be rooted in the continual discovery of such need if we are to share in building God's tomorrow.

But hunger and thirst always take place in time. Messianic feasts have not yet begun—and with good reason. God's future feasts require our present commitment to others. Future tenses are a normal part of God's promise, because so many still tenaciously cling to their present false abundance. What Christian who has prayed for his or her "daily bread" does not know this? St. Jerome reminded Christians of his day that Aramaic-speaking Christians prayed, "Our bread for tomorrow give us today."[32]

God's revelation of our hunger and thirst must urge us to commitment that will transform our sense of time. Joachim Jeremias sums it up well:

Only when one has perceived that the petition asks for bread in the fullest sense, for the bread of life, does the antithesis between "for tomorrow" and "today" gain its full significance . . . in a world of hunger and thirst, the disciples of Jesus dare to utter this word "today"— even now, even here—already on this day, give us the bread of life.[33]

LIMIT-EXPERIENCES OF OUR NEED

Many adults, recalling the first day of school in their young lives, might classify that event as a turning point. Through such events we learn something more about the fragile character of our identity and the surprising boundaries of our experience.

The child's safe world and its mythical figures are exploded by new expectations of teachers and new challenges of peers. We can continue to learn something about our needs from such experiences throughout our lives, as the example of Dr. Borg in *Wild Strawberries* illustrated.

We learn best to experience and speak of justification out of such events in our own lives, which may be identified as limit-experiences. Even the banal events of our stories (such as the first day of school) can dislocate the continuity of our lives as much as the years spent in the Nazi concentration camps of the thirties or the months spent as a hostage in the eighties dramatically ruptured the lives of others. It is not the details of an event but the paradox that it introduces into our lives that qualifies the event as a limit-experience. Such experiences contest our assumptions about our talents and tasks, and force us to question our place in the lives of others.

As Paul Ricoeur has brilliantly demonstrated, religious language aids us in perceiving the religious dimension of our ordinary human experience. We are invited to redirect our energies and vision as a result of experiences as diverse as the death of a friend, a diagnosis of cancer, the birth of a child, or the first awareness of love.

The human condition as such includes experiences which baffle discourse and praxis . . . religious language projects its radical vision of existence and ordinary experience makes explicit its potentially religious dimension. . . . But the Biblical text only finds its final referent when ordinary experience has recognized itself as *signified*, in its breadth, its height, its depth by the "said" . . . of the text.[34]

The result of a limit-experience, honestly dealt with, is a process of moving from the deepened awareness of our need and the service it reveals toward a redefined commitment to that service (for example, a new willingness to help the sick after we ourselves have experienced a serious illness). Limit-experiences test the meanings we have given to our lives. Ricoeur views Jesus' words as discerning the core of ordinary experience. Describing the "disclosing quality" of religious language, Ricoeur says that such language "dislocates our project of making a whole of our lives . . . a project which St. Paul identifies with self-glorification. . . ."[35]

This is not the place to restate the whole question of religious language and its use in worship. For our purposes, Ian Ramsey's now familiar insight supports our connection between limit-experience and the language of committed praise. In his classic *Religious Language,* he points out that such language allows for discernment and disclosure so as to permit response and commitment.[36] If we wish to appropriate rather than repeat, for example, the insight that "God is love," we must factor in our own experience of love (which is a limit-experience).

To say that "God is love" is thus to claim that the word "God" can be given in relation to a total commitment (alternatively labelled "love") which can be approached by considering these partial commitments which we normally describe in terms of the word "love."[37]

In other words, the use of such language is only possible because it is nourished by our symbolized experience that reveals our need and abundance as well as God's love.

The Christian experiences the disclosing quality of such religious language in, above all, parable and sacrament.[38] Yet very early in the Christian experience there was a tendency to hear parables and celebrate sacraments in a moralizing way. By moralizing a parable or sacrament, I mean that we narrow its meaning (for example, "The Good Samaritan parable teaches us to be compassionate," or "Baptism makes us members of the Church") and, therefore, the mystery of the Kingdom of God that the parable or sacrament symbolizes. We unconsciously mute the limit-expression of a parable ("Those invited were unworthy—call in the beggars and maimed") or a sacrament (celebrating "the death of the Lord until") so that its connection with the conflicts and limit-experiences of our lives is not perceived. With such muting, justification, need, and service tend to become privatized. Often enough, we avoid the higher cost of commitment that disclosure and limit-experiences demand.

Rituals of worship are dangerous unless they renew our awareness of the limits in our lives. Such limits teach us paradoxically the gift and purpose of the time and space we have left. Like Paul we are again taught the meaning of Christ's death and our justification through the life-experiences that pose questions previously unasked and, perhaps, suggest answers unexpected even now. The twentieth-century Christian begins to ask questions inspired by the parables and sacraments of his or her life: Am I among the unworthy invited guests or among the beggars and maimed who gladly go into the God's feast? Am I only a member of a church or a committed disciple of a Gospel way of life?

In brief, justification teaches us our need in the limiting experiences that are part of each life. Such limit-experiences provide us with a new religious vocabulary of praise and need.

SUMMARY

Justification enables individuals and communities to be honest editors of their complex experience. This unearned and continuing action of God in our lives discloses our limits and need and thus sharpens our response and commitment. But this process is symbolized in each stage of life where worthwhile conflict once more becomes the door to new religious meaning and commitment.

The psalms are a model for worship with their alternating cries of praise and frustration springing from life's situations. The parables complement such prayer because they insist on the unexpected mystery both of God's Kingdom and our lives. God's justifying action in our lives provides the material for the psalms and parables of our lives for these psalms and parables usually reflect crises that we have neither chosen nor anticipated. Here God's complexity meets ours. Some bless him, others curse. Some are strengthened for service, while others find only excuses for their stunted lives.

The retrieval of both parables and sacrament, with their unsettling call for commitment, will require a new openness to these crises for they invite us to pass through more than one cycle of orientation, disorientation, and reorientation. Since these events are played out on the changing stages of our lives, we will discuss in Chapter 3 the developmental nature of our religious experience and commitment.

NOTES

1. R. D. Laing, *The Politics of Experience* (New York: Ballantine Books, 1967), p. 28.

2. St. Augustine, *Confessions*, 5, ii, 2, as cited in P. Brown, *Augustine of Hippo* (Berkeley: University of California Press, 1969), p. 168.

3. Ibid, p. 165.

4. St. Augustine, *Confessions, 10, viii, 15, as cited in ibid, p. 168.*

5. M. Searle, ed., "Symbols of Abundance, Symbols of Need," *Liturgy and Social Justice* (Collegeville, Minn.: Liturgical Press, 1980), pp. 72–102; here, p. 76. Some of the material from that article appears throughout this chapter.

6. I. H. Marshall, *The Gospel of Luke: A Commentary on the Greek Text* (Grand Rapids, Mich.: W. B. Eerdmans, 1978), p. 681.

7. The Cardinal of Trent's sane reminder to his fellow theologians has been more forgotten than remembered in theological discourse: *Fides autem non est pars, sed janua, prout aliorum sacramentorum* ("Faith, however, is not a part but the door, as it were, of the other sacraments"). See *Concilii Tridentini Actorum Quartae Volumen Prius* (Fr. Brisgoviae: Societas Goerresiana, 1961), vol. 7, p. 293.

8. One has only to read John Hus' *On Simony* (1413) for a catalogue of sacramental abuses in that century. The translated text may be found in M. Spinka, ed., *Advocates of Reform: From Wyclif to Erasmus* (Philadelphia: Westminster, 1953). This does not deny the theological background of Luther's retrieval. Cf. B. Hagglund, *The Background of Luther's Doctrine of Justification in Late Medieval Theology* (Philadelphia: Fortress Press, 1971).

9. The Tridentine response to the theological and pastoral challenge of the question has been too narrowly evaluated on both Protestant and Catholic sides until recently. Küng's gentle reprimand to Barth in this respect remains, some twenty years later, valuable to us all. Cf. Hans Küng, *Justification: The Doctrine of Karl Barth and a Catholic Reflection* (New York: T. Nelson, 1964), p. 104.

10. For a discussion of the non-Pauline writings in this area, see K. Kertelge, *Rechtfertigung bei Paulus* (Münster: Aschendorff, 1967), p. 45; J. A. Ziesler, *The Meaning of Righteousness in Paul: A Linguistic and Theological Inquiry* (Cambridge, England: Cambridge University Press, 1972), pp. 142–46.

11. For a summary of this research and its implication, see R. A. Duffy, "Justification and Sacrament," *Journal of Ecumenical Studies* 16 (1979): 672–90. This chapter accepts the basic insights of Käsemann and his disciples and has benefited from some of the insights originally published in the above article.

12. E. Käsemann, "Justification and Salvation History," *Perspectives on Paul* (Philadelphia: Fortress, 1971), p. 75.

13. E. Käsemann, *Exegetische Versuche und Besinnungen* (Göttingen: Vandenhoeck und Ruprecht, 1960), I, p. 296.

14. D. Kelsey, "The Bible and Christian Theology," *Journal of the American Academy of Religion* 48 (1980): 385–402; here, 387.

15. C. Müller, *Gottes Gerechtigkeit und Gottes Volk: Eine Untersuchung zu Römer 9–11* (Göttingen: Vandenhoeck und Ruprecht, 1964), pp. 104, 107–8.

16. P. Stuhlmacher, *Gerechtigkeit Gottes bei Paulus* (Göttingen: Vandenhoeck und Ruprecht, 1965), pp. 205, 207–10.

17. Although R. Bultmann and H. Conzelmann have disagreed with Käsemann's position, the sharpest critique has come from G. Klein, *Rekonstruktion und Interpretation* (Munich: Kaiser, 1969).

18. G. Eicholz, *Die Theologie des Paulus im Umriss* (Neukirchen: Neukirchener Verlag, 1977²), p. 227.

19. P. Ricoeur, *The Symbolism of Evil* (Boston: Beacon, 1967), p. 278.

20. M. Barth, *Justification* (Grand Rapids, Mich.: Eerdmans, 1971), p. 69.

21. By the third century, the Sign of the Cross was used in Initiation rites in the West. Jungmann describes it as a bridge between Baptism and Eucharist; see *The Mass of the Roman Rite: Its Origins and Development*, 2 vols. (New York: Benzinger, 1950), vol. 1, p. 296.

22. See, in particular, P. Stuhlmacher, "Achtzehn Thesen zur paulinischen Kreuzestheologie," *Rechtfertigung: FS E. Käsemann*, eds. J. Friedrich, W. Pöhlmann, and P. Stuhlmacher (Tübingen: J. C. B. Mohr, 1976), pp. 509–25, esp. pp. 517–18.

23. For an excellent comparison of the two writers on this question, see M. Dibelius, *James*, rev. H. Greeven (Philadelphia: Fortress Press, 1976), pp. 174–80.

24. J. B. Metz deals with this brilliantly in "A Short Apology of Narrative," in J. B. Metz and J. P. Jossua, eds., *The Crisis of Religious Language, Concilium 85* (New York: Herder and Herder, 1973), pp. 84–96.

25. K. Rahner, for example, arrives at this same position from a metaphysical concern in his *Foundations of Christian Faith* (New York: Seabury, 1978), pp. 30–70.

26. P. Minear, *To Heal and To Reveal: The Prophetic Vocation According to Luke* (New York: Seabury, 1976), p. 61.

27. See J. Derrett, "The Rich Fool," *Heythrop Journal* 18 (1977): 131–51.

28. Ibid, 143–47.

29. Ibid, 137–38, esp. n. 36.

30. J. Jeremias, *The Parables of Jesus* (New York: Scribners, 1963), pp. 186–87.

31. See the comments of J. M. Ford, *Revelation: Introduction, Translation and Commentary* (Garden City, N.Y.: Doubleday, 1975), p. 128.

32. J. Jeremias, *The Prayers of Jesus* (Naperville, Ill.: A. Allenson, 1967), pp. 100–02.

33. Ibid, p. 102.

34. P. Ricoeur, "Biblical Hermeneutics," *Semeia* 4 (1975): 29–148; here, 128.

35. Ibid, 125.

36. I. Ramsey, *Religious Language* (London: SCM Press, 1957), p. 36. Complementary approaches will be found in C. Raschke, "Meaning and Saying Religion: Beyond Language Games," *Harvard Theological Review* 67 (1974): 79–116 (esp. 105–10) and M. H. Prozesky, "Context and Variety in Religious Language," *Scottish Journal of Theology* 29 (1976): 201–13.

37. Ibid, p. 52.

38. For a similar position, see E. Schillebeeckx, "The Crisis in the Language of Faith as Hermeneutical Problem," in Metz and Jossua, *The Crisis of Religious Language*, pp. 31–45; here, pp. 39–42.

CHAPTER 3

Conflict as Crossroads for the Christian

In his *Confessions,* Augustine retrieved his past experience so that he could serve God in the present. This was no sterile exercise, for he knew the value of memory: "Thus I will pass beyond memory; but where shall I find thee? . . . If I find thee without memory, then I shall have no memory of thee; and how could I find thee at all, if I do not remember thee?"[1]

One of the best places to watch Augustine as he uncovered his past experience and the message behind the facts of his story is in the Ninth Book of his *Confessions,* where he dealt with his mother's life. As if to illustrate Erikson's remark about how our life-stages "cogwheel" with those of others, Augustine re-examined incidents in Monica's life and their impact on him. Certainly few mother-son relationships have been recorded with such insight.

Augustine was thirty-three when his mother died (A.D. 387), at the age of fifty-six. Though he had shared a uniquely deep relationship with his mother, Augustine admitted: "I closed her eyes; and there flowed in a great sadness on my heart and it was passing into tears, when at the strong behest of my mind my eyes sucked back the fountain dry and sorrow was in me like a convulsion."[2] He fought the strong feelings within him throughout that day, but his attempt to intellectually master his sorrow only intensified it: "And so with a new sorrow I sorrowed for my sorrows and was wasted with a twofold sadness."[3] Only when Augustine once more reviewed the life of his mother within the frame of her death could he at last cry: "And it was a solace for me to weep in thy sight, for her and for myself, about her and about myself. Thus I set free the tears which before I repressed, that they might flow at will, spreading out as a pillow beneath my heart. And it rested on them, for thy ears were near me."[4]

Monica's death was a turning point for her son. She had played a significant and positive role on many levels of his life. While he had been aware of this influence, Augustine had not yet drawn out its full meaning so as to bless God out of his story. The conflict her death presented was revelatory to Augustine because it put his relationship with both his mother and God in a new light. His new perspective, gained from the vantage point of this conflict, is similar to Paul's: if people would only know themselves as people, then what songs would they sing to God.

What is consistently striking about our examined experience is the dimension of conflict and even crisis to be found there. Augustine's account of his mother's death and his reaction is but one example of such conflict. Each of us has similar examples, both dramatic and ordinary, of conflict to be drawn from each period of our lives.

The two operative words are experience and conflict. Experience has always been valued in Christian thought, but recent theological thinking and praxis has accorded it new importance.[5] The word *experience* is difficult to define because it includes both our attempts to work through the events of our lives and the actual paths we have taken. It entails no value judgment on whether these attempts and journeys were good or bad.

It is helpful to consider the Latin root of *experience: experior,* meaning "someone who knows by trying." Experience is at least the narratives of our shared story with our attempts and failures, decisions and indecisiveness, insights and blindness, commitments and irresponsibilities. Experience should ideally be revelatory, unfolding the implications of an event. Experience should be a door to the meanings, new and old, of our lives.

The words *conflict* and *crisis*, in current usage, have dramatic connotations. *Conflict* always suggests an unsettling event, while *crisis* refers to a decisive moment or a turning point. Conflict is, often enough, a prelude to crisis. In this chapter, we will use the conflicts and crises of our lives both to review our current commitments and to prepare for future ones. Like Augustine, we ought not to turn to these autobiographical events without discovering God's justifying action and the quality of our Gospel commitments. Charles Winquist describes this process:

Talk of God is deeply intertwined with the talk of self. Revelation is a problem for the self. That is, the vision of a new reality requires adjustment in self-understanding. The autobiographical form points to that knowledge which appropriates talk of transcendence into self-understanding. Augustine realized that before we can possess what we have seen and transform insight into understanding initial insight must be embodied in our living.[6]

ERIKSON'S LIFE-STAGES

Erikson's pioneering work in the study of life-stages has been treated extensively elsewhere.[7] My limited purpose here is to trace the broad outlines of his approach to life-cycles. Erikson learned much from Freud's insights, but actually developed his theory out of his clinical experience of listening to the life stories of his patients. He complemented his efforts to develop a cohesive theory with attempts to reconstruct the historical and psychological climate and mind-sets of complex historical figures such as Luther, Gandhi, and, more recently, Jefferson.[8]

Even in this following passage, Erikson underlines the element of conflict when he distinguishes two ways of analyzing a person's experience:

A genuine case history gives an account of what went wrong with a person and of why the person fell apart or stopped developing; it attempts to assign to the particular malfunctioning a diagnosis in line with the observer's psychodynamic views; and it arrives at therapeutic suggestions as to what could or can be done to reactivate a sounder development in this and in similar cases. A life history, in contrast, describes how a person managed to keep together and to maintain a significant function in the lives of others. . . . The hero of a life history, of course, usually has a chronic neurotic conflict as a significant part of his whole make-up but he becomes a case only insofar as the conflict has him.[9]

In analyzing the development of personality, we recognize three related areas of growth: the psychosexual, the psychosocial, and the cognitive. Broadly speaking, psychosexual development would recall Freud's work in uncovering the various relationships we must work through in order to achieve a healthy set of values and to love the valued people in our lives. Psychosocial or ego development theory points out the tasks that each growth period demands of us. The theory of cognitive development, particularly as advanced by Jean Piaget, traces the gradual ability to abstract, to intellectualize. Erikson's principal concern is psychosocial growth (although the psychosexual dimension cannot be entirely eliminated from consideration).[10]

The overall shape of the human life-cycle, according to Erikson, is a continuous process. There is a schedule of strengths or "virtues" to be achieved sequentially by working through certain tasks during each period of our lives. The virtues are a result of a synthesis of old experience and new needs and challenges.[11] The failure to integrate a needed virtue into our lives results in its negative counterpart: in the growing child, for example, trust versus mistrust, autonomy versus shame and doubt, initiative versus guilt; in the adolescent, industry versus inferiority and identity versus identity confusion; and in the adult, intimacy versus isolation, generativity versus self-absorption, and integrity versus despair.[12]

Each of Erikson's eight stages is characterized by the specific task it involves. The infant's first task, for example, is to acquire a basic trust that allows the mother to be out of sight momentarily without the infant becoming anxious. To fail or refuse such a task is to begin to develop mistrust.[13] By the time the growing child has worked through the tasks of autonomy and initiative, he or she is ready for the task of industry, that is, being productive in both school and simple work situations. Mastering this task prepares the adolescent for the struggle for identity which is "the accrued confidence that the inner sameness and continuity prepared in the past are matched by the sameness and continuity of one's meaning for others, as evidenced in the tangible promise of a 'career.'"[14]

The young adult then faces the challenge of intimacy: "the capacity to commit [oneself] to concrete affiliation and partnerships, and to develop the ethical strength to abide by such commitments."[15] The final two stages that should cap adult life are generativity ("the widening concern for what has been generated by love, necessity, or accident"[16]) and integrity (which demands a wisdom that is "a detached concern with life itself, in the face of death itself"[17]).

Although Erikson's stages of life provide a convenient starting point, life changes will be discussed here more in terms of motivated growth than in chronological age categories. More recent studies emphasize how individualistic growth is and how similar changes in people can be brought about by different events. Each historical epoch also makes its own demands on a particular age group. For example, we cannot easily equate the experience of an American twenty-year-old during World War I with that of an American twenty-year-old during the Vietnam War.

THE DYNAMIC OF CRISIS

The choice underlying the task of each life-stage is parent to crisis or conflict. "Such crises occur in man's total development sometimes more noisily, as it were, when new instinctual needs meet abrupt prohibitions, sometimes more quietly when new capacities yearn to match new opportunities, and when new aspirations make it obvious how limited one (as yet) is."[18]

In other words, just when we have finally achieved a certain equilibrium in our lives by succeeding in one life-task, new tasks (and, therefore, new demands) are presented to us. Our first reaction may be one of fear that we do not have the resources necessary for these new tasks. We have not yet perceived how previously acquired strengths have prepared us for the challenge of a new life-stage. To use a musical analogy, crises are the dissonances of our lives quietly prepared for well in advance and quite capable of eventual resolution.

Our life-stages are characteristically connected and intertwined with those of others. Autobiography always implicates the significant people in our lives. Their life struggles and strengths have often enough touched us. Erikson sums it up well: "For man's psychological survival is safeguarded only by vital virtues which develop in the interplay of successive and overlapping generations. . . . Here, living together means more than incidental proximity. It means that the individual's life-stages are 'interliving,' *cogwheeling with the stages of others which move him along as he moves them.*"[19]

Although the interdependence Erikson describes might seem rather obvious, it is often enough a dimension of experience missed in our interpretations. One can, for example, read St. Augustine's autobiographical *Confessions* and see his mother only in terms of her considerable influence in his life. But this would be to miss the fact that Monica's own growth and crises were part of Augustine's dialogue with his experience.

Against these broad descriptions of life-stages, the wider dimensions and purposes of conflict can be appreciated. Erikson's definition of change, already cited, should now take on new meaning: "True change is a matter of worthwhile conflict for it leads through the painful consciousness of one's position to a new conscience in that position."[20] The "painful consciousness" to which Erikson alludes is, in the main, the result of the unfinished nature of our growth and the seeming inadequacy of our gifts to confront each new period of our lives. The "new conscience," as we shall see, is the deeper sense of responsibility and the wider commitment we give to our world in the time left us. Within such a process, Erikson has every right to call this "worthwhile conflict."

Such an understanding of conflict, then, emphasizes the positive over the negative aspects of growth. Erikson has qualified these conflicts as moments of decision between integration and retardation and, therefore, as critical steps and turning points.[21] If honestly dealt with, such conflicts will help clarify and integrate our previous experience while opening up new possibilities for the new chapters of our story. For a new sense of identity is the result of many old ones, questioned and reshaped. Erikson sums it up well in this way: "And I would postulate that any new identity must develop the courage of its relativities and the freedom of its unconscious resources; which includes facing the anxiety aroused by both."[22]

Against the backdrop of this larger canvas, a more complete definition of experience is possible. Any comprehensive description of what we have lived must include the shape of crises and change in our lives with our resulting reassessment and repledging of our resources. It must trace both the continuity of our gained strengths and the discontinuity of our conflicts.[23]

Erikson firmly states that the ultimate test of the way we deal with our experience is the meaning we draw from it. "Any span of the cycle lived without vigorous meaning, at the beginning, in the middle, or at the end, endangers the sense of life and the meaning of death in all whose life stages are intertwined."[24] But experience does not always yield up its meanings easily. As already mentioned, experience must be symbolized if we are to begin to understand its meanings for our lives and its implications for our future.

At the heart of such a retrieval of our experience will be the way in which we deal with conflict. Although not always apparent at the time we experience it, conflict is a positive force that accurately reveals the focus and direction of our lives. Even when a personal crisis is framed by larger social or historical conflicts beyond the individual's control, it contains the potential for decision and growth. The victims of Nazi Germany of the thirties had to deal with the crises of their own lives within such a larger frame. Some were spurred on to greater achievement as human beings in this hostile environment, while others seem to have been crushed by it. We cannot always choose our conflicts, but we can usually emerge from them with greater integrity and vigorous meaning for our lives.

STORIES OF CONFLICT

Self-serving stories are not difficult to compose. They report experience, in general, and conflict, in particular, in ways that excuse us from responsibility for present or future tasks. In short, such storytelling does not find God's action in selected areas of our experience and, thus, misses the full meaning of the events remembered. Such partial narratives of our experience are a poor source of religious symbol and theological reflection.

Erikson has proposed three areas of identity which any exploration of our experience must include. First, there is the factual dimension of our story: the dates, events, background, and persons involved. A second area is the manner in which we are willing to experience the factual data we blithely set down. And, finally, the test of such a retrieval of our story is an emerging new sense of reality "that has visionary qualities and yet energizes in the most concrete tasks" (for example, Gandhi's leadership in the passive resistance movement against English colonialism in India).[25] But the process cannot stop here. The ultimate outcome should be "a new *actuality,* a new way of relating to each other, of activating and invigorating each other in the service of common goals."[26] The new sense of identity forged out of such insightful narration will inevitably encompass our "community," those core groups who both challenge and support us (such as our families, our professional friends, and the members of our religious community).[27]

A brief but insightful example can be found in 2 Corinthians 12. As Barrett comments, "Paul never wrote a more personal letter."[28] Paul had just given a lengthy account of the hardships he endured as an apostle in order to silence his adversaries. He then begins an autobiographical account of an ecstatic experience that he had fourteen years earlier. He is appropriately vague about the details of such a rapture and his humbling "thorn in the flesh, an angel of Satan to beat me" (2 Cor. 12:7), though the wording suggests the impact of the experience. The tension in Paul's narrative is related not to his remembered rapture but to the personal conflict he recounts, the "thorn in the flesh."[29]

Paul summed up the new perspective he gained in narrating the experience: God had taught him once again that his grace was sufficient for his work as an apostle, for "in weakness power reaches perfection" (2 Cor. 12:9). Paul concluded that, "When I am powerless, it is then I am strong" (2 Cor. 12:10). This insight and the commitment it elicited was the result of

Paul's confronting his conflict and learning to pray out of it ("Three times I begged the Lord that this might leave me"—2 Cor. 12:8). The result was that Paul took up his apostolic work with renewed meaning and vigor.

THE NATURE OF CONFLICT

In reframing their experience, Paul and Augustine underlined the dissonant features of that experience (Paul's "thorn in the flesh" and the disloyalty of his converts, Augustine's initial inability to express grief at his mother's death). The conflicts that emerged questioned their naively reported stories and urged them to examine their implications and the unassimilated areas of their lives. Such conflicts give new definition to the landscapes of our lives.

Paradoxically, conflict is a potential catalyst for strengthening the unity of our experience. For the very demands that are the result of conflict reveal the rich resources we bring from our past lives to our present and future work. We are forced to see the interlinking of tasks long ago worked through and the resulting commitments newly achieved. To trace such events may indeed be to realize that God writes with crooked lines, as Claudel suggested. We are shocked into the realization of how current dissonances of our lives were anticipated. It seems to be the very nature of experience, properly attended, to provide us with questions that crescendo in intensity over the intervals of our lives. (Well-known examples are easily found in Erikson's analysis of the lives of Luther and Gandhi.)

Conflict may reveal itself as a question of choice or change at a new crossroad in our lives as a result of a failed marriage, a second career, retirement, the decision to put a parent in a nursing home. In reviewing our experience, we begin to understand how conflict prepares the way for commitment. When the tension between the continuity of our experience and the shock of discontinuity can no longer be avoided, we are forced to decisions and choices. While thirty-three-year-old Augustine was forced by his mother's death to review the implications and directions of his conversion, Paul found he had to take a hard look at his future in ministry.

A forty-five-year-old Christian of today who has always thought of himself or herself as a motivated and responsible person (continuity) may sense a loss of motivation as a parent, in his or her work, or a loss of courage and purpose in the face of a serious illness or accident (discontinuity). This present conflict questions what priorities that forty-five-year-old person will maintain and how he or she will use the time that is left. Daniel Levinson describes a similar turning point:

Barnes felt that he had reached an impasse in his life. For some time now, he had been unable to make the critical decisions that faced him. Worse, he could not find a basis on which to make them. His Dream of becoming a scientist of the first rank had formerly given meaning to his life and provided clear goals. The enterprise of the first half of his life was now completed, but his Dream was unrealized and, as it seemed, unrealizable. Suddenly there was nothing to strive for. Life had no meaning.[30]

In responding to such conflict, we are asked both to adapt to a new situation and to summon up new resources. This involves dealing realistically with the affective dimensions of a conflict and knowing the limits of our tolerance (as Augustine did with his mother's death). It also requires the sabbatical or time out needed to reassess the new meanings in our lives and the courage to recognize that some conflicts may never be fully resolved this side of the Kingdom.[31] Above all, the invitation to grow into new roles and to internalize old values must be recognized. For Paul, this meant not only defending his apostolic role but being challenged in his ministry by the growth of the very communities he had founded.[32]

Simply stated, the very patterns in our lives that assure a certain regularity and direction also seminally contain the promise of painful growth. (Thus, in the life of Paul the very pattern of faithfulness and zeal for the Law provided continuity even in the jarring revelation on the road to Damascus. Through conflict, then, we can see the continuity of our lives in new depth because the unsuspected implications of those continuing patterns are revealed.

Dissonance and discontinuity are part of conflict. The unknown elements introduced into our lives are, in effect, a series of demands that we did not foresee and will not, at least initially, countenance. The immediate effect is the discovery of how incomplete the comprehensive symbols (religious and otherwise) of our lives are. This healthy but painful revelation can allow the "new" in our experience to be incorporated into these life-symbols and thus assure their continuing relevance.

Finally, conflict must force us to ask hard questions about how we are to pledge our remaining time and resources. Once the underlying assumptions of our lives are contested, we must return to basic questions that we thought had been settled, questions of personal giftedness and its meaning for others, and the complementary questions regarding the use of the space and time we have left. The young adult can afford to take some risks, for example, in making a career decision. The forty-five-older does not always have that luxury.

In brief, an individual's synthesis at each life-stage is bought at the price of new commitment engendered by conflict. This is most apparent in Erikson's later stages, where each needed virtue requires further commitment. For example, Erikson defines fidelity as "the ability to sustain loyalties freely pledged in spite of the inevitable contradiction of value systems."[33] Any responsible married couple knows the cost of such fidelity. "Sustaining loyalty" has demanded of each partner a continuing reassessment and recommitment to each other in view of different needs and values.

More recent research, in looking for the design of each person's life, has highlighted the crucial choices we must make. The challenge of each life-stage questions our presumptive meanings.[34] But the transition between life-stages affords us the time to answer questions, accomplish tasks, and make choices.[35] The process of modifying our life structures will not only touch all our roles and relationships. Such discontinuities and demands will call for a profound reappraisal of our shared meanings shaped in time.[36]

Again, Levinson provides us with a summary example:

By 45 Richard Taylor had created the basis for a new life and was entering Middle Adulthood. He and his wife had stabilized the marriage and started a family. He had established good adult relationships with the grown sons of his first marriage. Now a senior member of his writers' world, he was assuming various leadership and mentoring functions with the younger generation of Black writers . . . . While less driven by ambition, he looked forward to a creative, responsible life in the future. . . . Though he was a senior writer, he still had his mark to make. . . . His prospects were brighter than ever before, but the challenges and difficulties were greater.[37]

CONFLICT AND THEOLOGY

Paul and Augustine have been our mentors in helping us to see the conflicts of each particular life-stage as a doorway to new strengths and tasks in our lives. But the systematic theologian might legitimately question whether conflict is an adequate notion in the eventual development of a theology of religious commitment. This theological hesitation must be answered if we are to show the connection between symbols of experience and sacraments of the Kingdom.

First, however, I must state some of the limitations inherent in Erikson's approach. He has given us a cosmic and intuitive view of the growing person and seems to have captured, in its broad outlines, the complexity of human development. But from the viewpoint of the structural-developmental theories of Piaget, Erikson's concept of a "stage" is imprecise and vague.[38] In reading Erikson, we can easily forget, as Robert Kegan reminds us, that "persons are not their stages of development; persons are a motion, a creative motion . . . of life itself."[39] (As a result, there have been efforts recently to rethink the problem of growth in terms of life-span development.[40])

Ultimately, each of these approaches with its own special concerns has a certain validity. As Fowler points out, Piaget, Kohlberg, and Erikson are describing "the patterns of knowing, reasoning, and adapting . . . applicable to us all."[41] Our interest in religious symbols of growth and commitment parallels and benefits from such work.

In particular, I should point out the connections and differences between James Fowler's work on life-stages of faith and my own work. This demands, in turn, a brief review of the broad outlines of Fowler's work. Inspired by Piaget's work on cognitive development and Kohlberg's work on moral stages, Fowler began to investigate "faith as a patterned process of thinking and valuing" by means of the interview method.[42] He has proposed six nonevaluative stages of faith that are structural descriptions of the "long and painfully dislocating process of relinquishment and reconstruction."[43] He calls the structuring activity of this process of faith the "logic of conviction" in which the "knowing self is continually being confirmed or modified in the knowing."[44]

This process, according to Fowler, begins in early childhood with an intuitive-projective stage (in which the perceived faith of adults is key), moves through a mythic-literal stage two (in which the religious heritage of the community is appropriated, usually at the schoolchild age), and enters a synthetic-conventional stage three of adolescents and many adults (in which faith becomes a source of orientation, values, and identity). In stage four, the individuative-reflective stage, the individual takes responsibility for his or her commitments. (Fowler calls the independent, critical judgment behind these responsible choices the "executive ego."[45]) The conjunctive faith of stage five involves a reunion of the symbolic and conceptual in the believer's life, usually not before mid-life. Finally, six, the stage of universalizing faith, is best described initially by naming some examples: Gandhi, Mother Teresa of Calcutta, and Thomas Merton. Fowler's description of such individuals is challenging: "These persons embody costly openness to the power of the future. . . . Their trust in the power of that future . . . accounts for their readiness to spend and be spent in making the Kingdom actual."[46]

Erikson's stages continue to have a general influence in Fowler's thought.[47] But in his recent work, Fowler notes that a perfect correlation between advancement in Erikson's psychosocial stages and his own stages of faith does not exist. People can remain on stage two or three of faith, for example, throughout their whole adult lives. "This fact affects the way they experience and deal with the psychosocial crises Erikson has identified, but it in no way means that it will avoid or bypass them."[48] In other words, a young adult in stage two of faith will not bring the same depth and values to his or her struggle for intimacy as someone in stage three or four of faith.[49]

Fowler's stages are a major contribution to the discussion of the development of faith and the brief sketch just given can only hint at the richness of his thought. But he is dealing with faith as a universal dimension of human living and contrasts it with the traditions, revelations, and liturgies of particular religions.[50]

My concern is faith within the Christian tradition. This means that my ideas of experience, growth, and symbol are defined by the Pauline teaching on justification. In contrast with Fowler's search for universal characteristics of faith (applicable to Gandhi or Mother Teresa), my delineation of commitment in faith is influenced by Gospel service and mission. Above all, the eschatological vision that characterizes people in Fowler's stage six of faith is for me the inspiration of all faith and sacrament.

There are two important areas of shared concern in Fowler's thought and my own. The first is that of conversion and commitment. Fowlers defines conversion as "a significant recentering of one's previous conscious or unconscious images of value and power and the conscious adoption of a new set of master stories in the commitment to reshape one's life in a new community of interpretation and action."[51] This is no one-time event but a process that must continue throughout a lifetime and that may correlate in different ways with formal structural stage-change in faith.[52]

Secondly, Fowler correctly insists on the importance of imaging faith. ("Faith . . . gives form and content to our imaging of an ultimate environment."[53]) This imaging is tied to our "master stories," which "disclose the ultimate meaning of our lives."[54] Such imaging cannot be separated from the way in which we use symbols at each stage of faith in our lives.

Fowler has clearly established the connection between growth in faith and the stories of the many people he has interviewed. Our concern is with people who use the symbols of Christian worship and sacrament. How do the stories of their experience relate to their use of symbol? In Chapter 2, we summed up the Pauline teaching on justification as: God goes before us in our story. One writer has paraphrased it in this way: theology is always biography and biography at its best will always be theology.[55] From the Christian viewpoint, God's creative and gracious work constantly surprises us at the oddest times of our lives.

This is why life-conflict is revelatory for theology. In each life-stage, conflict is specifically revelatory of God's offer of salvation within the context of mission. But this call to mission is not a theme simply stated. Rather it is a theme whose full beauty and meaning is only achieved through development and, even, variation. If we were to trace Paul's idea of salvation, for example, from those first days after his conversion to his early years as a prophet in the church at Antioch to the final difficult years of his missionary efforts, we would see neat definitions of mission constantly contested and enlarged by the interlocking needs and gifts of the many people touched by Paul.

For mission is not only proclaiming what God has done to us but listening to what others can proclaim in turn. In such dialogue, assumptions are dismissed and apprenticeship in God's mystery of salvation is afoot once more. We tend to define mission, after all, in our own terms. Like Paul, however, succeeding generations of Christians have been forced by the unforeseen directions of their own and others' lives to reassess the service needed of them "on account of others." The very commitment we offer God in response is never adequate in terms of our gifts and needs or God's cosmic plan. Conflict can forcefully remind us of this.

Conflict is also revelatory of our radical sin which betrays itself during each life-stage in our life-style and value system. We often arrive at comfortable or despairing assessments of ourselves, but the result is the same: restricted and self-serving sharing of the meanings we carry for others. This flawed character of our lives allows us to refuse quietly any expanded demand for mission and self-gift. The "Johnny-one-note" of salvation is the outcome: those who do not awaken to development and dissonance are ill-prepared for the final resolution of a great theme.

Conflict, then, is a revelatory wedge, disclosing in our life processes the limited horizons that we too easily assign both to

God and to ourselves and the symbols that seem to demand nothing of us. Without such conflict, our minimal notions of being "justified," "washed in the blood of the Lamb," and "in the state of grace" let us remain content in both our stagnant commitments to God's work and our mindless rituals. Commitment, on the other hand, is the direct beneficiary of conflict that is attended to.

THE COMMITTED LIFE-STAGE

In the previous chapter, justification was re-seen as a powerful symbol through which God's loving, enabling action in our lives evokes our response from a specific context, our current life-stage. The worship in which we cry out to God is ultimately based on such a dialogue. But if the symbols of our hunger and thirst, as currently etched out in our lives, are not seriously attended to, then we will not hunger for the summary symbol, God's final and continuing feast of the Kingdom.

In the last analysis, even God's justification does not exist for our own or our church communities' private purposes. The overriding parable is that God's unwarranted and free gift will permit us neither to "earn our salvation" nor to stand in idle holiness and watch others build the peaceable Kingdom.

Paul's own awareness of the responsibility of mission is striking: "If the building a man has raised on this foundation still stands, he will receive his recompense; if a man's building burns, he will suffer loss. He himself will be saved, but only as one fleeing through fire" (1 Cor. 3:14–15).

Paul thus employs the analogy of building a house to outline the tasks and responsibilities of ministry. He is well aware that our works do not bring about our salvation. But he is equally insistent that the test of our belief is our service.[56] This service, in turn, is clarified by the needs of others, played out in a certain historical time and against a specific socio-economic background. For our service to remain committed, we must be willing to be instructed time and again by the conflicts of our own and others' lives.

OUR PARABLES

Such instruction comes by parable. A strong case can be made for parable as that which overturns our expectations.[57] Unlike in story or allegory, the dynamic of the parable revolves around the tension of the unexpected. The unlikely or, worse, the unacceptable become heroes of Jesus' parables. Because the present versions of these parables in the New Testament were redacted and allegorized in their early transmission, the original sharpness of the dissonance, left unresolved, can go unnoticed.[58]

Yet Jesus' purpose in telling such discomforting stories was to awake his listeners to their real need. The sinner is blind and deaf to God's vision of the future and how it should change the present. The messianic task is to make the blind see, the deaf hear, and to let the poor receive the Good News.

The choice of anti-heroes in Jesus' parables (a Samaritan, an unjust judge, a dishonest manager, etc.) made his audience uncomfortable. Behind such choices we hear the persistent Gospel questions: Who is my neighbor? What do the wise of this world know that we do not? Why are the tax-collectors and prostitutes going into the Kingdom of God before us? Thus, parable sets up conflict. This conflict is rooted in God's expectations being larger than our own and self-serving contracts blocking God's demands. Jesus took stories of his day and transformed them into parables of conflict.[59] In turn, our stories are the necessary material of any parable that recounts this same conflict. The implicit teaching of parable is, of course, God's justifying and enabling action, already providing an incipient experience of his reign. This is the hard edge of parable, cutting away our excuses and calling out for fresh answers to God's old questions.

The Christian community and its individual members have no choice but to find their own parables in their experience. Otherwise, true change and conversion will elude them. Erikson's definition of change, discussed earlier, parallels this process of parable. The worthwhile conflicts of our parables lead us invariably to a painful consciousness of our position. The reward of such an endeavor is a new conscience in our current life-stage.

This new conscience is the commitment to the new meanings of God's salvation, opened up by the parabolic process. As Ricoeur rightly emphasizes, metaphors "both gather and diffuse. They gather subordinate metaphors and diffuse new streams of thought."[60] But parable as metaphor does this through "the tension between the different patterns of crisis and response."[61] The very extravagance of Jesus' parables (what village, celebrating a marriage feast, would close its door on frivolous virgins? asks Ricoeur) intensifies the tension of crisis in the parable.[62]

Thus, all the parables that invariably answer the question, "What is the Kingdom of God Like?" re-orient us by disorienting us.[63] Here is where the limit-experiences and limit-expressions mentioned in Chapter 2 assume their full force. Once again there is a disclosure of God's purposes from a rereading of our own parabolic experience and an evoking of new commitment to those purposes.

Parables often enough begin where our reasonable expectations trail off. Let me offer one example of how a couple began to write a parable so as to incite the reader to deal with his or her own parables. A Christian couple in their mid-forties had successfully raised two children. Their seventeen-year-old son, however, became dependent on drugs. He eventually resorted to robbery to support his addiction and, late one evening, was caught by the police.

In trying to deal with this couple's bewilderment and pain, I suggested some parable writing. They could not write such a parable, of course, without including the strengths and conflicts of their current life-stage as well as their struggle to understand and empathize with their son's situation.

How did these parents begin their parable? The facts of their relationship with their son and the experiences underlying it had to be told. The tension and tasks of the current life-stage were factored in: "The onset of his adolescence was so abrupt and startling that we became confused." The final lines of the parable, while not resolving the tension, overturned the couple's expectations: "The mother recalled that when their son was only nine he had been invited to read St. Paul's letter to the

Corinthians at morning mass. 'Love is always patient and kind,' he began but interjected, 'Love isn't easy.'" The mother now came to the crucial, last line of the parable: "'Love never fails,' wrote St. Paul. 'But sometimes it does,' protested the child."

This last line was not a cry of despair but of insight. It did not provide answers but a challenge, retrieved from the ashes of these parents' experience: love must constantly be redefined. Here was the beginning of this couple's search for vigorous meaning at a new point of their lives. This Christian couple found such a parable no less surprising than the Jews found those parables that showed a Samaritan as loving his neighbor or the Prodigal Son as the Beloved Son. The pain of this couple's parable is not unlike that of the good-living Pharisee who did not go home justified or the righteous Elder Brother who had no party given for him.

Parable is always a symbol of God's future vision contesting our cherished blindness. We are tested and measured by the length and breadth of God's peaceable Kingdom. God justifies us, and Jesus tells us parables so that we might commit our time and resources to building that Kingdom. Parable can overcome the blindness of imperfect Christians who too easily excuse themselves from the tasks of the Kingdom because of their naive understanding of their own stories. We recapture our stories and their true meanings and surprises through parable. As Ricoeur suggested, parable as metaphor gathers the disparate themes of our lives into a new and liberating synthesis that enables new commitments in providing new meanings.

COMMITTED WORSHIP AND PARABLE

Pelagianism is the fear of parable. Technically, it refers to a fifth-century heresy that confused God's love and our flawed goodwill. Pelagius proposed that if we only tried harder, everything could be changed. Christians, he argued, are radically free to be perfect. Peter Brown has summarized this heresy as "the need of the individual to define himself, and to feel free to create his own values in the midst of the conventional, second-rate life of society. . . . For the Pelagians man had no excuse for his own sins, nor for the evils around him. If human nature was essentially free and well-created and not dogged by some mysterious inner weakness, the reason for the general misery of men must be somehow external to their true self. . . ."[64]

Pelagianism, in its contemporary form, describes liberals and conservatives, for example, who insist on their own brand of orthodoxy in order not to deal with orthopraxis ("right practice"). Pelagianism sums up the attitudes of people who "take sacraments" but do not take responsibility for what these sacraments signify (for example, parents who baptize their infant although they are not practising Christians). Pelagianism can explain why we find it easier to talk about the frequent reception of a sacrament (such as daily Mass) than about the cost of commitment of such symbols.

This naive view of human life and God's initiative in that life is exposed by parable. We see the flawed character of our goals and ambitions at the same time that we are reminded of what God enables us to do. The delicate balance between awareness and hope, between conscience and commitment are maintained in parable. This is why parable leads to true worship, while Pelagianism leads only to polite liturgical chortling. A Pelagian does not cry out to God out of real need, but speaks to him out of false strength.

The history of Christian worship has always been haunted by the fear of Pelagianism, and not without reason. Since the time of the prophets there have been constant reminders about the dangers of a self-justifying worship that promotes relevant ritual but irrelevant commitment. "I hate, I spurn your feasts, I take no pleasure in your solemnities . . . then let justice surge like water, and goodness like an unfailing stream" (Amos 5:21, 24).

Pelagianism, however, is usually a subtle temptation for good people. While theoretically admitting the need of God's justifying action, in practice it allows both the worshipping community and the individual to restrict the service and mission called for in a specific place and time. Luther and Calvin, for example, warned against abuses in medieval sacramental worship which were, in praxis, Pelagian. The obvious aspect of this type of worship is the quiet arrogance of good works performed or a too-facile "state of grace." The less obvious dimension of this attitude is the consistent refusal to allow worship to question what God has done in our lives and, consequently, what new service this calls for.

The fear of Pelagianism is a two-edged sword. It can be a prophetic warning against blithe worship. But such fear can also serve as a theological excuse for avoiding the question of religious commitment and worship. The result is an emphasis on what God does in worship (*ex opere operato*) with only a brief nod to what response God might expect of people gifted by so much love. (Both Roman Catholic and Protestant worship, as suggested in Chapter 1, continues to be touched by this problem in different ways and sometimes for different reasons.)

SUMMARY

It seems quite appropriate, at the end of a chapter on conflict and the Christian, to suggest a thesis: *worship, rooted in the gratuity of God's justification, is tested by ecclesial and eschatological responsibility*. Conflict is the vantage point from which we see the growing meaning of God's justification in our lives. The very genesis of the conflict for the Christian is the deeper commitments the reign of God demands of us. Although these demands are fleshed out in the usually banal incidents of a particular life-stage, this does not mute the challenge. In fact, it is our own parables, forged out of our experience, which correct our Pelagianism and lead us back to a worship in spirit and truth (John 4:24).

How, for example, does the couple whose parable we discussed earlier, receive sacraments more honestly as a result of their current crisis? Their theories and praxis of mutual love and how God's grace touches their lives have been called into question. Their worship and sacraments cannot remain unaffected by this.

Worship not only symbolizes God's presence but our response to it. Just as this worship must bear the marks of our current and past history, so too must it symbolize our new commitments to God's work wrung out of our conflicts. This is not Pelagian worship. After all, does the New Testament anywhere teach

that personal and communal responsibility for the building of
the reign of God in any way jeopardizes the unique and gratuitous nature of redemption?

But our worship cannot be limited to evoking private commitments. Mission and service have never been envisioned outside
the context of the church community we live in. Paul's advice is
still pertinent: "Since you have set your hearts on spiritual gifts,
try to be rich in those that build up the church: (1 Cor. 14:12).[65]
The effort to be a disciple community will involve a recommitment of our gifts in view of others' needs. Can there be honest
sacraments among teenagers, for example, if their Penance or
Eucharist does not demand new insight and care for the elderly
of the community?

In brief, true worship is animated by an obedient faith that
accepts the tasks of the reign now as Jesus did. Irresponsible
worship, on the other hand, like its Corinthian model, is a personal or communal self-justification that wants the reign of God
but not the work that must precede it. Worship in spirit and
truth cannot be separated from the eschatological accountability
that separates a Stoic ethic from a Gospel morality.[66] The ultimate test of this honesty is, as we shall see in the next chapter,
our own real presence, responding to that of a risen Lord among
us.

NOTES

1. St. Augustine, *Confessions*, 10, xvii, 26.
2. Ibid, 9, xii, 29.
3. Ibid, 9, xii, 31.
4. Ibid, 9, xii, 33.
5. In addition to the works of J. E. Smith, already cited in Chapter 1, I
   would add: E. Herms, *Theologie—eine Erfahrungswissenschaft* (Munich:
   Kaiser, 1978); *Revelation and Experience*, Concilium 113, ed. E. Schillebeeckx and B. Van Iersel (New York: Seabury, 1979), esp. D. Mieth,
   "What Is Experience?" pp. 40–53.
6. C. Winquist, *Practical Hermeneutics: A Revised Agenda for Ministry*
   (Chico, Calif.: Scholars Press, 1980), pp. 25–26.
7. For an excellent introduction to Erikson's work, see D. Browning, *Gener-
   ative Man: Psychoanalytic Perspectives* (Philadelphia: Westminster, 1973).
   For additional bibliographies, see L. D. Cain, "Life Course and Social
   Structure" in R. Faris, ed., *Handbook of Modern Sociology* (Chicago:
   Rand McNally, 1964), pp. 272–309; J. A. Clausen, "The Life Course of

Individuals" in M. W. Riley et al., eds., *Aging in Society* (New York: Russell Sage, 1972), vol. 3, pp. 457–514; W. Sze, ed., *The Human Life Cycle* (New York: Aronson, 1975), pp. 719–25.

8. E. Erikson, *Young Man Luther: A Study in Psychoanalysis and History* (New York: W. W. Norton, 1958); *Gandhi's Truth: On the Origins of Militant Nonviolence* (New York: W. W. Norton, 1969); *Dimensions of a New Identity* (New York: W. W. Norton, 1974).

9. Erikson, *Dimensions of a New Identity*, p. 13.

10. For a good discussion of this problem, see J. Loevinger, *Ego Development* (San Francisco: Jossey-Bass, 1976), pp. 78–79; 173. As Loevinger notes, there is a certain confusion built into Erikson's system because there is no clear delineation at any given point between the several related strands of development (ibid, pp. 173–74).

11. See Browning's remarks, *Generative Man*, pp. 160–61.

12. For the early statement of these stages, see E. Erikson's *Childhood and Society* (New York: W. W. Norton, 1950, 1963), pp. 247–74.

13. "Trust born of care is, in fact, the touchstone of the actuality of a given religion. All religions have in common the periodical childlike surrender to a Provider . . ." (ibid, p. 250).

14. Ibid, pp. 261–62.

15. Ibid, p. 263.

16. Erikson, *Insight and Responsibility*, p. 131; also, *Identity: Youth and Crisis* (New York: W. W. Norton, 1968), pp. 138–39; *Childhood and Society*, pp. 266–68.

17. Erikson, *Insight and Responsibility*, p. 133.

18. Ibid, p. 139; see also, *Identity: Youth and Crisis*, p. 95.

19. Erikson, *Insight and Responsibility*, p. 114.

20. Ibid, p. 30.

21. Erikson, *Childhood and Society*, pp. 270–71.

22. Erikson, *Dimensions of a New Identity*, p. 103; also, pp. 27–28.

23. There has been a certain questioning of the life-stage theory's underlying chronological age categories and implicit definitions of change and continuity. Life-span development would opt for a more individualistic definition of growth and for its study in terms of age cohorts; see O. Brim and J. Kagan, eds., *Constancy and Change in Human Development* (Cambridge, Mass.: Harvard University Press, 1980).

24. Erikson, *Insight and Responsibility*, p. 133.

25. Erikson, *Dimensions of a New Identity*, p. 33.

26. Ibid; see also, Erikson's *Toys and Reasons: Stages in the Ritualization of Experience* (New York: W. W. Norton, 1977), p. 61.

27. Erikson, *Dimensions of a New Identity*, pp. 27–28; see also, Erikson's *Life History and the Historical Moment* (New York: W. W. Norton, 1975), pp. 19–20.

28. C. K. Barrett, *A Commentary on Second Epistle to the Corinthians* (New York: Harper & Row, 1973), p. 32; see also, his discussions of this passage, pp. 305–18, with bibliography.

29. Ibid, p. 315. This might be compared with Erikson's own analysis of the "Vision" experience in Bergman's film *Wild Strawberries;* see Erikson, ed., *Adulthood* (New York: W. W. Norton, 1978), pp. 1–31.

30. D. Levinson, *The Seasons of a Man's Life* (New York: A. Knopf, 1978), p. 270.

31. G. E. Vaillant, *Adaptation to Life* (Boston: Little, Brown, 1977), p. 10.
32. See B. Holmberg, *Paul and Power* (Philadelphia: Fortress, 1978), esp. pp. 43–56.
33. Erikson, *Insight and Responsibility*, p. 125.
34. Levinson, *Seasons of a Man's Life*, p. 49. I employ the term *task* throughout this book in a broader sense than Levinson's use of *role*.
35. Ibid, pp. 18–19; 52–61.
36. Ibid, pp. 330–35; 86; 199. For a somewhat different perspective, see E. Weisskopf-Joelson, "Meaning as an Integrating Factor," in C. Bühler and F. Massarik, eds., *The Course of Human Life* (New York: Springer, 1968), pp. 359–83; see also, R. Kuhlen, "Developmental Changes in Motivation During the Adult Years," in B. Neugarten, ed., *Middle Age and Aging* (Chicago: University of Chicago, 1968), pp. 115–36.
37. Levinson, *Seasons of a Man's Life*, p. 293.
38. See J. Fowler, *Stages of Faith: The Psychology of Human Development and the Question of Meaning* (San Francisco: Harper & Row, 1981), p. 48. The author, in a fictional conversation among Piaget, Kohlberg, and Erikson accurately delineates the complementary and differing aspects of their positions.
39. R. Kegan, "There the Dance Is: Religious Dimensions of a Developmental Framework," *Toward Moral and Religious Maturity* (Morristown, N.J.: Silver Burdett, 1980), pp. 404–40; here, p. 407. This, in turn, brings out some of the limitations of the Piagetians: "Cognition to the neglect of emotion; the individual, to the neglect of the social; the epistemological to the neglect of the ontological . . . stages of meaning-constitution, to the neglect of meaning-constitutive process" (ibid, p. 406); see also O. G. Brim and J. Kagan, eds, *Constancy and Change in Human Development* (Cambridge, Mass.: Harvard University Press, 1980), p. 537.
40. Brim and Kagan, eds., *Constancy and Change*, pp. 12–14.
41. Fowler, *Stages of Faith,* p. 89.
42. J. Fowler and S. Keen, *Life Maps: Conversations on the Journey of Faith,* ed. J. Berryman (Oak Grove, Minn.: Winston, 1978), pp. 35ff.
43. Ibid, p. 38. Defining a life-situation becomes progressively more difficult at each stage, whether we are speaking of more advanced moral thought (Kohlberg) or commitment in faith (Fowler). Methodological approaches may account for some of these difficulties. See, for example, J. M. Murphy and C. Gilligan, "Moral Development in Late Adolescence and Adulthood: Critique and Reconstruction of Kohlberg's Theory," *Human Development* 23 (1980): 77–104; see also, P. J. Philibert, "Theological Guidance for Moral Development Research," *Essays in Morality and Ethics,* ed. J. Gaffney (New York: Paulist, 1980), pp. 106–25. In the higher stages of development of faith, an interviewer may have difficulty finding candidates; see Fowler and Keen, *Life Maps,* pp. 83–95.
44. Fowler, *Stages of Faith,* p. 102.
45. Ibid, p. 179.
46. Ibid, p. 211. These stages are described more fully in Fowler and Keen, *Life Maps,* pp. 39–99, and Fowler, *Stages of Faith,* pp. 122–213.
47. Fowler, *Stages of Faith,* pp. 106–09.
48. Ibid, p. 107.
49. "In some respects, we might say, it is not even the same crisis for persons at these three different stages" (ibid).

50. Ibid, pp. 9–15. Fowler, of course, sees faith and religion as reciprocal (ibid, p. 9).

51. Ibid, pp. 281–82. Fowler links his discussion of conversion to the contents of faith.

52. For the relation between formal structural stage change and conversional change in faith, see ibid, pp. 281–86.

53. Ibid, p. 24.

54. Ibid, p. 277.

55. J. S. McClendon, *Biography as Theology* (Nashville, Tenn.: Abingdon, 1974), esp. pp. 87–111.

56. See, for example, H. Conzelmann, *First Corinthians* (Philadelphia: Fortress, 1975), pp. 76–77.

57. See, for example, J. D. Crossan, *The Dark Interval: Towards a Theology of Story* (Niles, Ill.: Argus, 1975).

58. For an overall treatment of the problem and current liturature, see J. Roloff, *Neues Testament* (Neukirchen-Vluyn: Neukirchener, 1977), pp. 90–107.

59. For a typical example in the parable of the great feast (Matt. 22:1–10; Luke 14:15–24), see J. Jeremias, *The Parables of Jesus* (New York: Scribners, 1963), pp. 186–87.

60. P. Ricoeur, "Biblical Hermeneutics," *Semeia* 4 (1975): 94.

61. Ibid, 101.

62. Ibid, 114–19.

63. Ibid, 121–28.

64. P. Brown, *Augustine of Hippo* (Berkeley: University of California Press, 1969), pp. 346, 349.

65. See J. D. G. Dunn, *Unity and Diversity in the New Testament* (Philadelphia: Westminster, 1977), pp. 193–94; see also, J. P. Sampley, *Pauline Partnership in Christ* (Philadelphia: Fortress, 1980), pp. 67–68, for a more general statement.

66. A. Peters, "Systematische Besinnung zu einer Neuinterpretation der reformatorischen Rechtfertigungslehre," *Rechtfertigung im neuzeitlichen Lebenszusammenhang* (Gütersloh: G. Mohn, 1974), pp. 107–25; here, pp. 114–16; 124–25. No one has better expressed this than E. Käsemann: "At this point the doctrines of worship and Christian ethics converge. . . . The universal priesthood of all believers, called forth and manifested in the whole range of activities, now appears as an eschatological worship of God . . ."; see "Worship and Everyday Life, A Note on Romans 12," *New Testament Questions of Today* (Philadelphia: Fortress, 1969), pp. 191–92.

CHAPTER 4

A Question of Presence

In today's media language, we describe certain people as having "presence." Though such "presence" is hard to define, we know which people possess it. Pope John Paul II, for example, seems to be a person with "presence." In his world travels, he has impressed large groups of people with his forcefulness and charismatic personality. But such terms as *forceful* and *charismatic* do not satisfactorily define that elusive experience we call "presence." Our contact with such a person leaves an indelible impression on us, as if, in turn, some response were still expected of us.

Real presence is a rare experience for many people today. Perhaps that is why we are struck by the uniqueness of someone who has presence. It serves as a reminder of how easily we can work and play, live and even die with minimal demands made on us to "be present." Suddenly, we realize that we have gone for a long time without any effort to attend to others or even be aware of ourselves.

There are a number of reasons for this. Many people live and work at a faster pace than their parents did and under conditions that are often impersonal, if not depersonalizing. In social and professional situations, we find ourselves going through superficial public rituals that seem designed to act as buffers against any real contact or presence with others. We learn to cherish anonymity, which, after all, is an escape from presence.

Ralph Keyes has expressed it this way: "Thus do we become more free of each other as we also grow less known. We cherish this freedom and loathe it. We curse the loneliness of anonymity, yet crave its power. We want to stand revealed to each other, and do everything possible to avoid it."[1]

When Mother Teresa stood up to speak at the Eucharistic Congress in Philadelphia a few years ago, she took some bread, broke it, and extended it to the audience, saying: "This is the bread of the poor." This simple action and explanation was transformed by her presence into a prophetic action-word that challenged her listeners to a response in presence and service. In much the same way, the prophets of the Old and New Testaments performed an action and gave its explanation. The message was always the same: a call to covenant people to come back to God. This action-word of a prophet is called an *oth* in Hebrew—literally, a "sign."

Isaiah, for example, walked naked around Jerusalem and explained the meaning of this act: God will strip Egypt and Ethiopia of its power (Isa. 20). Agabus, a New Testament prophet, performed a similar action-word in tying himself up with Paul's garment and prophesying the apostle's imprisonment (Acts 21:11–14). Such action-words are filled with the power and presence of God to alert his people to their lack of covenant presence.[2] Here we find God's presence calling out the presence of his people. These are no idle rituals but effect what they signify.

Jesus' presence made a powerful impression on his contemporaries. Mark described it this way: "The people were spellbound by his teaching because he taught with authority and not like the scribes" (Mark 1:22). The temple guards, sent to arrest Jesus, returned empty-handed and excused themselves, saying, "No man ever spoke like that before" (John 7:46). Jesus is described in the New Testament in terms of real and prophetic presence that included both actions and words inviting us into God's presence.

Symbols and presence go together. Presence has already been defined as our gathered resources attending to others as well as to ourselves. Presence is shaped in symbol and enhanced by conflict and crisis. Symbols alone are capable of dealing with the complexity of experience that forms the core of presence.

All of this remains quite vague until we attach names to presence: God, Moses, Paul of Tarsus, Augustine of Hippo, and our own first names. To say a name is, after all, to sum up a history of experience. It is to tell of conflicts met and commitments made. To be called by name is to be called to presence.

In the previous chapters, we have looked at committed people like Paul, Augustine, and Teresa of Calcutta. God's justifying action in their lives is most apparent in their conflicts and crises. In working through the unsettling events of their lives, they opted for deeper meaning and wider service. Their "presence," in itself, was a Gospel message to their world. In this chapter, we come to the central theme of this book: real presence. Roman Catholics use the term almost exclusively for Christ's presence in the Eucharist. But an even older usage defines real presence as a covenant presence. When Israel "remembers" (ZKR) her God, she participates in his current redemptive action/presence. As Brevard Childs aptly phrases it: "The covenant history of Yahweh with his people continues. The role of Israel's memory here is not to relive the past, because much of what is remembered is painful, but to emphasize obedience in the future."[3] Traditionally, covenant people have used worship and sacrament to escape the responsibility of covenant presence.

We described the Corinthians' problem, in fact, as just such an escape. A careful look at the Sunday morning worship situation should remind us that this temptation is still with us. If, during the preceding week, our familial and professional lives have permitted us to be only minimally aware of and responsive to our own and others' presence, there is no theological reason for supposing that this situation will suddenly change in church. This chapter continues the discussion of religious commitment in our worship and sacrament by examining more closely the rituals of absence and the process of presence.

TWO SCENES OF PRESENCE

Paradigms are not hard to find. Two will be offered here: Moses and Paul. In Exodus 3, Moses' "calling" is narrated. While watching his father-in-law's sheep, Moses willingly entered into an encounter in which he would not be able to remain indifferent. God set a new task for Moses: "I will send you to Pharaoh that you may bring forth my people" (Exod. 3:10). The tense dialogue, centering around this task, is colored by Moses' prophetic resistance.[4] For Moses, to accept this new task was to turn in a radically new direction, one requiring resources not much in evidence in his life up to that point.[5]

In a final effort to hedge, Moses raised the question of God's name.[6] The response given is in the language of presence, using the verb *to be* in an active sense. Whether God's reply is translated as "I am who I am," "I am what I am," or "I will be what I will be," the name describes his active presence in our world.

Furthermore, this is a classic instance of name and "remembering" (ZKR) being coupled. In Hebrew thought, name is associated with presence. To "remember" the name of God in worship is not, as in Western thought, to call it to mind or to recite it, but to praise and proclaim it.[7]

Implicit throughout this account of Moses' "calling" is the question of Moses' own presence before such a God of presence. Startled by the demands of God, Moses raised a series of objections, culminating in the exasperated cry, "Oh, my Lord, send I pray, some other person" (Exod. 4:13). The reluctant prophet had to painfully gather his resources to be present in this new stage. This task would both clarify Moses' past experience and stretch the dimensions of his experience. To "remember" such a God in worship was to accept his tasks in life: "This is my name forever, and thus I am to be remembered throughout all generations. Go and gather the elders of Israel together . . ." (Exod. 4:15–16).

Although Paul's conversion story does not seem to have been modeled so much on Moses' call as on later prophetic examples,[8] the general dynamic is the same. Paul was called by name and challenged to an unforseen task by the Lord (Acts 9; 22:5–21; 26:12–18). God's style of asking for prophetic service had not changed: "Be on your way. I mean to send you far away from here, among the Gentiles" (Acts 22:21)—"to open the eyes of those to whom I am sending you, to turn them from darkness to light and from the dominion of Satan to God" (Acts 26:18).

Paul is pictured as having readily accepted this radically different vision, though the unexpectedness and gratuity of it would remain with him throughout his life (Gal. 1:15–16).[9] The conflict elements of the episode have perhaps been muted to conform to the Lucan picture of apostleship, but they can be authentically reconstructed without too much difficulty.

Once more, as in the story of Moses, there is a question of mutual presence, that of the Lord and Paul. The latter's response of presence was focused by the tasks of mission that were the very doorway to his conversion. These tasks not only sprang from God's initiating and enabling presence but presented unanticipated choices that deeply disturbed the self-serving visions of Moses and Paul.

Whether the reader of these stories is sophisticated in the methods of form and redaction criticism or simply a searcher for religious meaning, one constant stands out: the question of presence. There is no attempt to define the presence of Moses' God or Paul's risen Lord. Only the impact of such a presence is depicted. The presence of a Moses or a Paul must be enlarged to meet the needs of a peaceable reign not yet fully established. In contrast to the version in Acts 9 and 26, Acts 22 shows Paul receiving the call to mission after his baptism, while praying in the Temple. This Lucan choice underlines the revelatory presence of God, associated with the Temple, and the vision of Jesus.[10]

In biblical categories, faith is never reduced to intellectual affirmation and assent. Rather, it is a response to the living God. Empowered and liberated by his presence, we become more "present" in the deepest sense of the word. This growing willingness and ability to be present will inevitably touch the lives of others and be expressed in symbol. The dynamic character of symbol, however, rests not only on the liberating and gratuitous quality of God's presence, but in its ability to transform our experience. Symbol and the story of our own shared experience cannot be celebrated separately.

We have already developed some of the crisis aspects of this process in Chapter 3. It is now time to analyze the rituals of absence, the result of flight from crisis and commitment.

RITUALS OF ABSENCE

Anyone who travels a good deal knows how ritualized air travel has become. Before even entering the plane we have had to choose between smoking and nonsmoking sections of the aircraft. Once in the plane, we are subjected to acted-out instructions on emergency exits, oxygen masks, and seat-belts. While we believe we ourselves could give these demonstrations from memory at this point, we feel obliged by courtesy to look at the stewardess during her familiar explanation, though our minds are elsewhere. We go through the verbal and nonverbal rituals that signal the stranger in the seat next to us whether or not we are interested in making his acquaintance. In brief, we do not have to read Erving Goffman's *Behavior in Public Places* to be aware that many of our social rituals of "presence" (from inquiries about people's health to conversations at cocktail parties) are designed to keep others at a safe distance.[11]

This phenomenon is understandable, up to a point. We cannot hope, for example, to have a responsive presence to a hundred fellow passengers whom we will probably never encounter again. Many of our social and familial rituals afford us the necessary distance we periodically require so that we can return to even our simplest rituals of presence (such as a kiss or a handshake) with more honesty and investment.

Part of the problem is that we assume that our rituals (for example, of greeting) always mean what they are supposed to mean. We sometimes use the same ritual in different situations with varying intentions. The handshake, for instance, when used as a greeting ritual at work is not the same as a handshake between close friends. Yet even when we are quite sure what we intend by the ritual of the handshake, we must still invest ourselves in that ritual.

Rituals of absence are usually the result of naive assumptions about our intentions. The consequence is a lack of self-investment. "Amen" in the Christian liturgy, for example, is a verbal ritual by which we usually commit ourselves again to God and his work. In the course of a forty-five-minute liturgy, we may have said "Amen" a number of times. "Amen" becomes a ritual of absence when it is only a "response" to a prayer that we have duly given. "Amen" means little when we do not have to give something of ourselves in response. The argument here is not that every "Amen" must be an intense experience but that there must be an aware intention behind those forty-five minutes of ritual.

The intentions and self-investment we bring to any ritual form part of our "presence." In a practical way such intentions and self-investment summarize values, decisions, and commitments of our lives. To keep our "Amen" from becoming a ritual that staves off, rather than welcomes, the presence of God, we must examine both the theory and praxis of our lives. Our renewed intentions and self-investment are the result of such re-examinations. Many rituals of absence, on the other hand, are born of a mindless reading of our stories and what they tell us about our theory and praxis.

The periodic awareness of how much we block out in the narratives of our experience suggests with new force our redemptive problem and its sometimes ambiguous cultic expression. The experience of the "sacred," rooted (as it must be) in presence, is always the first victim of our dishonest stories.

In contrast to the person struggling to work through the conflicts and demands of a certain period of life, the "absent" person uses ritual and time as an escape from presence. The very fear that provokes such flights from reality is grounded in the partial, fragmented ways of being present to which such a person has become accustomed. Rituals, both secular and religious, are used as a buffer zone, excluding uninvited reality and feared conflict.

In place of experiences that invite us to be more present, rituals of absence demand nothing of us and hinder any potential transition and transformation in our lives. They assure us a world of delusions in which lived experience is ignored and symbols of presence are barred. R. D. Laing, in describing the paranoid's world, suggests the more general results of such rituals and their underlying attitudes:

Unable to experience himself as significant for another, he develops a delusionally significant place for himself in the world of others. . . . Instead of real-izing a sense of his own presence for others, he developed a delusional sense of his presence for others.[12]

To concretize this connection between our rituals and our stories, we return to an example offered in the previous chapter: the teenager who does not want to go to Mass or worship on Sunday. The argument of the young person is, often enough, one of honest ritual: why go to Mass "just to be there"? Such an argument begs the real question: *how much connection must there be between our stories and our intention before our rituals are honest?*

When we ask what the teenager's intention must be using a ritual honestly, we are asking a question about his or her meaning and commitment.[13] As Rollo May has cogently argued, intentionality "refers to a state of being and involves, to a greater or lesser degree, the *totality* of the person's orientation to the world at that time," including both our conscious and unconscious intentions.[14] I may, for example, have a conscious intention to say "Amen" externally. But May is asking what are my unconscious intentions in regard to the meaning and commitment demanded by an internalized "Amen"?

We cannot separate our intentions and our acts. "The separation of intention and act is an artificial posture and does not accurately describe the human experience. The act is in the intention, and the intention in the act."[15] Rollo May, as a practicing therapist, then goes on to show how crucial intentionality is in the healing process. "What such a patient is doing is precisely taking the *intentionality* out of the experience. . . . What we want the patient to do is to genuinely experience the implications and meaning of his intention. . . . If I have faced my intentionality, I can hope to make the decision in the outside world."[16] May's persistent thesis is that we can only be responsible for our presence if we are willing to see how it is shaped by our explicit and implicit intentions.

The teenager who wishes to be honest in ritual must be honest in intention. But honest intention is a result of owning our experience again. Part of the teenager's "unowned" experience, for example, may be the connection between religion and parents in his or her mind. Whether this connection is considered good or bad by the teenager, it must be experienced and acknowledged. Otherwise, the teenager cannot decide if this Sunday ritual is what he or she truly intends.

To put it another way, contact with and responsibility for our experience must precede and accompany our rituals. Rituals of absence only reflect their users: those who are strangers to their own experience. The parents' first concern should be with the teenager's intentions, not with his or her rituals. (The background issue here is the theological principle that the celebrant of any sacrament must "intend what the Church intends," which, in turn, hinges on Christ's "intention.")

THE AFFILIATION PROCESS

Our presence involves our enabled choices and reconsidered experience. This is always demanding and sometimes frightening. (Put another way, an artist trying to recreate the Moses and Paul episodes discussed earlier might paint their faces full of anxiety rather than rapture and joy.) God's presence has been presented as justifying, that is, as an enabling presence that allows us to review our intentions and commitments. But God's presence must overcome our fears if we are to do this. There seems to be a certain dynamic in such enabling presence that I prefer to call "affiliation."

The Latin root of the word *affiliation* suggests the process of becoming a son or daughter. We did not originally choose our parents, nor, for that matter, did they choose us. Parents choose to have a child, little knowing all the ramifications of that choice. In a healthy environment, however, we spend the rest of our lives choosing one another. A son at forty-five is still choosing, in deeper ways, his mother of seventy, and vice versa. This choice ought not be made out of guilt but out of a freely given love. Such continuing choice in relationship is a further investment in presence. In Christian thought, God is the model for such a process.

Both theology (1 John 4:10) and current therapy models[17] identify the beginning of the affiliation process as an individual's *unconditional acceptance* (by God or the healer/therapist). This kind of acceptance is not to be confused with approval. Approval refers to the (good/bad) quality of our actions, while acceptance includes the continuing understanding and love that others give us. (The parent or spouse can disapprove the selfish action of a child or partner, but continue to love and value the unique doer of the selfish action.)

Such unconditional acceptance by God is not measured by our performance, but is the result of a gratuitous love that values us in ways we cannot match. The experience of such acceptance will evoke such grateful expressions as, "Not that we have loved God but that he has loved us" (1 John 4:10) or Augustine's "Because you loved me, you made me lovable."

The fear of presence stems, in good part, from the conditional acceptance that we experience in our day-to-day living. In both obvious and subtle ways, we serve the ideal self others may expect us to be. Their love is conditioned by their expectations, reasonable or unreasonable. Our response to such significant people in our lives is affected by such conditional love. When our life-praxis cannot match the expectations of others, we may be tempted to filter out such experience.[18]

The result is parents who cannot admit that they feel both love and hate for their teenage child; a wife who cannot admit even to herself that she is deeply disappointed with the husband she loves; an older man who fears death but whose grownup children will not permit him to verbalize that fear. There is a breakdown in communications with both ourselves and others. Once this happens, as we have seen, our real intentions become blurred.

In the beginning of Chapter 2, we cited Laing's dictum about the self-destruction that results from distortion of our experience. Laing also speaks of the "reciprocal terrorism" that we can exercise on one another.[19] Our mutual and self-serving expectations can make us prisoners of one another. The immediate corollary is a lack of communication with our own and others' experience. ("I cannot admit to myself a point of experience which, I am sure, you could never accept in me.")

The first result of unconditional acceptance is the second stage of affiliation: *creative communication*. Once we are in the presence of someone who accepts us without condition, we can sometimes show to them what we cannot even admit to ourselves. The reason is obvious. In dealing with such negative experience, the other will accord us the love and respect we would deny ourselves at that moment because our negative experience contradicts our ideal self-image. Areas of our story are once again opened up. What were the restricted archives of our experience now become the source of more comprehensive and clarifying symbols of communication for ourselves and others. Carl Rogers' words then ring true in our experience: "What is most personal and unique in each of us is probably the very element which would, if it were shared or expressed, speak most deeply to others."[20]

In Chapter 3, the need to symbolize conflict and limit-experience was stressed. The obstacle to such symbolization is the overriding fear of nonacceptance. The creative communication being described here is the ability to image and clarify our experience with its conflicts so as to arrive at new meaning and more reliable presence in a certain stage of our lives. And it is the presence of the other which has freed us for this new moment of unity with our experience. The prophetic resistance of Moses is but one example of this process in which God's presence evokes our presence and the experience we denied becomes the experience out of which we symbolize.

When such a process is set in motion, a new possibility—*creative confrontation*—presents itself. This is the third stage of affiliation. Many of the challenges in our life can seem to come from false prophets who know what is wrong in our lives, but give us no strength to change it. Thus, they only confirm our worst fears about ourselves.

True prophets are the model of creative confrontation. By definition, they are filled with the spirit or presence of God. When there were no prophets in Israel, the spirit was silent and Israel could only hear the "echo of his [God's] voice."[21] By contrast, the prophet was the paradigm for communication and challenge between God and his convenant people. No prophetic challenge was given that could not become a reality. No prophetic call to convenant presence was proclaimed that could not be answered (Jer. 11:1–5).

The true prophet perceives the footprints of God in our story and its implications. Such persons call out of us new commitment. They enable us, by their acceptance and communication, to assume responsibility for a broader view of ourselves as people gifted for the new tasks as well as the old in our lives. Their challenge is not negative but therapeutic: the blind do see again and the deaf hear; young people see visions and the old dream dreams (Joel 2:28; Acts 2:17).

Creative and prophetic confrontation for the Christian, then, is the call to commitment and the final test of presence. It is the final step in the continuing process of becoming affiliated once more, of reappropriating a relationship with God and others. We can only bring to such a relationship what we are, our self fully present. But affiliation permits us to symbolize and be challenged to further commitment out of our experience. It is not Moses or Paul but we ourselves who now stand on holy ground and are challenged to new commitments by God.

PRESENCE AND TRANSFORMED EXPERIENCE

Our resources for developing a more balanced statement about the complexities of redemptive presence and its cultic expression have been considerably enlarged since the times of Augustine, Aquinas, Luther, and Calvin. The problem of avoiding God's presence by the use of mindless rituals is as old as the history of unredeemed alienation, though its expressions may change according to epoch and culture. One contemporary resource for analyzing the cultural effects of such ritualism is a psychosocial study of our personal experience and its structured expression in social interaction. If we are to recognize our rituals of absence, we may well need the insights that only an interdisciplinary study can afford.

Several statements about the symbols of presence will be proposed. These are minimal descriptions of what our presence in worship must be if it is not to degenerate into ritualism. I will test the comprehensiveness of these theses against the insights of Erving Goffman whose sensitive sociological analyses of public experience and its rituals reward attention.[22] The assumption of such a methodology is older than the scholastic axiom that God's grace builds on our nature. It rests on the theological fact that God's redemptive purpose gives eschatological direction to his creation and that only naive rituals tend to forget this.

First, if we wish to enter honestly into the meaning of any symbol (such as the Eucharist), we must be willing to deal with our complex experience more perceptively. Symbols are only transforming when they have a whole person to transform.[23] Ritualists can be satisfied with the external actions of symbol (kneeling, singing, etc.) and the resulting satisfied feelings. Ritualists bring carefully selected excerpts from their stories to their worship (for example, people who present themselves before God as imperfect but loving parents, while carefully filtering out their forty-hour-a-week professional lives with their perhaps questionable business ethics and unbridled ambitions). Ritualists oversimplify their experience and, thus, their need for redemption. Finally, ritualists' "intention" in worship is limited by restricted and self-serving readings of their own experience.[24]

To "proclaim the death of the Lord until" (1 Cor. 11:26) in such a way that it cannot call into question our continuing need for redemption, or provide us with new reasons for that need, is to have evaded the Pauline experience. Better than any dogmatic text, our shared stories substantiate our models of absence and presence and give depth to a worship in spirit and truth.

Goffman would put some hard questions to us about such an ideal. The fact that most people spend a good part of their lives maintaining social roles may tempt us to confuse these roles with their personal identities. The working person in our society who spends forty or more hours each week in a situation where rituals and roles have little or nothing to do with that individual's real identity cannot be expected to enter readily into participatory symbols on Sunday. In fact, such a person will probably feel tempted to use sacramental rituals for some of the protective space, security, and assurance that our weekday rituals guarantee. In such situations, "presence" can be reduced to convenient interpretations of our experience. Do our celebrations of God's presence consistently contest such partial identity?

Our current ability and willingness to be "present" has been shaped, in part, by the interaction of our story with that of others. We are all careful editors of our autobiography when we present it to others.

It is apparent that two persons who are much together have an opportunity to create something of a privately shared world for themselves. Each supplies the other with details of prerelation personal biography and they begin to develop a new phase of their biography jointly.[25]

This "new phase" of shared biography requires us to give deeper importance to the symbols of presence in others' lives. (Erikson's efforts in psychohistory, mentioned in Chapter 3, are an example.) In interacting with the lives of others, we return to our own experience with new insight. The Christian sees the life of Jesus, for example, as more than biography. The Gospels also represent the response of early Christian communities to the meaning of Jesus' life for them.

If we return to an incident in our lives which occurred years ago and involved a parent or classmate, we may discover that we know little more than the "facts" of the story. We may feel that we know what meaning and importance we attach to that incident. But we may never have grasped the real intentions and perspective of the other person in our story. If this old story is to assume new meaning for our current living, then the real presence of the other in that story must be re-evaluated. This is one practical way in which we can clarify our complex experience so that we may be present.

This process of re-evaluation underlines the role that others may have in the way we relate our stories and, thus, implicitly argue for our rituals of presence or absence. Goffman reminds us that we have "versions" of our personal experience that "replay" because of our "audience." In other words, we build potential listener-participation into the telling of our experience.[26] And, like a good detective fiction writer, we set our scenes so that they will both explain and condone our ecclesial irresponsibility. (The teenager we cited earlier as an example may use previous interactions with his or her parents as the reason why he or she "cannot" go to Mass in a honest way now.)

Anyone familiar with the experience of counselling or the process of therapy will recognize the similarity. The therapist's presence alters the telling of the client's story in many ways. One of the hallmarks of growing congruence may be the new versions of an old story in which the client has integrated elements once discreetly laid aside.[27] The new versions of the experience will then be characterized by the deeper admission of uniqueness and consequent responsibility, based on a less filtered awareness.[28] This less filtered awareness will recognize the part that others have played (or been made to play) in the experience. Complexity will have returned to the telling of the experience and symbol cannot fail to be the richer for it.

One sign of this heightened awareness of multidimensional experience is a more nuanced use of the personal pronoun *I* in our own religious narratives. The personal pronoun at the heart of autobiography represents presumably a unified and unique person. But it is the very complexity of that person's experience that both shades and changes the significance of the many *I*'s of presence in our stories.[29] The factual statement, "I began high school in 1948," may need the subsequent explanation, "I couldn't afford to attend a private high school," and its current evaluative comment, "I guess my parents just couldn't afford it."

The personalized character of cultic canticles in the Bible, for instance, reflects the need to respond to God's presence out of our own currently experienced presence, imperfect as that may be. Religious symbols have an impact, not only because they bespeak God's power-filled presence, but also because they contest our lack of presence, betrayed in the bland and undifferentiated *I*'s of our own experience. Ira Progoff has expressed this well:

Beyond symbols there is a dimension of reality which does not depend upon the symbols at all but rather uses them. It uses symbols as media through which it can unfold its latent meanings and participate in the lives of persons . . . for reality is not a symbol separate from you to be reverenced and interpreted. Reality, like man's relation to truth, grows as the tissue of his life.[30]

Quite correctly, Progoff insists that the prophetic symbolized awareness of God's presence cannot be separated from the collective and personal warp and woof of our own life story of presence.[31]

In brief, when we oversimplify the data and perspectives of our own shared stories, we betray the whole question of our lack of presence. For our religious creeds may then have no connection with our lived experience. The central question of why we need a savior may find no corroboration in our story. We have discarded the very dimensions of our narratives that would show

how absent we can be and how present God needs to be to us.
Our definitions of redemption are incomplete because the reading of our experience is superficial.

Sacramental symbol as the saving presence of God must deal
with such defective definitions of presence and salvation. In effectively sharing symbolic action, we, too, return to our redemptive definitions and their autobiographical references. We once
more integrate the developments and aberrations of our lives
that both explain our uniqueness and expand our responsibilities for the Kingdom.

Redemptive symbols, liturgically celebrated, can evoke our responsible presence. But this depends, *ex opere operantis,* on an
increasing willingness and ability to deal with our lived experience. Ritualism re-enforces the self-serving and consistent misreading of that same experience. Our current theological analo-
gies of "presence" may limp badly because our current
conceptions of experience do not include important layers of our
story. "Presence," the core of any notion of worship, then remains a theological mirage because our notion of experience is
both limited and naive.

FRAMING OUR EXPERIENCE

A second statement about presence can now be offered: *religious symbol always calls us to redemptive presence by deepening the meaning we give our experience and revealing God's
action there.* If God's presence is genuinely welcomed in our
lives, the eventual result must be a new perception of the meaning of our presence and that of others. This insight will not
easily tolerate the divisive meanings and values that keep us
from God and others. Ritualism falsely reassures the worshipping Christian that objective religious meaning and value become ours when the externals of worship have been performed.
This begets a theological counterpart: theories of sacramental
causality that seem to thrive on static notions of both God's
presence and our own. These theories can render God's redemptive presence and gracious action literally incredible if they do
not challenge our own presence.

This second statement is more telling than it might appear at first. We sometimes choose to hastily interpret our experience and its meaning because, as Goffman has pithily observed, "We tolerate the unexplained but not the inexplicable."[32] In describing how we involve ourselves in structuring meaning into our life-situations, Goffman employs the term *frame*. To analyze a frame is to deal with the organization of our experience.[33]

Goffman's work on frames reminds us that we are always in search of control over whatever might impinge on our lives. This is part of the socialization process and includes our public and private worlds of experience. Even the most bizarre behavior may, if properly "framed," reveal rituals that support a perspective that is consistent and personally meaningful. For it is our perspectives that determine our reading of events and thus contribute to their structure.

A primary frame is a basic meaning that allows us to cope with an event. People seldom explicate their primary frames, even though these frames are operational throughout an ordinary day. (Polanyi's dictum that we know more than we can tell is exemplified by such framing.) Because these frames organize our incessant and complicated experience into manageable packages, we tolerate very little ambiguity or doubt. (I will assign a reason for misplacing my car keys, even though it may be neither satisfactory nor helpful.) The need for "orderly" experience is indeed great, and thus framing is the regular mode of perceiving ourselves and others.[34]

A more honest framing of our experience leads to insight about our real intentions in the rituals of both living and worship. This is the "homework" we must constantly do if our participation in religious symbol is to be "present" and responsible.

The understanding of symbol within the Christian tradition has always tried to safeguard the unique action and meaning that God's presence provokes. When symbolic action is analyzed from the viewpoint of "framing," therefore, the dimensions of God's work among us must remain intact. Throughout this book, we have been dealing with the *response* aspects of presence, symbolically celebrated. God's presence in ritual gives meaning to redemptive events, not in a social vacuum but in contexts that affect (as well as potentially effect) our response. Symbols of worship and sacrament, in inviting us to redemptive and objective meaning, must deal with the very frames that would render our response difficult, if not impossible.[35] These frames, in turn, are affected by our story and the experience it both represents and filters.

Sacramental symbol, then, contests our fragmented presence because it clarifies the results of the framing of our stories. Our decisions and their underlying values are exposed. In the Corinthian situation, Paul lays bare the Corinthians' enthusiastic transposition of the meaning of the death and resurrection of Jesus to a key more comfortable to them. This in turn explains their distorted liturgical celebration of the Eucharist. Paul knows that it is not God's presence that is at stake but the Corinthians' lack of presence. Ritualism stems from a denial that our frames play any role in symbolic response in presence. Once this is accepted, then it is a short step to uncommitted rituals and a new Corinthian situation.

COMMITTED PRESENCE

A third statement about presence is the culmination of our preceding two statements: *symbols of presence evoke new communal and individual commitment to God's Kingdom from those who are not yet fully redeemed.*

Moses and Paul were not invited to be spectators at God's appearance, nor are we. God's presence is enabling so that our presence may be serving. But such service is not demanded of us apart from our experience.

If our stories are more honestly recounted, then the profile of our stages and conflicts will be revelatory. We will begin to see that the new tasks and strengths of each life-stage, and the new meanings that accompanied them, have prepared us for the current challenge to service in our present stage.

The problem of commitment, however, lies in the telling of our journey. Because we are not yet fully redeemed (we are "at one and the same time sinners and saints," as the classical axiom has it), our narratives tend to be affected by the fear of new commitments and tasks. But God's justifying presence can allow the clarity of new visions and the courage of reconsidered purpose to accompany us in our stage of life.

Ritualism, as might be expected, does the opposite. Ritualists, arguing from their current incongruence, plead for sacramental consolation but no deeper accountability for God's Kingdom. Further, a widening credibility gap between the eschatological message of sacrament (Paul's "until") and our misframed experience allows us to redefine "presence" in increasingly minimal terms. In other words, our symbolic response is in jeopardy because our experience is literally not in question.

God redeems us, we have argued, out of our experience, not despite it. But if we fabricate our experience, what then of God's redemption? Is our worship response qualitatively different from our fabrication? Goffman used the term *fabrication* to describe the deceptive contexts of experience. Fabrication invites misinterpretation from at least some of the participants in an experience.[36] It provides a viable, if deceptive, explanation, as if false reassurance were better than none. Self-delusion can accompany fabrication, and it can be self-imposed.

Presence can be corrupted by fabrication. Reality-testing is, I submit, a necessary corollary of any adequate symbol of presence. Fabrication, on the other hand, blocks such a function. It prevents us from seeing others in our story as they really are and distorts our true intentions. Ultimately, willfully fabricated experience is both misinterpreted and misleading because it tampers with our own presence.

CAN YOU BERAK?

In biblical times, to ask someone whether he could "berak" was to pose a highly personal question. "Berakhah" (BRK or its verb form, "berak") is a Hebrew word that is usually translated "blessing."[37] The translation, however, is a disservice to the richness of the idea this word was meant to convey. For to the Hebrew, to bless was not to recite a ritual, but to improvise praise of God based on the current realities of one's life. In other words, a berakhah was a prayer form that drew directly from one's retrieved experience.

Standing in the midst of an unfinished story, the believer

blesses God in new ways because his or her experience has disclosed the presence of God's action. The young Mary is pictured as responding to Elizabeth's blessing with one of her own: "My being proclaims the greatness of the Lord. . . . God who is mighty has done great things for me" (Luke 1:46, 49).[38] Shortly afterwards, Zechariah, Elizabeth's husband, also improvised a blessing, occasioned by the birth of his son: "Blessed be the Lord God of Israel because he has visited and ransomed his people . . ." (Luke 1:68).[39]

Although the berakhah later tended to develop into fixed forms, the original style of the prayer was extemporized. Classically, improvisation, whether in jazz or other styles, begins with the announcement of a theme, often a familiar one. At first glance, that theme may seem very banal. The performer-composer then proceeds to unfold its rhythmic and melodic richness. And, often enough, there is a reprise at the end in which the original theme is once more played, as if to say to the audience, "You thought you knew that tune. See what can be done with it."

The berakhah is an improvised response to the presence of God. Its seemingly banal and oft-repeated "Blessed be God" takes on new resonance as the specific context and particular events of our lives are seen as marked by that presence. The inherent complexity of our experience makes a careless refrain once more a song of credible praise. Christians who can see the process of justification etched out in their lives are empowered to pray such a prayer of presence, responding to the marks of God's presence.

Matthew gives us a fine example of such prayer in the last days of Jesus' life when his mission and ministry had already been definitively rejected by the leaders of Israel. The sacred writer offered this berakhah of Jesus: "Father, Lord of heaven and earth, to you I offer praise; for what you have hidden from the learned and the clever you have revealed to the merest children" (Matt. 11:25). Joachim Jeremias sums up the meaning of that improvised prayer: "From the ruins Jesus gives thanks."[40]

This prayer mirrored both the conflict and commitment of Jesus' experience as described in Hebrews: "In the days when he was in the flesh, he offered prayers and supplications with loud cries and tears to God . . . and he was heard because of his reverence" (Heb. 5:7). The result is the presence of someone "on account of others," someone recommitted to the work of the peaceable reign of God. In a similar way, the credibility of worship and sacrament must reflect the honesty of our dealings with the stories of our conflicts, commitments, and presence.

SUMMARY

God's presence is always a question of his meaning challenging ours. Whether we think of Moses, Paul, or ourselves, an honest experience of God has always called into question the intentions, values, and commitments that make up the meaning of a person's life. But such meanings also constitute shared presence and community. For God's presence in the Old Testament is a covenant presence which proposes meanings that will unite a divided, alienated people. The new covenant people are brought together by the meaning of Jesus' life and death. To speak of presence, then, is always to speak of meanings that bridge our divisions.

But both presence and its meaning are played out in a definite space and time and include all the biological, psychological, sociological, and theological factors that affect us. Robert Kegan has suggested an evocative image for this process of meaning—"the human dance." He says: "Any developmental framework, taken as a whole, should be a kind of attention to the human dance—the changing form through time in space."[41]

The berakhah is a model of prayer that sums up the new intentions and meanings in our lives. Its expression originates from a definite time and place in our lives when new meanings and commitments are built on our old experience. This prayer reflects the price of growth, our willingness to move past the narrower confines of a previous period of our lives.[42] If we are to bless God, individually and communally, then we have no choice but to deal with our story more honestly.

Here is where the difference between symbol and ritual can be most easily perceived. God's symbols are full of his meaning and power and, therefore, effect what they signify. Rituals are an invitation to symbol. When we ritualize out of our experience in response to God's presence, then symbol is in play.

A paradigm for symbol is the prophetic action-word (*ôth*). The Jew believed that when the prophet broke a vase, for example, and then explained, "And thus will God do to you, O Israel," what had been signified had already begun to happen.[43] The prophetic action word did not ignore but rather invited response from God's covenant people at a definite time and place in their history. Once more both God's presence and that of his people were framed by a very precise moment in their shared story.

Walter Brueggemann calls this task in the community "prophetic energizing," a hope-filled action-word that speaks of real presence. In recalling how faithful God has been in the story of the community, the prophet forges a language of amazement "that engages the community in new discernments and celebration just when it had nearly given up and had nothing to celebrate. . . . Indeed, the language of amazement is the ultimate energizer in Israel, and prophets of God are called to practice that most energizing language."[44]

The question of presence, then, recapitulates the discussion of commitment, justification, and crisis of the previous chapters. Dorothy Day and Mother Teresa strike us as committed people who have worked through a series of conflicts and crises with the help of God's justifying action in their lives. In turn, they continue to fulfill a prophetic role in the Christian community and the world at large. Their worship and sacrament affect even the nonbelieving onlooker because they sum up the meaning and presence of their lives.

In the following chapters, specific sacraments will be discussed in the light of committed presence. Robert Kegan has captured the larger issue behind such a discussion:

In a community worthy of the name there are symbols and celebrations, ritual, even gesture, by which I am known *in the process of my development,* by which I am helped to recognize myself. Intact, sustaining communities have always found ways to recognize that persons grow and change, that this fate can be costly, and that if it is not to cost the community the very loss of its member, then the community must itself be capable of "recognition."[45]

In the twentieth century, we are tempted, as those were before us, not to hope and, therefore, not to change. God's presence continues to address our own faltering presence as he once addressed a wavering early Christian community: "So strengthen your drooping hands and your weak knees . . . we who are receiving the unshakable kingdom should hold fast to God's grace, through which we may offer worship acceptable to him in reverence and awe. For our God is a consuming fire" (Heb. 12:12, 28–29).

NOTES

1. R. Keyes, *We, the Lonely People* (New York: Harper & Row, 1973), p. 15.
2. For an overall discussion and bibliography, see F. J. Helfmeyer, "oth," *Theological Dictionary of the Old Testament*, ed. G. J. Botterweck and H. Ringgren (Grand Rapids, Mich.: W. Eerdmans, 1974), vol. 1, pp. 167–88.
3. B. Childs, *Memory and Tradition in Israel* (London: SCM Press, 1962), p. 51.
4. See B. Childs, *The Book of Exodus* (Philadelphia: Westminster, 1974), p. 45. Childs' translation of the passages cited from Exodus has been used here. For a somewhat similar treatment, see S. Terrien, *The Elusive Presence* (New York: Harper & Row, 1978), pp. 118–19.
5. Childs, *Exodus,* p. 73.
6. For the difficult form-critical background, cf. ibid, pp. 64–70.
7. Childs, *Memory and Tradition,* pp. 50–54.
8. See Childs, *Exodus,* pp. 83–84, where he suggests that the model might be more the servant of Deutero-Isaiah because of the suffering and willing acceptance dimensions.
9. See, for example, E. Haenchen, *The Acts of the Apostles* (Philadelphia: Westminster, 1971), p. 328; G. Eicholz, *Die Theologie des Paulus im Umris* (Neukirchen: Neukirchener Verlag, 1977²), p. 168.
10. Thus, Haenchen, *Acts of the Apostles,* p. 627.
11. E. Goffman, *Behavior in Public Places* (New York: Free Press, 1963); see also his *Interaction Ritual* (New York: Doubleday, 1967).
12. R. D. Laing, *Self and Others* (New York: Pantheon Books, 1969), pp. 118–19. Compare this with Erikson's thought in D. Browning, *Generative Man: Psychoanalytic Perspectives* (Philadelphia: Westminster, 1973), pp. 201–07.
13. R. May, *Love and Will* (New York: W. W. Norton, 1969), p. 230.
14. Ibid, p. 234.
15. Ibid, p. 242.

16. Ibid, pp. 260–61.
17. For brief description of this therapeutic process, see D. Delaney and S. Eisenberg, *The Counseling Process* (Chicago: Rand McNally, 1972), pp. 50–59. A classic statement will be found in Carl Roger's *Client-Centered Therapy* (Boston: Houghton Mifflin, 1951).
18. Rogers, *Client-Centered Therapy,* pp. 520–21.
19. R. D. Laing, *The Politics of Experience* (New York: Ballantine Books, 1967), pp. 88–90.
20. C. Rogers, *On Becoming a Person* (Boston: Houghton Mifflin, 1961), p. 26.
21. See J. Jeremias, *New Testament Theology* (New York: Scribners, 1971), pp. 78–82.
22. E. Goffman is somewhat ironic when it comes to the possibility of analyzing religious experience; see his *Frame Analysis: An Essay on the Organization of Experience* (New York: Harper & Row, 1974), pp. 27–28, 448. I take responsibility for the application of his model to our present concerns.
23. For the patristic understanding of symbol and its liturgical expression, and the subsequent deterioration of this concept, see J. P. de Jong, *Die Eucharistie als Symbolwirklichkeit* (Regensburg: Pustet, 1969), pp. 15–81.
24. To examine this from Goffman's viewpoint, we might use his idea of "keying" in which an activity that has a primary meaning and context is transformed into something quite different. "A keying, then . . . performs a crucial role in determining what it is we think is really going on" (*Frame Analysis,* p. 45). The quiet purpose of such transformations of experience is to reduce personal responsibility (*Frame Analysis,* p. 541).
25. Ibid, p. 458. Cf. also E. M. Zuesse, "Meditation on Ritual," *Journal of the American Academy of Religion* 43 (1975): 517–30; here, 522.
26. Goffman, *Frame Analysis,* pp. 503–04, 541, 559.
27. See, for example, N. Hobbs, "A New Cosmology," in B. Berenson and K. Carkhuff, eds., *Sources of Gain in Counseling and Psychotherapy* (New York: Holt, Rinehart and Winston, 1967), pp. 114–25, esp. 117–20.
28. Compare this with R. D. Laing's description of counterfeited experience in *The Divided Self* (New York: Pantheon Books, 1965), pp. 44–45.
29. Goffman, *Frame Analysis,* pp. 519–20.
30. I. Progoff, *The Symbolic and the Real* (New York: McGraw-Hill, 1963), pp. 211–13. Similarly, B. Lonergan says: "Affective development, or aberration, involves a transvaluation and transformation of symbols. . . . Inversely, symbols that do not submit to transvaluation and transformation seem to point to a block in development"; see *Method in Theology* (New York: Herder and Herder, 1972), p. 66.
31. Progoff, *The Symbolic and the Real,* pp. 217–18.
32. Goffman, *Frame Analysis,* p. 30.
33. Ibid, pp. 10–11. The term is Bateson's, but it has been much developed by Goffman.
34. Ibid, pp. 305, 338. Goffman would follow such a discussion with his idea of "keying" (cf. n. 24).
35. I accept C. Raschke's argument that the meaning of religious language must "convey man's total involvement in his world and his experience of commerce with the highest powers of the universe"; "Meaning and Saying Religion: Beyond Language Games," *Harvard Theological Review* 67 (1974): 109.

36. Goffman, *Frame Analysis,* pp. 83–84. As usual he is ingenious in detailing an assortment of such fabrications; cf. ibid, pp. 87–123.

37. I am using the word in a nontechnical sense. For discussion of the complexities of the usage of BRK, see J. P. Audet, *La Didachê: Instruction des Apôtres* (Paris: Gabalda, 1958), pp. 375–410; R. Ledogar, *Acknowledgment. Praise-verbs in the Early Greek Anaphora* (Rome: Herder, 1968); J. Guillet, "Le Langage Spontané de la Bénédiction dans l'Ancien Testament," *Recherches de Sciences Religieuses* 57 (1969): 163–204; J. Scharbert, "berakhah," *Theological Dictionary of the Old Testament,* vol. 2, pp. 279–308.

38. Technically, Mary's song is best described as hymn; see I. H. Marshall, *The Gospel of Luke: A Commentary on the Greek Text* (Grand Rapids, Mich.: W. B. Eerdmans, 1978), pp. 77–79.

39. For a discussion of the berakhah and hymn sections, see ibid, pp. 86–87.

40. Jeremias, *New Testament Theology,* p. 190.

41. R. Kegan, "There the Dance Is: Religious Dimensions of a Developmental Framework," *Toward Moral and Religious Maturity* (Morristown, N.J.: Silver Burdett, 1980), p. 410.

42. "Growth involves a separation from an old system of meaning. In practical terms this can involve both the agony of felt meaninglessness and the repudiation of commitments and investments" (ibid, p. 439).

43. G. von Rad, *Old Testament Theology* (New York: Harper & Row, 1965), vol. 2, pp. 95–98.

44. W. Brueggemann, *The Prophetic Imagination* (Philadelphia: Fortress, 1978), pp. 69–60.

45. Kegan, "There the Dance Is," p. 426.

CHAPTER 5

The People in the Water

On-the-job training is a familiar experience for many people beginning a new position. The best way to train people for certain types of work is to give them the necessary instruction in the situations in which they will be working. New workers ask the right questions about their job because they have a firsthand experience of its problems.

In a sense, the early Christian Church seems to have taken much the same approach when dealing with interested inquirers about Christianity. Jews, Romans, and Alexandrians became Christian by living, praying, and dying among other Christians. They learned the challenges and commitments of Gospel life by living in the unfavorable climate of the Roman Empire, which was the antithesis of the life-style and many of the values demanded by the Gospel. Newcomers in a Christian community could usually find Christians there who had already suffered for their convictions and could see the various ministries of the community firsthand.

By the second century, however, these informal methods of preparing an inquirer to become a Christian had become more structured. This processs of structuring seems to have been the reaction to heresy among some Christian teachers, as well as a response to a desire on the part of the Christian community to supervise more carefully the training of its candidates.[1] The process of becoming a Christian is called the "catechumenate." Although historically short-lived, the classical catechumenate was an extraordinarily successful solution to the pastoral problems involved in helping someone follow the Gospel way of living and praying.[2] In the Christian Church today, we are more familiar with infant Baptism, and the adult converts we receive sometimes have an extended acquaintance with Christianity. As a result, it is more difficult for us to appreciate the pastoral problem of how adult converts were to be welcomed in the second or third century.

To illustrate the problem, let us imagine the spiritual journey of a twenty-five-year-old Roman soldier who wished to become a Christian. (The example is more common than the reader might expect. The number of early Christian martyrs who were Roman soldiers is impressive.) This soldier had been raised in the Roman world whose moral values and life-style were often diametrically opposed to the Gospel way of life. Paul's description of the moral climate of his time is not overdrawn: "God delivered them up in their lusts to unclean practices; they engaged in the mutual degradation of their bodies, these men who exchanged the truth of God for a lie and worshipped and served the creature rather than the Creator" (Rom. 1:24–25). The young man's experience with the brutalizing elements that formed part of military service would have been a major obstacle to Gospel living.

Yet, perhaps because of the influence of a fellow Christian soldier, this young man became interested in the Christian way of living. How was the Christian community to elicit commitment to Christ from this soldier? How was it to teach such a man to tell his story and discern his deeper needs? How might the community teach him a Christian morality that would demand radical change in so many areas of his life? The answer was the catechumenate.

In its classical form, the catechumenate required a cautious admission and lengthy duration because of the nature of the process: a reassessment and realignment of commitments in terms of the Gospel. The typical lists of unacceptable occupations were a practical example of this concern.

The early third-century *Apostolic Tradition* (which perhaps represented the praxis of a Roman Christian community) gives a precise list of jobs and professions that were to be abandoned if someone wished to become a catechumen—for example, pimps and prostitutes, artists who illustrated the pagan gods, actors, and gladiators. Soldiers were not to kill another person.[3] Hippolytus did not pretend that the list was all-inclusive: "If we have omitted something, the professions themselves will instruct us, for we all have the Spirit of God."[4] From the beginning, a catechumen learned that Christianity is a living commitment with practical consequences that touch every area of life. In Hippolytus' community, the candidate spent at least three years learning to hear God's Word and to pray.

As the time drew near for deciding which candidates were ready for the sacraments of Initiation, the practical questions of commitment were asked: "Have they lived honestly while they were catechumens? Have they honored widows and visited the sick? Have they been engaged in good works?"[5] The *Apostolic Tradition* represents the effort of one Christian community to specify the commitments of faith in terms of its age and society.

The seminal writing of Cyril of Jerusalem, John Chrysostom, and Theodore of Mopsuestia on the catechumenate reveals a pervasive concern with the shaping of religious affections and, thus, with the convenanted, committed response of the candidate for Initiation.[6] In a similar way, Cyprian and the North African church's strong position on apostasy cannot be separated, for example, from the commitment expectations of the community.

All of this is of more than historic interest. The overall success of the catechumenate was proved by the number of people who, even before their Baptism, witnessed their faith under torture and even to the death. With the restoration of the *Rite of Christian Initiation of Adults,* not only is the catechumenal structure retrieved but its implicit theology of Church, Initiation, and commitment is put into question.[7]

There are Christian communities today that have many people who, though ritually baptized as infants and confirmed as young children, have not yet appropriated their faith. Their first need is evangelization, that is, a hearing of the Gospel within the context of a witnessing Christian community, much as that young soldier experienced it centuries ago. The catechumenate provides a model of Christian community, both for candidates and for those already initiated. The catechumenal process is a challenge to the baptized and nonbaptized within the Christian community.

Our concern in this chapter will be the sacraments of Christian Initiation (Baptism and Confirmation[8]). Normally, Initiation is the first test of religious commitment. Although infant Baptism and children's Confirmation are the usual pastoral experience, it is the adult faith and Initiation that serve as the norm for a theology of this process. Unlike the infant, the adult is capable of active choice and commitment. The catechumenate is once again the normal process in which the adult is assisted in responding to God's call to faith. It is also the most effective guide for re-evangelization of uncommitted Christians. Our discussion of Initiation, therefore, will be framed by the catechumenal process. Before explaining this theology, however, we must analyze the interaction process and the rites of passage implicit in such conversion.

MUSICAL CHAIRS

Victor Turner's anthropology has featured the model of *communitas* as one of its principal insights.[9] He uses the Latin term to distinguish his model from the sometimes superficial contemporary usage of the word *community*. Turner agrees with Martin Buber's contention that community is more than sharing common space or even common goals.[10] Turner expresses it in this way: "For communitas has an existential quality; it involves the whole man in his relation to other whole men."[11]

Notice this total response that both distinguishes communitas from social structures and makes it difficult to actualize. Static definitions of ourselves and the focus of our gifts will inevitably generate partial responses to the communities of family, church, and work in which we operate. We have noted more than once that the function of crisis in each life-stage is to invite us to redefine ourselves in terms of our larger community and its changing needs. This alone can ensure a more holistic response.

True communities provide us with rites of passage as we attempt to redefine our roles and goals. In turn, communitas is only a continuing normative experience when those same rites of passage revitalize the group's purpose and vision and invite its renewed commitment. (Augustine, for example, uses the "begetting" image to suggest the shared response of the whole Christian community in the Initiation process.[12]) To stay with the pleasures of one phase of shared life and not move into the hardships of the next phase is to endanger communitas.

Rites of passage are the ways in which the community invites its members to assume new meanings and roles within its circle. The rites of puberty are the most obvious example. Whether these puberty rites take the African form of temporary survival outside the community, followed by gradual re-integration, or the American form of presenting the car keys to the teenager, such rites represent a transition point, not only for the candidate but for the whole community.

Within the process of passage, the initial phase psychologically involves separation from the familiar securities of our current stage. Thus, survival in the jungle or any similar experience would divide the child from the play world he or she has known and demand that the individual assume a new responsibility for self-maintenance. In a post-industrialized society, a young person's "getting out on his own" may have the same effect.

The next phase, the liminal, is well-named. The Latin word *limen* means "a threshold," which suggests both an entrance into a new area or space and the extra effort required to function there. The liminal phase is a new period in our life because there are new expectations and roles that the community has in mind for us. Our life will never again be quite the same, nor, for that matter, will the life of the community be the same.

In a more basic society, the new expectations of the community may result in the young person joining the hunting party of adults from now on. In our Western society, entering the liminal phase may require a young person to become at least partially responsible for his or her financial needs. The follow-up period provides time for readjustment needed by both the initiate and others who will be affected by this change. An older hunter, for example, would become a mentor to the younger man. And any family that has had to adjust to a teenager's newly acquired driver's license and all its implications will need no further explanation of this phase. In brief, the lives of everyone in the community are affected by these rites of passage.

The effects of these rites of passage on the community may be better understood through an analogy. "Musical chairs" is a birthday game that many of us well remember. If ten play, then nine chairs are set out. As we circle the chairs, the musical accompaniment becomes faster and faster and suddenly stops. The object of the game is to get to one of the chairs. But the successful players must once again leave the hard-earned security of their seats and chance another turn around them with the possibility that they might not succeed next time.

The catechumenal model delineates a process of community renewal in which both the candidates for initiation and the baptized leave the security of their "positions" and move together once more. Each person inevitably begins to redefine "mission" within the context of his or her life-stage and the crises that accompany it. But in the initiation process of catechumenate, one person's newly found or reshaped commitment contests the self-serving definitions of commitment of the rest of the community. A young convert's willingness to devote part of their leisure time to working in legal services for the poor challenges those baptized lawyers in the Christian community who have never donated their professional services to aid the less privileged.

In evoking the candidate's commitment to the Gospel, the Christian community has to be challenged by it. For liminality is not only the threshold over which the candidates must step into a new stage of the community's widened expectation. It is also the dynamic response of the community, reassessing its old roles and shaping new resources. In other words, the new resources of the candidates will question what new roles and gifts are needed from the older members. Such rites of passage, while not strictly aligned to chronological age, cannot be divorced from life-stages.

In effect, the communal and individual change involved in rites of passage accurately reflects the process of conversion and commitment that our Initiation calls us to throughout a lifetime. We now turn to this theology of conversion and Initiation as developed in the early Christian Church.

A PAULINE MODEL

Paul never set out to write a theology of Church, but his ongoing problems with communities such as the Corinthians forced him continually to sharpen his image of the Church and its mission. Unlike some recent ecclesiologies that deal with the tension between the institutional structures and the more spontaneous, charismatic elements of the Church,[13] Paul emphasized the "mission" or the work of the Gospel, as a key element of any Christian community.

Mission is, first of all, the result of God's justifying work in us, making us his covenant "flesh" in this world for the sake of others. Such a perspective shapes all the aspirations, symbols, and actions of such a community. Mission does not deny the institutional dimension of the Church, but prophetically reforms it. It encourages the charismatic elements in community, but discerns their appropriateness and purpose.

Mission is the appropriate starting point for any praxis theology of Church and sacrament.[14] It reminds us that God does not give us sacrament for our private purposes. Such a perspective also suggests a more dynamic idea of why the Church may be called the basic sacrament.[15] Christ's saving and healing action is present in the community to continue his prophetic work. In each historical epoch, however, the Christian communities have had to discern their mission within the complexities (historical, socio-economic, psychological, etc.) of their world.

In Paul's time, "mission" included the missionary and local ministries of the Christian community, as well as the care of widows and the one-to-one evangelization that Priscilla and Aquila carried out, for example, in instructing Apollos in greater detail about Christianity (Acts 18:26–27). If Paul were with us today, his vision of "mission" would be equally wide-ranging. Mission is not only the missionary and religious education activities of the Church. Lobbying for legislation that is sensitive to social justice, donating one's professional expertise to the poor, and assisting in programs for the elderly are a few obvious examples of how diversified mission must be.

True and false Christian communities are distinguished, in part, by their actual definitions of mission. False ecclesial communities give us enough security to insure our continuing membership, but not enough prophetic and eschatological challenge to grow with. In this situation, sacramental celebrations may be used as a substitute for, rather than an incitement to, more practical Gospel service. True ecclesial communities afford us both the necessary security and the challenge of mission so that God's tomorrow does not happen without us. Sacramental celebrations and worship in such communities call out a deeper sensitivity to the different kinds of poverty (intellectual, emotional, moral, economic, etc.) that abound in our communities and countries. They help us to discern our mission, in much the same way that Mother Teresa saw her new task in the familiar slums of Calcutta.

In Paul's mind, the praise of God was not separate from his gracious desire that all people be saved. "For if you confess the Lord Jesus with your lips and believe with your heart that God has raised him from the dead, you will be saved. For man believes with his heart and is justified, and confesses with his lips and is saved. ... The same Lord is Lord of all and he makes all who call on him righteous" (Rom. 10:9–10, 12).[16] Käsemann also underlines this Pauline connection in commenting on the above verses: "The Lord of the community is also the Lord of the world which has received both its goal and judgment through the event of the resurrection. ... Paul often speaks of riches as the fulness of eschatological grace. ... The community which is growing in all the world has been set in this fulness which points beyond itself."[17]

The Pauline theology of Initiation begins, then, with this cosmic view of God's gift of salvation. Our praise of God springs from this gift, and our service is enabled by it.

THE IDENTIFICATION PROCESS

Paul expressed the process of becoming Christian in an unsettling formula that can be summarized this way: *as Christ, so we*

(Rom. 6:4). In understanding the implications of this formula
for us, its first part is key. What does the summary phrase, "as
Christ," involve?

"As Christ" sets up a christological comparison. Prescinding
from the matter of "high" or "low" christologies, how did
Christ deal with his identity? The New Testament answers this
question in diverse but complementary ways. One revealing way
in which Christ's identity is unfolded is in what he did. Seeing
the actions and contours of his life, we can come in contact with
his self-awareness as revealed in statements about his growing
in wisdom and knowledge (Luke 2:52), and learning obedience
(Heb. 5:8).

Francis Fiorenza has insightfully suggested that Jesus' life-
praxis profiled his radical obedience. Not only did this obedience make him one with his Father, it involved solidarity with
the marginal society of his time, the outcasts and the poor. The
meaning of Jesus' death was shaped by this obedient praxis.
Profiting from Irenaeus' insight, we can say that the "radical
obedience of Jesus to his self-identity with God the Father and
to his fellow persons expresses not only who he is but also mani-
fests the radical integrity of his life to the extent that he was
killed for being who he was."[18]

The startling phrase "killed for being who he was" explains
"as Christ." Jesus' life-praxis forcefully contested the radical,
pervasive evil of his time. That challenge was so telling that it
could not be ignored. That challenge cost Jesus his life and gives
meaning to his resurrection. Paul's identification of Jesus' death
and resurrection with our own logically presumes this dynamic
praxis: "For our faith will be credited to us also if we believe in
him who raised Jesus our Lord from the dead, the Jesus who
was handed over to death for our sins and raised up for our
justification" (Rom. 4:24–25).[19]

What does the Pauline identification process cost us in terms
of commitment? It will involve our own self-identity being
shaped and clarified in our life-praxis. To identify with Christ
is to contest radical evil in our own lives to the extent that we
ourselves might be considered worthy "to be killed." That is,
our witness to Gospel values will be evident to our contempo-

raries. This is a radical doctrine, but essential to Paul's understanding of how we become Christian.

"To be baptized into the death of Jesus," "to be united with
him through the likeness of his death," "to be buried with him"
(Rom. 6:3-6) are all Pauline attempts to describe the participation required of Christians. Commenting on this last passage, G.
R. Beasley-Murray says: "Paul's first thought in this passage . . .
is not that the believer in his baptism is laid in his own grave,
but that through that action he is set alongside Christ Jesus in
His."[20] In Paul's thought, the Christian has the same radical
experience of self-gift as Christ.

"As Christ, so we" is a continuing experience, colored by the
particular life-stage in which we find ourselves. In Chapter 3,
we stressed the positive growth that can come from the conflicts
and crises of any life-stage. The new gifts that emerge from this
period of our lives point out in practical ways what identification with Christ and mission will mean in our current life-cycle.
In Fowler's thought, this is the crucial distinction between
structure and *content* in faith. While the contents of a person's
faith (their ideas of sin and salvation, Church, etc.) are obviously important, their day-to-day intentions, decisions, and outlook
on life represent the actual structuring of that same faith.[21]

To be obediently one with God and the marginal people of
our time is not a static posture but the response of a growing
person. Within such a development, both faith and conscience
will have to review and deepen their commitments to living out
such an identification.[22] This process by which our answers to
God's action become more committed in no way denies justification. In fact, it shows the connection between Paul's teaching on
justification and being initiated into the death and resurrection
of Jesus.

Identification, as a continuing Initiation process that shapes
our life-praxis, underlines the Pauline logic of how we become
Christian. Bornkamm, in noting the parallel structuring of Romans 6:5-6 and 8-10, says: "The baptismal event and the
Christ-event are not only related to each other in terms of analogy but are identical with each other."[23] The Christian community that struggles to implement such an event time and again

for its members begins to realize the full force of Paul's summary phrase for Initiation: "united with him through *likeness to* (*to homoiomati*) his death" (Rom. 6:5).[24]

PAULINE METAPHORS OF RADICAL SURPRISE

When struggling to clarify God's mystery in Jesus as it touches us, Paul resorted to metaphor. As Ricoeur reminds us, a metaphor is more than a figure of speech. A metaphor tells us something new about reality by applying "a familiar label to a new object which first resists and then surrenders to its application."[25] To understand the challenge of identification, two Pauline metaphors are helpful: "new creation" (2 Cor. 5:17) and "image of God" (2 Cor. 3:17–18).

An initiated person, a Christian, is a "new creation." A first reaction to such a description might be to regard it as "rhetorical," "speculative," and even "utopian." In context, however, Paul was attempting to sketch the dynamics of how God reconciled us so that we might share his deeply rooted confidence. "New creation," of course, is an English translation that tries, if inadequately, to reproduce a complex Greek thought: we are a *kaine ktisis.*

In contrast to other adjectives Paul could have used, *kaine* expressed something radically new.[26] In this context, it certainly does. The message of *kaine* is: "You have never seen anything like this." "Creation" (*ktisis*) can be a very static word in English, but it was not static in the Pauline text we are studying. Reconciliation, for Paul, was a passage from one world to another. The individual who has made such a trip has entered a new world of eschatological possibilities.[27]

Justification, which makes our reconciliation possible, is a dynamic process, as we have seen. It is this process that helps us understand "new creation" as an ongoing event whose radical surprise unfolds throughout a lifetime. Paul's metaphor for the ongoing Initiation of a Christian has its fullest extension only when seen within the demand for new commitment in each lifecycle. Further, these demands are made on us "for the sake of others." Each of us is a "new creation" in the function of our mission within our church community and the larger community.

Another startling Pauline metaphor that describes the continuing results of Christian Initiation is "icon" or "image of God." In what seems to be a familiar hymn to the Christians in Asia,[28] the letter to the Colossians calls Christ the visible likeness (*eikon*) of the invisible God (Col. 1:15). The visibility of God is revealed in Christ. The community views Christ as "image" so that they can "praise him as the first in whom God reveals himself."[29]

The Pauline extension of this idea is startling. In 2 Corinthians 3:17–18, after connecting the Spirit of the Lord and freedom, Paul says: "All of us, gazing on the Lord's glory with unveiled faces, are being transformed from glory to glory into his very image [*eikon*] by the Lord who is the Spirit." The gradual transformation of a Christian ("from glory to glory") results in the visibility of the Risen Lord in that person. Because this change is worked out in the complexity of our staged lives, only God's creative renewal of us could enable the constant conversion that is needed.[30]

To say a Christian is the "icon," the image of the Lord, is another Pauline way of describing the identification process discussed earlier in this chapter. Although the emphasis in these passages is on God's action, the Pauline context draws out the implications for our response to this transformation. Paul's ideal of what the local church community and its mission should be and his ethical teaching rest on the new possibilities of God's creation in us. Those new possibilities can be summarized in the term *commitment*.

If examined closely, Paul's metaphors of "new creation" and "icon" are the results of God's eschatological gift, given for the sake of proclaiming that salvation. Such a proclamation is called mission. There is no reason why Christians so freely and continually enriched should attribute this initiative of God (justification) to themselves. On the contrary, as God goes before us in our experience, we see more clearly the connection between our own redemption and that of others.

The identification process shapes the emerging self-awareness of a Christian whose self-gift is challenged within the changing demands of his or her own and others' life-cycles and that of their larger socio-political world. Several Pauline metaphors describe God's saving action in us: for example, "in his name" and "in his death." The images "new creation" and "icon" stress the vital and constant nature of conversion, Initiation, and its corollary, commitment.[31] Our renewed effort to be "on account of others" in each stage of our lives specifies our mission and commitment as Christians. Such efforts, rooted in God's power, become a quiet challenge to the radical evil that makes people lose hope in God's presence and their own meaning.

The radical character of Paul's teaching on Initiation reflects his appreciation of the Cross of Christ and its meaning. But over the centuries, with the praxis of infant Baptism and children's Confirmation, the elements of commitment and mission in Paul's teaching have not been a major concern in the theology of Initiation. We see the results of this one-sided, objective treatment of Initiation in the pastoral situation: the Baptism of infants whose "nonpractising" parents have not yet appropriated their own faith or confirmation is treated as a social rather than religious rite of passage in some countries. The underlying problem is not infant Baptism, nor even the chronological age of candidates for Confirmation. The question is this: if faith is both the gracious gift of God and the gift of our whole self in free response to him (as cited earlier from the teaching of Vatican II), then what consequences does this have for the praxis and theory of Initiation?

IN THE WATER WITH JESUS

This identification process of "as Christ, so we" as service is powerfully symbolized in Jesus' Baptism in the Jordan. A careful comparative reading of the four Gospel accounts of the event (Mark 1:9–11; Matt. 3:13–17; Luke 3:21–22; John 1:29–34) reveals a gradual muting process in which John the Baptizer recedes into the background and the character of Jesus' Baptism is subtly altered. This is understandable as early christologies were developed and heresies were combatted. Questions such as, "Did Jesus really need Baptism (or forgiveness)?" and "Was

Jesus subordinate to John?" could not be as readily answered then as today.[32]

More central to our concerns is the recent exegetical analysis of this scene in terms of a "meaning-vision"("deute-vision").[33] Within such a frame of reference, the central elements of Jesus' Baptism, common to all the Gospels, take on new significance for Initiation theology. A "meaning-vision" externalizes what was originally an internal response, in this case, Jesus' experience as he was baptized. In other words, the "meaning-vision" interprets the symbols of the event (the voice from heaven and its message, the dove, etc.) so that *new meaning* emerges. It is a way of answering the question, "What did Jesus' Baptism mean for him?"

Key to the meaning of this scene is the heavenly voice's description of Jesus as "my beloved son." The phrase has many Old Testament resonances[34] that center around the traditions of "messiah," "king," and "servant."[35] The meaning of Jesus' Baptism is framed by a rich collage of these different traditions, which gives new depth to his role as servant, son, and gatherer of God's convenant people.[36] Unlike the static Renaissance tableau of "the humble Jesus" being baptized with sinners, this forceful interpretation of his Baptism shows him being commissioned on account of others.

This scene, a favorite for the patristic commentaries on Initiation,[37] remains a norm for our own Initiation process of identifying with Jesus. Tertullian provided a clue to the significance of this event in one of the earliest monographs on Baptism: "But we, being little fishes, as Jesus Christ is our great Fish, begin our life in the water, and only while we abide in the water [*in aqua permanendo*] are we safe and sound."[38] He cited the alternative as well: killing the fish by taking them out of the water. In other words, the challenge of this word-event is to determine how the Christian may stay in the water, remain constantly committed to Christ. It is a concern raised by the long-range view of conversion and Initiation.

The "meaning-vision" suggests an answer: as Christ, so we are sons and daughters, servants and covenant-gatherers in our mission on account of the others. It is our life-praxis, summing up our life-style and mind-sets, that is the practical test of that mission. There we, too, externalize our internal experience of God's justifying and enabling action in us. It is there, in our life-praxis, that Initiation commitment is constantly refocused by the demands both of those remaining in the water with us and those still on the shore. Like Jesus, our own specific identity as Christian is shaped within this process that makes us one with the marginal people of our time and with the Father. Only such Christians are indeed "worthy to be killed."

Furthermore, only such an understanding of Initiation, it seems to me, allowed Paul to bridge the chasm between Christ's death and our own lives. In the sixth chapter of Romans, we have the classical explanation: "Are you not aware that we who were baptized into Christ Jesus were baptized *into his death?* Through baptism into his death we were buried with him, so that, just as Christ was raised from the dead by the glory of the Father, we too might lead a new life" (Rom. 6:3–4). In the background, there are the older Hebrew ideas about burial and going down into the "sea of death."[39] But more important is the way in which Paul was working out the theological problem of how Jesus' death could possibly touch us. Among the dense complexities of these verses,[40] the phrase "into his death" is perhaps most germane to our discussion.

Paul was making a connection between the experience of Initiation and the saving death of Jesus.[41] That death can touch us because it was "for us," "for all," "for our sins." These prepositional phrases assume the corporate and covenant nature of both our redemptive situation and God's redemptive promises (Rom. 5:12–19).[42] They reflect the martyr terminology of the Fourth Book of Maccabees, where the martyr-witness intercedes for the whole people, as well as the atonement theologies that proliferated after the Exile. These phrases also demonstrate that the early Christian community saw the Servant's mission to others in Isaiah 53 as a clarifying image of Jesus' own role.[43]

Paul, with masterful theological insight, brought these traditional elements into a new synthesis: Jesus' obedience even to death is redemptive for the whole family.[44] The unexpected result of this action is "so that we might lead a new life" (Rom.

6:4). The Christian commitment to mission and its ethical corollaries are premised on this new and unearned possibility.[45] As with the Pauline phrase "a new creation," "new life" reflects the dynamic nature of a conversion that never ceases this side of the Kingdom.

At this juncture, we touch upon a question that theologically troubled the Reformers and pastorally affected the first Christian communities: faith versus works. In other words, in introducing commitment into the discussion of Initiation, are we forgetting that God's salvation is sheer gift?

This question is not prompted by a concern for theological niceties, but by the continuing Pelagian temptation to justify ourselves by what we do. Luther, for example, saw much in the sacramental praxis of his day which encouraged some to believe that they could "earn their salvation" by the number of Masses they attended. A few observations may help us deal with this question.[46]

Reviewing our treatment of justification as the root of all faith and sacrament, we saw that it empowers us to accept the tasks of the Kingdom which cannot be separated from their ecclesial context. Faith is more than intellectual assent. It is the ongoing answer we give to God's enabling invitation to be as Christ.[47] This obedient faith allows the Christian to follow Christ's example of self-gift for the sake of the Kingdom and "on account of the others."

On such a basis, Paul could establish the connection between justification and Baptism.[48] This connection, already apparent in the pre-Pauline teaching, was given more precision by Paul. Baptism is a privileged symbol of God's justification of "the impious." However, having occurred in the past, it must be complemented and continued in a faith that responds obediently now.

The baptismal event initiates a process that constantly invites the Christian into the Christ-event. This is why there is a connection between the "new person in Christ" and the justified person. For Paul, the Crucified One's gift of salvation had to have real consequence for the life of the Christian. To be baptized, then, into such a death is not a ritualization of some theological notion of justification. The communities of baptized Christians, by their ongoing faith, actualize the symbolism of their Baptism. They recommit themselves to a "faith, which expresses itself through love" (Gal. 5:6). The test of honest faith and redemptive works is, once more, the Pauline "as Christ, so we" and its corollary, being a "new creation."

But if these new possibilities are available, why does the Christian presence seem to have so little impact on the radical evil of our world? Bornkamm responds: "For the baptismal event cannot be presupposed as a foregone conclusion which is effective naturally. Rather, baptism itself must constantly become the object of proclamation" that repeatedly calls Christians to the obedience into which they have been taken in Baptism.[49] That obedience, of course, is modeled on Jesus' obedience, concretized in his life-praxis. "To remain in the water with Jesus" is, in effect, to live out such obedience at each stage of our lives.

And this ongoing commitment is all too rare. Again, it is not the theory of Initiation but our praxis which is in question. What degree of practical commitment should the local Christian community, for example, ask of parents who present their infants for Baptism? In an interesting response to the query of the African hierarchy about just such a question, Rome gave a somewhat surprising reply. While reiterating the traditional teaching that infants of practising Christian parents should be baptized within a reasonable time after birth, Cardinal Šeper, in the name of the Congregation of the Doctrine of the Faith, insisted that the local church must judge, in the case of nonpractising parents, what assurances of a Christian upbringing can be given.[50] If these assurances are insufficient, then the infant's Baptism may be postponed while the local church continues to have further pastoral contact with the parents.

This document calls for some minimal commitment on the part of adults who are capable of giving it. The question is not infant Baptism but the responsibility that Augustine spoke of: it is the whole church that begets each and all of the baptized.[51] The "faith of the Church" cannot be and should not be used as a substitute for the faith of the parents whose privilege and responsibility it is to give their children their own unique and crucial witness to the meaning of the Gospel life and service. This response from Rome, in turn, suggests a related question: what minimal commitment must the Christian community ask in any sacrament? Christian Initiation has always been thought of as a prerequisite for the reception of other sacraments. But how can the commitment required for Initiation be a guideline for the question of commitment in the reception of other sacraments? If the principles applied to nonpractising parents in the Roman response were used, for example, in discerning whether a couple is prepared for the celebration of Marriage within the Christian community, how would this change the current praxis and theory of that sacrament?

THE CATECHUMENAL MODEL

Phrases such as "initiation into Jesus' death" or "as Christ, so we" may be theologically compelling but their implications for day-to-day living can remain quite vague. At the beginning of this chapter, I proposed the catechumenate as a model for the praxis and theory of Initiation. Victor Turner's insights on communitas revealed the dynamic behind such a model. We do not receive candidates for Baptism and Confirmation into an international organization or a set of church buildings but into a community of Christians. That community does not have to be perfect, but it must be credible. Christian credibility involves continual renewal of Gospel commitment in the practical issues that are the warp and woof of our daily lives: the whole range of affective needs and practical assistance that we require of one another. Our Christian communities usually do not lack generous people, but we sometimes need to learn how to play "musical chairs" again, that is, to rethink our commitments and roles as Christians.

This is the ideal of the catechumenate. "The initiation of catechumens takes place step by step *in the midst of the community of the faithful. Together with the catechumens, the faithful reflect upon the value of the paschal mystery, renew their own conversion, and by their example lead the catechumens to obey the Holy Spirit more generously.*"[52] Erikson's image of how our own and others' life-stages "cogwheel" is pertinent here. The growing commitment of a few catechumens, interacting with a group of baptized Christians, provides the necessary dynamic for a mutual Christian re-evaluation of intentions, priorities, and goals.[53]

The catechumen goes through a series of stages that facilitates this interaction. The initial precatechumenate or inquiry stage is a period of evangelization and conversion in which members of the Christian community (usually a catechumenal team composed of priests, religious educators, and other community members) explain the Gospel to a candidate. It is also a time for the catechumen to meet Christian families and groups. As a result of "the first sense of repentance and the practice of calling on God in prayer, and the first experience of society and spirit of Christians,"[54] the candidate may seek admission into the catechumenate proper.

Catechumens have always been considered part of the "household of Christ."[55] During this second extended catechumenal period, their journey of conversion continues. Once again, the active role of sponsors, the catechumenal team, and the whole community is emphasized.[56] The Christian maturity envisaged in the rite is brought about by four factors: a theological formation, a prayer-life that will result in "a progressive change of outlook and morals . . . with its social consequences," the constant experience of the liturgy, and learning how to "work actively with others to spread the Gospel."[57]

This ambitious program relies on the process of "musical chairs" in which the catechumenal team is constantly interacting with the catechumens. The touchstone of this interaction is the frequent celebration of the Word of God and the telling of each one's story in response to that Word. As the catechumens learn, like Paul and Augustine before them, to pray out of their own stories, the baptized members of the group re-learn that same process. As the catechumen works out the moral and social implications of Christian living, already initiated Christians will find their own commitment once again called into question.

In fact, the third catechumenal stage—the immediate preparation of the catechumens for the Initiation rites of Baptism,

Confirmation, and Eucharist—is also the Lenten preparation of the whole community to renew their baptismal commitment. If, however, renewal is restricted to ritual, then another Corinthian community is in the making. R. M. Kanter has demonstrated how such renewed commitment is the heart of any continuing and successful religious community.

The search for community is also a quest for direction and purpose in a collective anchoring of the individual life. Investment of self in a community, acceptance of its authority and willingness to support its values, is dependent in part on the extent to which group life can offer identity, personal meaning, and the opportunity to grow in terms of standards and guiding principles that the member feels are expressive of his own inner being. . . . For this to occur, the group must first provide ways for an individual to reassess his previous life, to undo those parts of himself he wishes to change, and to perceive that identity and meaning for him lie not in an individualistic, private existence but in acceptance of the stronger influence of the utopian group.[58]

It is this cathechumenal model which has served as a practical guide to the renewal of half-hearted Christian communities.[59] It is this same catechumenal process which spells out, for each Christian community and for its individual members, what "as Christ, so we" means in an affluent, white Christian community in suburban Houston as opposed to a poor, minority group of Christians in the Bronx or Los Angeles. One Christian's commitment becomes another's challenge to commitment. The commitment of a Mother Teresa, a Dorothy Day, or a Father Damien has called out the commitment of many others in response to the specific needs of specific groups of people. This process of Christian Initiation is still at work among those who were baptized perhaps a long time ago, but who once more renew their "likeness to Christ."

The Christian family with teenagers is a case in point. As indicated earlier, the most pressing question for such a family is not whether the teenagers will "go to Sunday Mass," but whether they will begin to take responsibility for the Gospel that is proclaimed there. Both the parents and their teenage children are once more working though the conflicts and crises that will determine how much vigorous meaning they will bring to their next stage of life. Ideally, with one another's help, they will achieve new intentions and commitments. Erikson has forcefully described the interdependance of this process of life-stages and their tasks: "Without old people in possession of such integrity, young people in need of identity can neither rebel nor obey."[60]

From the Christian viewpoint, each member of such a family has a role to play in the new commitment of the others. A teen-age son, for example, in interacting with his father, may not only help the latter to reassess his professional and personal priorities in his middle years but also begin to see his own gifts in relation to others' needs. After all, at what age should the teen-ager learn the meaning of Jesus' saying, "As often as you did it for one of my least brothers, you did it for me" (Matt. 25:40)? Christian Initiation continues as both father and son perceive this test of their Gospel commitment fleshed out in each other's needs.

SUMMARY

Christian Initiation as a life-long process of commitment can be costly. We can draw courage, however, from the situation of a group of New Testament Christians addressed in 1 Peter. The letter has a number of baptismal themes (1 Pet. 1:3–5, 23; 2:2, etc.), but the specific purpose of the letter is summed up in the third chapter: "Who indeed can harm you if you are committed deeply to doing what is right?" (1 Pet. 3:13). This community of Christians paid a high price for its Initiation.

The writer of 1 Peter repeatedly drew the connection between suffering and baptismal commitment: "The reason why Christ died for sins once for all . . . was that he might lead you to God. . . . You are now saved by a baptismal bath. . . . This baptism is no removal of physical stain, but the pledge to God of an irreproachable conscience through the resurrection of Jesus Christ. . . . Therefore arm yourselves with his same mentality" (1 Pet. 3:18, 21; 4:1).

David Hill summarizes that connection between suffering and Initiation: "When a writer seeks to strengthen and encourage a body of Christians in distress, it is not surprising that his exhortation should, from time to time, recall or imply that critical moment of their responsible commitment to God to live uprightly and unashamedly in his service and way, which is, in the view of the authority of 1 Peter, the real meaning of baptism."[61]

Like the Christian communities that have preceded us, we can draw back from the sometimes painful and costly implications of becoming Christian at a new stage of our lives. The complex problems of our international, national, and local communities and the interlocking conflicts of our families and personal lives can leave us paralyzed with doubt and fear. Our honest attempts, communally and individually, to reconsider and renew our commitments in view of the needs of God's world will make us "a witness of Christ's sufferings and sharer in the glory that is to be revealed" (1 Pet. 5:1).

NOTES

1. For a succinct treatment of the historical origins of the catechumenate and its connection with the problem of orthodoxy, see A. Turck, "Aux Origines du Catéchumenat," *Revue de Sciences Philosophiques et Théologiques* 48 (1964): 20–31. For general historical outlines of the question, see M. Dujarier, *A History of the Catechumenate* (New York: Sadlier, 1979); and T. Maertens, *Histoire et pastorale du rituel du catéchumenat et du baptême* (Bruges: Biblica, 1962).

2. The classic delineation of this complex history is to be found in *Leiturgia* 5 (1970): 1–348, in G. Kretschmar's work on the early Church's Initiation process and theology. See B. Jordan's work (ibid, 350–640) for the medieval and more recent developments.

3. Here we have followed the excellent critical edition of Dom Bernard Botte, *La Tradition apostolique de Saint Hippolyte: Essai de Reconstitution* (Münster: Aschendorff, 1963), pp. 34–39.

4. Ibid, p. 39.

5. Ibid, p. 43.

6. J. Bernsten, "Christian Affections and the Catechumenate," *Worship* 52 (1978): 194–210. The same concerns might help solve the problem that R. Murray deals with in "The Exhortations to Candidates for Ascetical Vows at Baptism in the Ancient Syriac Church," *New Testament Studies* 21 (1974): 59–80.

7. The rite was restored in 1972; see *Rite of Christian Initiation of Adults* (Washington, D.C.: United States Catholic Conference, 1974).

8. Actually, the Eucharist is part of the triad of Initiation sacraments. Throughout this chapter, we will use the term *Initiation* to refer to the

entire process of becoming Christian. The unity of Baptism and Confirmation has been reaffirmed by *Rite of Christian Initiation of Adults,* par. 34 (p. 8).

9. V. Turner, *The Ritual Process* (Chicago: Aldine, 1969); and V. Turner, "Passages, Margins, and Poverty: Religious Symbols of Communities," *Worship* 46 (1972): 390–412; 482–94.

10. M. Buber, *Between Man and Man* (London: Fontana, 1961), p. 51, as cited in Turner, *Ritual Process,* pp. 126–27.

11. Turner, *Ritual Process,* p. 127; cf. also his *Worship* article, 402–03.

12. Letter 98, par. 5 in *St. Augustine: Letters,* trans. Sr. W. Parsons (New York: Fathers of the Church, 1953), vol. 10, p. 134. The context is the question of infant Baptism.

13. The extent to which this is still a problem in the speculative Roman Catholic models of ecclesiology is treated in M. Kehl, *Kirche als Institution: Zur theologischen Begründung des institutionellen Charackters der Kirche in der neueren deutschsprachigen katholischen Ekklesiologie* (Frankfurt-am-Main: J. Knecht, 1976).

14. For a similar position, see R. Haight, "Mission: Symbol of the Church Today," *Theological Studies* 37 (1976): 620–49.

15. For typical Roman Catholic statements, see K. Rahner, *The Church and the Sacraments* (New York: Herder and Herder. 1963). esp. pp. 76ff. For a perceptive and sympathetic Protestant critique of this position, see V. Vajta, *Evangile et Sacrement* (Paris: Cerf, 1973), pp. 29–33.

16. I follow E. Käsemann's translation here; see *Commentary on Romans,* trans. G. W. Bromley (Grand Rapids, Mich.: W. B. Eerdmans, 1980), p. 283.

17. Ibid, pp. 291, 292.

18. F. Fiorenza, "Critical Social Theory and Christology," *Catholic Theological Society Proceedings* 30 (1975): 63–110; here, 107.

19. This is not to say that Paul had an explicit praxis model in mind, but to emphasize his connection between Jesus' Resurrection by the Father and his self-gift, which was revealed in his life and symbolized in his death. For further discussion, see K. Kertelge, ed., *Der Tod Jesu: Deutungen im Neuen Testament* (Freiburg: Herder, 1976).

20. G. R. Beasley-Murray, *Baptism in the New Testament* (Grand Rapids, Mich.: Eerdmans, 1962), p. 130. For conplementary aspects of these verses, see H. Frankemölle, *Das Taufverständnis des Paulus* (Stuttgart: Katholisches Bibelwerk, 1970), pp. 52–56. My discussion in no way precludes the corporate dimension of Paul's thought as in G. Eicholz's discussion in *Die Theologie des Paulus im Umriss* (Neukirchen: Neukirchener Verlag, 1977), pp. 209–11. The possible Hebrew origins of this image are also helpful here; see J. Ysebaert, *Greek Baptismal Terminology* (Nijmegen: Dekker and Van De Vegt, 1962), esp. pp. 53–56.

21. J. Fowler, *Stages of Faith: The Psychology of Human Development and the Question of Meaning* (San Francisco: Harper & Row, 1981), p. 48.

22. The developmental work of J. Fowler on faith and that of Kohlberg on moral judgment, touched on in previous chapters, is germane here.

23. G. Bornkamm, *Early Christian Experience* (New York: Harper & Row, 1969), p. 75.

24. For a discussion of this much disputed phrase, see ibid, p. 78, and Beasley-Murray, *Baptism in the New Testament,* p. 135. For somewhat different

positions, see J. D. Dunn, *Baptism in the Holy Spirit* (London: SCM Press, 1970), pp. 142–43, and E. Käsemann, *Commentary on Romans*, trans. G. W. Bromley (Grand Rapids, Mich.: W. B. Eerdmans, 1980), pp. 168–69.

25. P. Ricoeur, "Biblical Hermeneutics," *Semeia* 4 (1975): 80, 86.
26. Ysebaert, *Greek Baptismal Terminology*, pp. 89–90; 131–35, where there is also an interesting discussion of how Paul seems to have coined verb forms with this same root in attempting to express this process.
27. J. Behn, "Kainos," *Theological Dictionary of the New Testament* (Grand Rapids, Mich.: Eerdmans, 1965), vol. 3, pp. 447–50. "Thus *kainos* becomes a slogan of reality of salvation which we know already in Christ" (p. 449).
28. E. Lohse, *Colossians and Philemon,* trans. W. R. Poehlmann and R. J. Karris (Philadelphia: Fortress, 1971), p. 46; cf. p. 47, n.163 for bibliography, as well as U. Luz, "New Testament Perspectives of the Image of God in Christ and Mankind," in P. Benoit et al., eds., *The Presence of God,* Concilium 50, (New York: Paulist, 1969), pp. 80–92.
29. Lohse, *Colossians and Philemon,* p. 48.
30. For discussion in a somewhat similar vein, see C. K. Barrett, *A Commentary on the Second Epistle to the Corinthians* (New York: Harper & Row, 1973), pp. 124–25.
31. Dunn, (*Baptism in the Holy Spirit,* pp. 110, 158) speaks of the "constant conversion" language of these lines.
32. For some of the background, see J. Schmitt, "Le milieu baptiste," *Revue des Sciences Religieuses* 47 (1973): 391–407, and R. Brown, *The Gospel According to John (I-XII)* (Garden City, N.Y.: Doubleday, 1966), pp. 63–65.
33. F. Lentzen-Deis, *Die Taufe Jesu nach den Synoptikern* (Frankfurt-am-Main: J. Knecht, 1970).
34. Cf. ibid, pp. 183–91.
35. By way of comparison, see the work of R. Longenecker, *The Christology of Early Jewish Christianity* (Naperville, Ill.: A. Allenson, 1970), esp. pp. 95–99.
36. Lentzen-Deis, *Die Taufe Jesu nach den Synoptikern,* pp. 278–79.
37. For a summary of this patristic commentary, see A. Hamman, *Baptême et Confirmation* (Paris: Desclée, 1969), pp. 92–93; 95–96.
38. E. Evans, ed., *Tertullian's Homily on Baptism* (London: SPCK 1964), pp. 4–5. There is a play on words in the Latin text where *pisciculi* ("little fish") is contrasted with the Greek word *ichthus* (literally, "fish"), the early symbol for Christ (cf. pp. 48–49, n.10).
39. See Ysebaert, *Greek Baptismal Terminology,* pp. 53–56.
40. In addition to the works of Beasley-Murray and Dunn, already cited, see that of Frankemölle, *Das Taufverständnis des Paulus,* pp. 38–60.
41. Ibid, pp. 52–53.
42. For the distinction between solidarity and corporate personality, see Beasley-Murray, *Baptism in the New Testament,* pp. 135–38; for the "messianic affliction" as another possible element in these verses, see C. K. Barrett, *Letter to the Romans* (New York: Harper & Row, 1968), pp. 122, 80.
43. Cf. K. Kertelge, "Das Verständnis des Todes Jesu bei Paulus," in *Der Tod Jesu,* pp. 114–36, esp. pp. 116–24.
44. For a balanced position on this complex question, see ibid, pp. 119–22.

45. See the emphatic statements of Beasley-Murray, *Baptism in the New Testament,* pp. 142–45, and Bornkamm, *Early Christian Experience,* p. 74.

46. I have treated this question at greater length in "Justification and Sacrament," *The Journal of Ecumenical Studies* 16 (1979): 672–90.

47. F. Hahn, "Taufe und Rechtfertigung," *Rechtfertigung* (Festschrift für E. Käsemann), pp. 95–124; here, pp. 120–21.

48. Ibid, p. 121.

49. Bornkamm, *Early Christian Experience,* p. 81; see also, K. Kertelge, *Rechtfertigung bei Paulus* (Münster: Aschendorff, 1967), pp. 228–36, 248, for the exegetical positions on this question.

50. *Notitiae* 61 (1971): 64–73. The Roman response lists among those considered "nonpractising" people in polygamous situations, parents who want their children baptized for social reasons, and those who do not receive the sacraments regularly (ibid, 69).

51. To my mind, L. Ligier stresses the infant Baptism dimension to the neglect of the question of adult commitment in sacrament; see his "Débat sur le baptême des petits enfants," *Gregorianum* 57 (1976): 617–57; here, 642–43; cf. P. Vanbergen, "Baptism of the Infants of 'non satis credentes' Parents," *Studia Liturgica* 12 (1977): 195–200.

52. *RCIA,* par. 4, italics mine.

53. Space does not permit a detailed description of the catechumenal process. For a liturgical and pastoral discussion of the catechumenate, see M. Dujarier, *The Rites of Christian Initiation* (New York: Sadlier, 1979); A. Kavanagh, *The Shape of Baptism: The Rite of Christian Initiation* (New York: Pueblo, 1978), pp. 126–49; R. Kemp, *A Journey in Faith: An Experience of the Catechumenate* (New York: Sadlier, 1979); *Becoming a Catholic Christian* (New York: Sadlier, 1978).

54. *RCIA,* par.15, p. 4.

55. For example, catechumens are married and buried with the rituals of the Christian community (ibid, par. 18).

56. Ibid, par. 19, p. 4.

57. Ibid, p. 5.

58. R. M. Kanter, *Commitment and Community: Communes and Utopias in Sociological Perspective* (Cambridge; Mass.: Harvard University Press, 1972), p. 73.

59. G. Zevini, "The Christian Initiation of Adults into the Neo-Catechumenal Community," in *Structures of Initiation in Crisis: Concilium* 122, ed. L. Maldonado and D. Power (New York: Seabury, 1979), pp. 65–74.

60. E. Erickson, *Insight and Responsibility* (New York: W. W. Norton, 1964), p. 95.

61. D. Hill, "On Suffering and Baptism in I Peter," *Novum Testamentum* 18 (1976): 181–89.

CHAPTER 6

Servants at Table

Eating on a plane is quite different from having a meal at home. The first is functional; the second, familial. The flight personnel serve the passengers' dinner in a polite, efficient, and impersonal way. The family dinner is potentially a time of sharing, mutual service, and recommitment. The context of a meal is important because it frames the meaning we attach to it. We have not chosen our meal companions, for example, for our in-flight meal, nor does our eating together imply any commitment to our fellow passengers. Often enough, we find ourselves eating alone in a crowded plane, separated from our family and friends.

Since Vatican II, we have once again begun to speak of the Eucharist as both meal and sacrifice. In contrast to pre–Vatican II days, the majority of people at Sunday celebration receive the Eucharist. After some initial confusion with new eucharistic rituals, the average community of Christians now appears to have a certain unity of meaning and purpose as it celebrates the Sunday liturgy.

We should, however, exercise a certain Pauline caution. Under the unity of our rituals, we may discover a confusion of meanings, some of which would certainly earn Paul's comment, "You are eating and drinking judgment to yourselves" (1 Cor. 11:29). Just as a group of air passengers can share common rituals and the same dinner menu but remain strangers, so too can the post–Vatican II community in its eucharistic celebration. And just as a family can have a meal that is replete with rituals of love and shared commitment but fail to actualize those meanings, so too may the Christian community evade the needed intentions and crucial meanings of the Eucharist and settle for the comfort of familiar rituals. There are, unfortunately, Corinthian communities in every age.

The young Roman soldier of the third century whom we discussed in Chapter 5 would probably have had an extended catechumenal experience before his first Eucharist, received in his Initiation. The cost and ecclesial context of honest Eucharist would have been part of his long training as a catechumen. In this post–Vatican II period, however, initial satisfaction at the sight of large numbers of communicants should be balanced by the sober question about the commitment of these communicants. Again, my contention throughout this book bears repeating: we are not discussing the commitment of perfect people, but the need of imperfect people to be committed.

Eucharist is one of the most frequently employed religious symbols of commitment in the contemporary Christian Church. Participation in the Sunday liturgy may demand more obvious commitment of a Polish or Hungarian Christian than of an American one. But Paul's clear teaching applies to Christians of all ages and nationalities: "He who eats and drinks without recognizing the body eats and drinks judgment on himself" (1 Cor. 11:29).

OUR MEANINGS FOR EUCHARIST

The meanings that communities and individuals give to their Eucharists cannot be discerned by simply analyzing their creedal statements. Doctrinal labels like "real presence" and "sacrifice of the Mass" can camouflage disparate communal and personal meanings of participants. To compound the difficulty, we find ourselves in a post–Vatican II period in which there is a mixture of old and new attitudes about the Eucharist.

Erving Goffman would have a fertile field for investigation in observing the adult who suddenly reverts to childhood rituals in receiving the host with eyes closed, hands crossed on the breast,

and fear of "biting the host" an obvious concern. My purpose
here is not so much to criticize these rituals as to question their
underlying meaning for the communicant. The person educated
in the post–Vatican II era may have similar problems of meaning, if dissimilar ritual instincts. Having been brought up with
the Eucharist-as-meal model, any aware person might ask
whether this model corresponds to anything in their own American experience of a meal in a "fast-food" culture or, for that
matter, to any of the typical nonmeal settings of Eucharist in
their parish.[1]

Any praxis theology of Eucharist, then, must deal with the
implicit but unclarified meanings of Eucharist as betrayed in the
rituals of participants as well as the time-locked cultural trans-
lations of the eucharistic tradition of the New Testament. In
both instances, our pastoral concern is the same: that our Eucharists be the occasion and cause of deeper commitment to the
work of the Kingdom and not a flight from such commitment.

As indicated in earlier chapters, this confusion of eucharistic
meanings was part of the problem at Corinth. These Christians,
under the guise of relevant rituals, celebrated a Eucharist that
excused them from commitments to the Cross so that they could
rejoice in their private and unearned salvation. As Paul indicates, they had been given correct doctrine (1 Cor. 11:23). However, "meaning" encompasses much more than correct statements of belief. It involves self-investment which is tested in the
shared decisions of our lives. Here is where the Corinthians betrayed themselves.

This chapter, therefore, will not try to duplicate the available
discussions of the Lord Supper's from a scriptural, historical, or
systematic viewpoint.[2] Rather, we will draw out the corollaries
for commitment from this rich heritage. First, recent exegetical
work on the eucharistic texts will be examined for their implications. Then an historical overview of some eucharistic theologies
and praxis will suggest how the meaning of Eucharist is tied to
the problem of symbol. Finally, a proposal will be made about
the Eucharist as a continuation of the identification process of
Initiation examined in the previous chapter.

CONTEXTS FOR EUCHARISTIC TEXTS

The most basic context for the Last Supper and its meaning has already been proposed. The symbols of eating and drinking assume a privileged meaning in the Old Testament and directly prepare for "hungering and thirsting for righteousness" (Matt. 5:6; Luke 6:21) in the New Testament. As we saw in Chapter 2, God's "poor ones" long for his feast at the end of time. The meal symbols of good food and fine wine sum up the need for salvation and God's gracious answer, his Kingdom pictured as the final feast.

But there are two other contexts in the New Testament that develop this symbol of meal. The first is Jesus' meals with sinners. In the Gospel of Mark, for example, Jesus' meals seem, at least sometimes, to have a messianic context of joyful news to the needy.[3] The importance of such meals with the marginal people of his time can easily be lost on our Western sensibilities. As Jeremias says, "The oriental, for whom symbolic action means much more than it does for us, understood immediately that the acceptance of religious and moral outcasts into table fellowship with Jesus signified the offer of salvation to the sinner and the declaration of forgiveness."[4]

Only against such a background can the outraged reactions of the Pharisees be appreciated: "When the scribes who belonged to the Pharisee party saw that he was eating with tax collectors and offenders against the law, they complained to his disciples, 'Why does he eat with such as these?'" Jesus' response emphasizes the purpose of such meals: "I have come to call sinners, not the self-righteous" (Mark 2:16–17). In this context, the conversion stories, such as that of Zacchaeus, take on new meaning.[5] Jesus invited himself into the tax collector's home (Luke 19:1–10). The presumption was (as it is even today in the East) that Jesus would eat there. Luke comments: "Everyone began to murmur: 'He has gone to a sinner's house as a guest'" (Luke 19:7). But the meaning of Jesus' offer was not lost on this sinner. In response, he stated, "If I have defrauded anyone in the least, I pay him back fourfold'" (Luke 19:8).

The undeserved and universal gift of salvation eventually was told in parable: "A man was giving a large dinner and he invited many" (Luke 14:16–24). The "undesirables" replaced the originally invited guests who proved ungrateful: "'Go out quickly into the streets and alleys of the town and bring in the poor and the crippled, the blind and the lame'" (Luke 14:21). Long before Jesus told this parable, he had lived it with many of the marginal people of his time.[6]

A less obvious development are the meals Jesus had with his disciples before and after his Resurrection. The Master educated his disciples, in part, by showing them how to eat with sinners. In this way they saw the redemptive compassion of Jesus evoking commitment from people of whom nothing had previously been asked. Further, the master-disciple relationship required that the disciples justify Jesus eating with prostitutes and tax-collectors, the outcasts of Jewish society.[7] They could have done this only because they had witnessed the results of such meals time and again.[8] Certainly the formative effect of these meals on the disciples should not be underestimated.[9] The disciples learned the meaning of salvation by watching the Master as he moved among the outcasts and called out of them the gifts they had never given.

In the post-Resurrection accounts, the sinner-disciples are the primary test and proof of a Risen Lord. These are also conversion stories, often enough with a meal element that represents a certain continuity with accounts of earlier meals with sinners (for example, Luke 24:13ff, 41ff; John 21:12ff). Whether or not there are eucharistic shadings in these accounts, they seem to contain the meal symbol with all its promised reconciliation and hope.[10]

Healing and new commitment are always important elements in these post-Resurrection stories. Disappointed disciples, after recognizing Jesus in the breaking of the bread at Emmaus, say to one another, "'Were not our hearts burning inside us as he talked to us on the road and explained the Scriptures to us?' They got up immediately and returned to Jerusalem . . ." (Luke 24:32–33). There they witness to a Risen Lord. Jesus himself prepares an early morning meal for his dispirited disciples by the shore of the Sea of Tiberias and then commissions a repentant Peter to "'Feed my sheep'" (John 21:17).

These meals of a Risen Lord with sinner-disciples are not

poetic imagery for some future salvation. The results are more impressive than any such meals in the lifetime of Jesus. Flawed men who had never really understood the price of commitment that the Gospel would entail accept healing for themselves and mission to others. This is the first result of Jesus' Resurrection: disciples healed for the service of others.

THE SERVANT-AT-TABLE THEOLOGY

The fact that the Last Supper account immediately precedes the Passion account in the Scriptures is not simply a matter of chronology. The early Church struggled with the question: how is the death of Jesus saving for us? An early response to that question is the careful connection made between the last meal of Jesus with his disciples and his death on the Cross.[11] To appreciate how the early Church arrived at this connection, we must briefly trace the idea of Jesus' death as saving, in several stages.

A key phrase in the Last Supper texts describes Jesus as "on account of the many" (Mark 14:24; Matt. 26:28) or "on account of you" (Luke 22:19–20; 1 Cor. 11:24). The application of this Old Testament phrase to Jesus is one way of explaining why Jesus is savior: he is someone "on account of others." Recent exegetical research has suggested that this insight is a result of a three-stage development in awareness of Jesus' death as saving for us.[12]

In the first stage, the Church saw Jesus' death as the result of ignorant or wicked people, but his Resurrection as the work of God (as in Acts 4:10). In a second stage of development, God is seen as willing Jesus' death for us (as in the Synoptic Passion accounts). Indeed, over the centuries, many Christians' awareness of the meaning of Jesus' death for them started with and never left this second stage.

But closer examination of the New Testament shows that a third stage of meaning had been arrived at fairly early in Christian thinking: Jesus is "someone on account of us." The image that carries and clarifies this meaning is that of a servant.[13] Mark 10:45 gives us an early classical statement of this theology: "For the Son of Man also came not to be served but to

serve and to give his life as a ransom for many." Even a casual
reading of the text reveals the sharp transition from a theme of
"service" to one of "ransom." This leap can only be justified if
"servant" has already become a clarifying metaphor for Jesus'
salvific work.[14]

Luke framed the meaning of the Last Supper account with
this servant-at-table metaphor (Luke 22:26–27). After presenting his version of Jesus' Last Supper words for the bread and
wine, Luke pictured the disciples as fighting among themselves
about seniority. The meaning of Jesus' death as the ultimate
service, symbolized in the Last Supper, was lost on these first
participants in Eucharist.

In an earlier passage, Luke had stressed the image of Jesus as
servant: when the Lord returns and finds his disciples waiting
and alert, "he will put on an apron, seat them at table, and
proceed to wait on them" (Luke 12:37b). Luke took up the
same image of servant-at-table in this new context of the Last
Supper. He said to his disputing followers, "Let the greater
among you be as the junior, the leader as the servant. Who, in
fact, is the greater—he who reclines at table or he who serves
the meal? Is it not the one who reclines at table? Yet I am in
your midst as the one who serves you" (Luke 22:26b–27).

To such servants, Jesus repeated the Old Testament eschatological promise: "In my kingdom you will eat and drink at my
table, and you will sit on thrones judging the twelve tribes of
Israel" (Luke 22:30).[15] This eschatological meal motif both
summarizes and transposes the themes of service and salvation.
The disciples in Luke's account would learn the meaning that
bridges the Last Supper and the Cross if they could see Jesus as
"the one who serves," that is, someone "on account of others."

The background for the Last Supper as a symbol of the
meaning of the Cross has been our concern here. Jesus' saving
work is portrayed in the New Testament in his meals with sinners and in the servant-at-table image. Salvation begins when
the sinner hopes in God's Kingdom (the eschatological meal
symbol) and, like Jesus, is willing to help bring it about (the
servant-at-table image). As we saw in Chapter 2, this process
entails the recognition of our own need linked to that of others.

With that recognition comes the possibility of service and commitment to God's work. This seems to be the point of the reconciliation scenes in the post-Resurrection accounts: sinner-disciples are healed "for the sake of others."

The meal and servant motifs are powerful symbols, for they not only clarify the meaning of Jesus' death but invite us to appropriate its consequences. Salvation is not an automatic event like a cassette tape that is plugged into the believer and simply starts playing. Rather, the Christian notion of salvation is summed up in the Pauline formula we discussed in the previous chapter: as Christ, so we. The gift of reconciliation and the power to serve others is always God's free and justifying action, but the consequent ability to serve as Jesus did is our response to that gift. There is no clearer explanation of this salvation than in the prophetic action-words of the Last Supper.

READING MENUS?

The Last Supper texts, in one form or another, are familiar to Christians because of the celebration of the Eucharist. That fact is of small consolation until we see what meanings and commitments those texts elicit. One suspects that, for some, these accounts read like sacred menus of an important meal. They invite our interest but not our commitment.

There are several levels of meaning in the Last Supper texts. The first level of meaning, the *historical,* involves legitimate questions of fact about the Last Supper (such as, did Jesus actually celebrate a paschal meal as the Last Supper?). Such historical questions have the important task of moving us to a second level of meaning, the *theological.*[16] (Therefore, even if Jesus did not historically celebrate the Last Supper within the context of the Passover meal, what was the *theological purpose* of these accounts?)

There is still another level of meaning: the Last Supper accounts reflect the life and self-understanding of different faith communities in the early Church. In reading these texts we are brought into contact with the very faith life of a community.[17] (Therefore, how does the paschal meal context provide a passage to new meaning and commitment for us?)

Within the Christian tradition, the celebration of the Eucharist is much more than an historical recollection or a theological commentary. For Paul and the contemporary Christian, Eucharist is a proclamation of the death of the Lord (1 Cor. 11:26). We *symbolize* the Last Supper, that is, we actualize the meaning of that meal so that we may be enabled to accept the consequences of the Cross.[18] In traditional language, we call the Eucharist a sacrament because it effects what it promises: participation in the death of the Lord "until he comes" (1 Cor. 11:26). But, as we saw in the first half of this book, participation in such symbols can only be effective for us when we symbolize out of our experience.

These remarks are an important preface to an insightful reading of the Last Supper texts. These texts are obviously the result of some textual, liturgical, and theological development. It is not my purpose to simplify the problems such developments present. I will summarize positions on various aspects of the Last Supper accounts which I regard as the most plausible and persuasive so as to be able to comment in more systematic fashion on our concerns of commitment.

Two traditions, based on certain textual and thematic similarities, are usually distinguished in the Last Supper texts: first, Paul (1 Cor. 11:23–26) and Luke (22:15–20), then, Mark (14:22–25) and Matthew (26:26–29).[19] But, given the complexity of these texts, is it even possible to reconstruct the "original" text? Both traditions have details that are older than their counterpart. Liturgical influence certainly accounts for some developments, but to what extent remains a disputed question. Hans Conzelmann simply says, "'The' original form can no longer be reconstructed. It is doubtful whether there was ever a uniform wording in general circulation."[20] What can be suggested is an early seminal wording that would allow for the eventual liturgical and theological shaping of these texts.

Helmut Merklein proposes two such basic texts: "This is my body being given on account of many" and "This is the cup, the new covenant in my blood."[21] How are we to regard these texts—as an already developed christology of the early Church or as more directly grounded in the words of Jesus himself? A technical, systematic answer to that question is outside the scope of this chapter. We can say, however, that these texts and their recounted events were not recited, but celebrated in the first faith communities. The theological meaning of these texts pointed to Christ's self-gift and how it enabled and transformed that of the first Christian communities. Once again, we find the same implicit praxis suggested in the texts of the Last Supper: *to understand the Cross, celebrate the Eucharist.*

This emphasis on the meaning rather than the text is illustrated by the fact that the Last Supper event, as described in the earliest extant liturgies[22] and in the post–Vatican II liturgies[23] combines the two traditions (Mark/Matthew and Paul/Luke). It is this liturgical form of the words of institution that Christians are usually more familiar with: "Take this, all of you, and eat it: this is my body which will be given up for you. . . . Take this, all of you, and drink from it: this is the cup of my blood, the blood of the new and everlasting covenant. It will be shed for you and for all so that sins may be forgiven. Do this in memory of me."

EMERGING LAST SUPPER THEMES

What background themes in the Last Supper accounts can clarify the meaning of the Cross for us? The setting of the last meal provides the first such theme. In the Synoptics (Matt. 16:17; Mark 14:12; Luke 22:7) and John (13:1), the Last Supper is described as the Passover feast. The historical question of whether Jesus could have celebrated an actual Passover meal is of secondary importance. There are, however, theological themes that might explain why the early Church described that night as a Passover meal.[24]

Passover is the best example of Israel's duty "to remember" (in Hebrew, ZKR), not in the sense of an historical souvenir, but as an actualization of God's saving work in a cultic context. At Passover, Israel is "to be present" to the God who now liberates this new people from bondage as he had their ancestors.[25] Secondly, not only is the past made present in liberating ways at Passover but the "blessings" (*berakoth*), properly improvised, praise God in view of the participants' present life so that they might be ready for his future, coming toward them.[26] Passover is, therefore, an eschatological feast.

Thirdly, Passover had a sacrificial character. Even in Jesus' time, the head of the house still sacrificed the Passover lamb (which would be eaten later at home) in the Temple, a remnant of the earlier domestic setting of the ritual. The father of the family was indeed a priest on this occasion.[27] This sacrifice with its shedding of blood sealed the covenant that Passover summarized.[28] But Passover's primary ritual in its earlier form was the covenant meal, understood as sacrifice.[29]

Sacrifice is a question of God's presence and that of his covenant people.[30] This is clearly seen in Exodus 24 where the older form of a covenant meal frames the newer covenant rituals of sprinkling blood over the people and the altar. The elders ate and drank before the face of God (Exod. 24:11) so that they might have a shared and covenant presence with him. As Samuel Terrien describes it, "Before the exile, 'to worship' was 'to have mirth before Yahweh.'"[31] A central concern of covenant presence and its sacrifices was the commitment of Israel to their ever-faithful God.

Whether or not the Jews of Jesus' time still understood their Passover as a covenant sacrifice, there is, as Notker Füglister notes, "an astonishing correspondence" between the traditional Passover elements with their underlying theology and the New Testament description of the Last Supper.[32] With this frame of reference, the consistent "covenant" themes in our texts ("new covenant" in 1 Cor. 11:25 and Luke 22:20; "blood of the covenant" in Mark 14:24 and Matt. 26:28), associated with the cup-word, assume their full meaning as the blood of a covenant people.[33] It is this cup that is sent, with good reason, to absent members of the family. The genesis of this new covenant may have been the radical Jeremian idea (Jer. 31:31–34) that new attitudes and not new treaties with God are needed. The appropriation of this idea by the early Christian community represents the "conviction that God had acted in a new way through Jesus."[34]

In addition to the Passover motif, there are a number of other elements that emphasize God's future promises and their impact

on the present.[35] The most dramatic of these eschatological motifs is the prophetic action of Jesus in refusing to drink the cup
(Luke 22:16, 18; Mark 14:25; Matt. 26:29).[36] Luke describes
Jesus at the Last Supper as saying, "Take this and divide it
among you; I tell you, from now on I will not drink of the fruit
of the vine until the coming of the reign of God" (Luke 22:17–
18). Since wine is an Old Testament symbol of God's future
Kingdom, Jesus' refusal of the cup would then be, if not a prophetic action-word, at least a powerful commentary on how the
disciple "waits" for the Kingdom.[37] The early Christian communities seemed to have learned this lesson early, if we understand correctly the eschatological import they gave to the "mara-
natha" cries ("Come, Lord Jesus, quickly") in their Eucharist.[38]
To call out for God's future reign is to commit oneself to its
building in the present.

BREAD AND WINE—SYMBOLS OF WHAT?

For centuries, the theological idea of symbol was deprived of
its original force (as a mediator of reality so that we might share
in it) and connoted something less. Symbol became synonymous
with sign. For Ambrose and Augustine, the Eucharist as symbol
meant much more than it did for ninth-century debaters on Eucharist like Paschasius and Ratramus and eleventh-century her-
etics like Berengarius.

If symbol is honestly encountered, it moves us to thought (Ricoeur) and, eventually, to commitment. Therefore, sacrament as
symbol does not simply reproduce salvation history but actual-
izes it. Symbol does not say, "This is the way it was and it can
be now," but rather, "This is what can begin now but it is not
yet complete." (The possible abstention of Jesus from the Last
Supper cup, as noted above, would highlight this meaning:
God's reign is beginning, but is not yet completed.)

The bread and wine are independent but complementary and
cumulative symbols. They are independent in that each, in itself, is complete in the Hebrew usage. Both the bread and wine
texts (when reconstructed in their probable, original Semitic
form) emphasize *the whole person of Jesus as self-gift*. In Paul
and Luke, this self-gift is articulated in language ("My body

. . . given . . . on account of you") that may reflect the Servant of Deutero-Isaiah or martyr terminology of a later date.[39] As we noted earlier, the servant-at-table theology may also explain an early connection made between Jesus' death as serving self-gift and its symbol, the Last Supper's bread and wine ("blood . . . poured out").

What does seem fairly certain is that behind these developed texts was an experience, rooted in the actions of Jesus himself. He gave new meaning to familiar meal actions (possibly in the style of a prophetic action-word, discussed earlier). In such a prophetic context, what was signified had already proleptically begun to happen: Jesus' self-gift on the Cross. But, as in all prophetic contexts, the symbols are participatory; their meaning becomes our challenge. The post-Resurrection stories, with their eucharistic overtones, are not "recognition" stories, in the passive sense, but "conversion" stories, orchestrated in the commitment terms of Cross/Eucharist. In the same way, we are no longer dealing with a question of bread and wine, but with the self-gift of Jesus and how it implicates us.

Whatever explanation for the development of the Last Supper texts is accepted, it is certain that their complementary and cumulative meaning was important for the eucharistic celebration of the early Christian communities. For them, the Lord's Supper was the symbol of redemptive process. It was not chronology, first of all, but the Christian community's concern with a praxis theology of redemption that inspired the juxtaposition of the Passion and Last Supper accounts.

Once again, it seems that the symbol of Jesus as "servant-at-table" sums up this theology of self-gift. Such a symbol provides a frame within which later developments (perhaps of martyr terminology, later extended into more cultic sacrificial terminology) are possible. Such suggestions retain their tentative character. But this does not preclude a theology of Eucharist that is grounded in the saving life, death, and Resurrection of Jesus. Rather, we are reminded that the strongest evidence for the efficaciousness of Jesus' redemptive work is its grateful appropriation by the early Church, whose faithful response resulted in the complex Last Supper tradition.

GUIDELINES FOR A EUCHARISTIC PRAXIS

My purpose in reviewing some of the complexity in the Last Supper accounts was to indicate the rich theology and faith-experience behind them. If there is to be some deepening of a eucharistic theology *ex opere operantis* (that is, from the subjective side), it must be guided by the response of those who first experienced the results of Christ's saving death and Resurrection. (Our more informed perception of the role of the early Christian communities played in the formation of these accounts only emphasizes this all the more.) We can derive some guidelines for a honest praxis and theology of Eucharist from these same Last Supper accounts.

The first guideline involves respect for the complexity of the mystery we celebrate in the Eucharist and try to live out in our daily lives. Theologies which insist on the "elements" of the Eucharist in a simplistic way that slights the biblical contexts discussed above lack such respect. More important than *how* bread and wine become the real presence of the Lord (a concern that did not become prominent in theology until Berengarius' heresy in the eleventh century) is the liturgical injunction to the Christian community after the consecration, "Let us proclaim this mystery of faith." This mystery includes God's unearned love and our enabled response to serve as Jesus did.

A second guideline that emerges from our texts is a relational one, that is, a question of mutual response. It has already been suggested that the presence of God is an implicit theological context of Passover, sacrifice, "remembrance," "blessing," and covenant. God's presence, if one may generalize, is not statically conceived in Scripture, but ever-evocative of the presence of his creatures. Due to a number of historical and theological factors, this theology of mutual and covenant presence was replaced by a praxis and theology of Eucharist that sometimes separated the "real presence" from the "sacrifice of the Cross."

The dynamic symbol of "presence" was then transposed (for example, in the unsymbolic controversies of Paschasius and Ratramus) into rituals that emphasized the "state of grace" but were not always understood as demanding commitment to the work of Jesus, the Servant. If we wish to develop the *ex opere operantis* dimension of Eucharist, we must re-examine the one-sided, sometimes unecclesial, and eventually uneschatological understanding of the sacrament among us, both in praxis and in theory.

A third guideline is the ecclesial emphasis that Paul himself made: "Because the loaf of bread is one, we, many though we are, are one body, for we all partake of the one loaf" (1 Cor. 10:17). Bornkamm's paraphrase of this verse is accurate: "For the body of Christ offered to us in this bread and given up for us is one, and just for this reason we, the many, are one body, namely the body of Christ."[40] The reason was demonstrated in Paul's choice of words. He spoke of "participants" of the body and blood of Christ (1 Cor. 10:16) and of "partaking" of the one bread. In the original Greek, these words had a strong connotation of responsible presence.[41] Paul used such language to correct the selfish, privatized notions of Eucharist in the Corinthian community. One can argue that Paul's concern was "not that the Corinthians are profaning a holy rite but that they are fragmenting a holy society."[42]

In Paul's question, "The cup of blessing which we bless, is it not *participation* in the body of Christ?" (1 Cor. 10:16), we do indeed have "the only authentic commentary in the New Testament itself on the words of institution."[43] It is commentary that refuses to dichotomize "real presence" from its ecclesial and ultimately eschatological purpose. When such purposes are acknowledged, the corollaries for an eventual ecumenical Eucharist and for a theology, spelling out our response as well as God's action, are significant. When such purposes are refused, it is then that Paul's judgment theme (1 Cor. 11:27–29) becomes operative. It is addressed to the eschatologically irresponsible, to the ecclesially naive, to the "enthusiastic" Christians who do not discern the complex reality of the "body of Christ."[44]

A fourth guideline, flowing from our texts, is the eschatological emphasis. This prescinds from the question of Jesus' own awareness of the eschaton and allows for the gradual adjustment of the early Church's understanding of this event. The so-called "renunciation" of the Last Supper cup, discussed above, stresses such a view of God's future, not yet fully realized among us. The Pauline "until he comes" (1 Cor. 11:26) not only corrects the naive "enthusiasm" of the Corinthian Eucharists, but demands eucharistic accountability for the "in-between" time. We are challenged by such an eschatology to redefine the relational and ecclesial dimensions of our Eucharist that already symbolizes the final unity of God's future feast.

SUMMARY

The Eucharist as sacrifice is the privileged symbol of Christ's death for us. In the Last Supper texts, the total commitment of Jesus ("given/poured out on account of the many"), as saving for us, is the unifying theme underlying the bread and wine words. But Jesus chose to symbolize, not recite, this meaning. Recitation allows us to repeat the meaning of the Cross without necessarily being committed to its cost. If we honestly symbolize the meaning of Christ's death for us in the Eucharist, then we will "participate" in the service it requires.

Vatican II expressed this same theology in more practical terms: "Pastors of souls must therefore realize that, when liturgy is celebrated, more is required than the mere observance of the laws governing valid and licit celebration. It is their duty also to ensure that the faithful take part *knowingly, actively, and fruitfully*."[45] The words suggest the attitude, style, and results of response to God's enabling gift in us.

Authentic Eucharist will not allow us to be consumers of grace and yet avoid service to others. The Pauline formula "as Christ, so we" applies equally to our Initiation and its test, our Eucharist. Conzelmann put it another way in asking whether "there are two ways into the Kingdom of God, through martyrdom and through sacrament and the latter represents an appropriation of the Passion."[46] Knowing, active, and fruitful participation of the Eucharist is the ongoing appropriation of Jesus' sacrifice on the Cross.

None of this would be possible if all participation were not founded on the living Word of God. Ricoeur has suggested that the Passion accounts contextualize the parables to such an extent that they become the parables of the Crucified.[47] Yet this is true of all Scripture, which the Christian Church has always read in the light of the Cross. It is this Word that challenges the eucharizing community and individual and enables our response out of the lived contexts of our need. It is this Word that prepares us for honest participation.

Self-gift (or its opposite, radical sin) is always played out in the arena of our lives. In the opening chapters of this book, we considered lived experience in the frame of life-stages, punctuated by crises. These crises not only make us re-examine our experience but draw out the implications of it for new and deeper commitments in our next life-stage.

Needs are at the center of our crises. Our own new and enlarged self-definition will be the result, in part, of finding within ourselves the resources with which we can respond to our own and others' need. This is not a "secular" process. It is this self-gift that the Word of God enables and the Eucharist evokes.

The self-gift of a Christian, directed to building the peaceable Kingdom, is a response to Jesus as someone "on account of others." But our Gospel service cannot ignore the specificity of our current life-stage and its crises. New commitments reshape our awareness of why and to whom "we are sent." We recommit ourselves as we struggle to perceive the old and new gifts of others as well as our own gift.

Patristic commentators have often focused on Judas' reception of the Eucharist so that Christians might learn to avoid a similar action at the same table. Augustine, commenting on the Johannine reference to the Evil One entering Judas at that Last Supper, adds, "not because he received the bad [in the Eucharist] but because the bad one [Judas] received the good [the Eucharist] badly."[48] In other words, our intentions and commitments, based on a realistic assessment of current situations, make all the difference at the table of the Eucharist.

DISCIPLE GROUPS AND EUCHARIST

With the eucharistic symbol of Christ's sacrifice on the Cross, we find ourselves at the same table with other would-be disciples. The covenant sacrifice-meal of the Old Testament united people because God's presence, when attended to, invited their shared, obedient presence. Eucharist is described as new covenant sacrifice because it enables us to be part of a disciple-group that shares the tasks of the Master. We become one body of disciples in eating this one bread, and, in doing so, we keep proclaiming the death of the Lord until he comes. Then the Church will definitively be replaced by the Kingdom.

In Eucharist, we are drawn into the very disciple formation that Peter, James, and John had in eating with sinners and sinner-disciples at the Last Supper. In our own faith-situation, the Risen Lord invites us, as he invited the disciples in the post-Resurrection accounts, to a more aware and committed discipleship. We begin to grasp the meaning of justification for our current lives because the Eucharist will not allow us to remain indifferent disiciples. Real presence, then, is a question of mutual presence and communication that permits us to see the need of God's people with the eyes of the Master.

"Come, Lord Jesus" seems to have been an early and realistic liturgical cry because the example of Jesus had not been lost on those earlier Christians.[49] The test of their Eucharist was a growing love for today's mission and service in view of tomorrow's feast.

The well-to-do Christians of Corinth may not have intended to offend their poorer fellow Christians. But Paul cited the actual situation: "When you assemble it is not to eat the Lord's Supper, for everyone is in haste to eat his own supper. . . . Would you show contempt for the church of God, and embarrass those who have nothing?" (1 Cor. 11:20–22).[50] The Pauline question is still with us.

Faced with the immensity of our world's problems (for example, ruthless and widespread oppression of human rights and continuing famine in Third World countries), we Christians may too easily excuse ourselves from the service that Eucharist entails. Even within our own public and family communities, we may be quite insensitive to the needs of others, much as the Corinthians were. Honest Eucharist begins with our asking Pauline questions about the needs of our world and the gifts we have not yet given.

There are affluent Christian communities, for example, who demand nothing more of their members than the weekly collection and a vague sense of sin and contrition as conditions for participation in worship and sacrament. Yet such communities usually have a number of professional people whose services would benefit the poor. Such communities have the ability to help finance local self-help programs for the less privileged. Above all, such communities could exercise a collective influence in dealing with human rights, environment, the education of minorities, and other, similar problems. In other words, how does the Christian community link the symbol of abundance and service, which the Eucharist is, with the need of God's world all around us?

If Jesus ate with sinners as a witness to God's offer of reconciliation, how can his Church do any less? Today we use the term *outreach* to describe service that extends past our usual boundaries. This is the lesson the Eucharist constantly teaches the community: to reach out creatively to the "unacceptable" and the "undesirable" with a compassion and service that bespeaks a Master criticized for his table-companions.

NOTES

1. For example, the work of M. Douglas situates such rituals within the specific social structures of a family and its application to the Eucharist; see *Natural Symbols* (New York: Pantheon, 1970), pp. 46–51.
2. Cf., for example, H. Feld, *Das Verständnis des Abendmahls* (Darmstadt: Wissenschaftliche Buchgesellschaft, 1976); A. Gerken, *Theologie der Eucharistie* (Munich: Kösel, 1973); G. Martelet, *The Risen Christ and the Eucharistic World* (New York: Seabury, 1976).
3. Joachim Jeremias has argued that Mark's description of Jesus reclining at table (Mark 2:15) should be seen in such a context; see *The Eucharistic Words of Jesus* (London: SCM, 1966³), pp. 48–49.
4. J. Jeremias, "This Is My Body," *Expository Times* 83 (1972): 196–203; here, 197.
5. E. E. Ellis, *The Gospel of Luke* (London: Nelson, 1966), pp. 222, 192, 250–51; L. Dussaut, *L'Eucharistie: Pâques de Toute La Vie* (Paris: Cerf, 1972), pp. 101–03.
6. See F. Hahn, "Das Gleichnis von der Einladung zum Festmahl," *Verborum Veritas* (*Festschrift für G. Stählin*) (Wuppertal: R. Brockhaus, 1970), pp. 51–82.
7. D. Daube, "Responsibilities of Master and Disciples in the Gospels," *New Testament Studies* 19 (1972): 1–15; here, 11.

8. *Pace* W. O. Walker, "Jesus and the Tax Collectors," *Journal of Biblical Literature* 97 (1978); 221–38.

9. V. Taylor, following Bultmann, has suggested an intriguing insight in this regard: Peter would have never even considered eating with the Gentile Christians of Antioch (Gal. 2:12) if his own experience with Jesus had not prepared him for this ministry; see *The Gospel According to St. Mark* (London: Macmillan, 1966²), pp. 203–04.

10. C. Vogel, "Le Repas sacré au Poisson chez les Chrétiens," *Eucharisties d'Orient et d'Occident* (Paris: Cerf, 1970), vol. 1, pp. 83–116; esp. pp. 86–91, 116; R. Brown, *The Gospel According to John (xiii–xxi)* (Garden City, N.Y.: Doubleday, 1970), pp. 1093–94; 1098–1100.

11. R. Feneberg comments on some of the current exegetical efforts to determine the relationship between the Last Supper and Passion accounts; see *Christliche Passafeier und Abendmahl: Eine biblisch-hermeneutische Untersuchung der neutestamentlichen Einsetzungsberichte*, SANT, 27 (Munich; Kösel, 1971), pp. 97–117.

12. J. Roloff, "Anfänge der soteriologischen Deutung des Todes Jesu (Mk. 10. 45 und Lk. 22.27)," *New Testament Studies* 19 (1972): 38–64. For further discussion of Jesus' and the early Church's attitudes on the meaning of the Cross, see A. Vögtle, "Todesankündigungen und Todesverständnis Jesu" (pp. 51–113) and K. Kertelge, "Das Verständnis des Todes Jesu bei Paulus" (pp. 114–36), in Kertelge, *Der Tod Jesu.*

13. Although there are suffering servant references, early theological reflection on the New Testament may not have applied them to the death of Jesus; cf. Roloff, "Anfänge der soteriologischen Deutung des Todes Jesu," 44–45; cf. also, F. Hahn's discussion, *The Titles of Jesus in Christology* (New York: World, 1969), pp. 54–67. A second possible explanation is the extension of the Maccabean martyr terminology to the meaning of Jesus' death; cf. S. Williams, *Jesus' Death as Saving Event: The Background and Origin of a Concept* (Missoula, Mont.: Scholars Press, 1975).

14. See Vögtle, "Todesankündigunden und Todesverständnis Jesu," pp. 100–04, for further discussion.

15. For a technical discussion of the text, see I. H. Marshall, *The Gospel of Luke: A Commentary on the Greek Text* (Grand Rapids, Mich.: W. B. Eerdmans, 1978), pp. 814–18.

16. Feneberg, *Christliche Passafeier und Abendmahl,* pp. 41, 76–77.

17. Ibid., pp. 86–115.

18. Also, J. Murphy-O'Connor, "Eucharist and Community in First Corinthians," *Worship* 51 (1977): 56–69; here, 60–61; see also, H. Conzelmann, *First Corinthians* (Philadelphia: Fortress, 1975), pp. 201–02.

19. For the bread-word, Mark and Matthew have the action of "praise" (*eulogein* in the Greek text) rather than "thank" (*eucharistein*) as do Paul and Luke. Some commentators see this as Mark's earlier and more "correct" translation of the *berakhah* idea as compared with that of Paul and Luke. Mark and Matthew omit the qualifying expression for "body" ("given . . . on account of you"), which the other tradition cites. See H. Merklein, "Erwägungen zur Überlieferungsgeschichte der neutestamentlichen Abendmahlstraditionen," *Biblische Zeitschrift* 21 (1977): 88–101; 235–44; here, 93; L. Ligier, "From the Last Supper to the Eucharist," in L. Sheppard, ed., *The New Liturgy* (London: Darton, Longman, and Todd, 1970), p. 118. R. Ledogar has suggested some sound explanations for the change

from one verb to another; see *Acknowledgment: Praise-verbs in the Early Greek Anaphora* (Rome: Herder, 1968).

In the cup-word, there is a different kind of problem. The Mark/Matthew texts have "blood" as the key word while Paul/Luke have "cup" with a qualifying "in my blood." An underlying question is the integrity of the Lucan text; for a summary of the problem, see Ellis, *Gospel of Luke,* pp. 253–55; H. Schürmann, *Der Einsetzungsbericht Lk. 22.19–20* (Münster: Aschendorff, 1970), vol. 2, pp. 133–50; M. Rese, "Zur Problematik von Kurz- und Langtext in Luke XXII. 17ff.," *New Testament Studies* 22 (1975); 15–31. There are both textual (cf. Schürmann, *Der Einsetzungsbericht Lk. 22.19–20*) and theological reasons (Merklein, "Erwägungen zur Überlieferungsgeschichte der neutestamentlichen Abendmahlstraditionen," 95–96, but cf. P. Neuenzeit, *Das Herrenmahl: Studien zur paulinischen Eucharistieauffassung* [Munich: Kösel, 1960], pp. 118–19) which might favor Luke's cup-text as older than Mark's. However, the opposite view has also been able to muster some fairly strong arguments (R. Pesch, *Das Abendmahl und Jesu Todesverständnis* [Freiburg: Herder, 1978], pp. 34–38; 93–101).

20. Conzelmann, *First Corinthians,* p. 201; H. Patsch, *Abendmahl und historischer Jesus* (Stuttgart: Calwer, 1972), pp. 69–89.

21. Merklein, "Erwägungen zur Überlieferungsgeschichte der neutestamentlichen Abendmahlstraditionen," 88–98 (*Touto estin to soma mou to huper pollon didomenon/Touto to poterion he kaine diatheke en to haimati mou*); cf. J. Betz, "Eucharistie als zentrales Mysterium," *Mysterium Salutis,* eds. J. Feiner and M. Löhrer, IV/2 (Einsiedeln: Benziger, 1973), pp. 185–313; here, pp. 191–92.

22. See J. Jungmann, *The Mass of the Roman Rite: Its Origins and Development* (New York: Benzinger, 1950), vol. 2, pp. 194–201.

23. Cf. J. H. Emminghaus, *The Eucharist: Essence, Form, Celebration* (Collegeville, Minn.: Liturgical, 1978), p. 184.

24. Even if one argues with Conzelmann's position that "the construing of the Lord's Supper as a Passover meal is a secondary piece of interpretation" (*First Corinthians,* p. 99, n. 50) and that 1 Cor. 5:7 has no connection with the Last Supper, Paul's description of Christ as a sacrificed paschal lamb is a pre-Pauline symbol of covenant and Passover sacrifice and might well explain the use of Passover as a theological interpretation of that night.

25. B. Childs, *Memory and Tradition in Israel* (London: SCM Press, 1962), pp. 67–85; N. Füglister, *Die Heilsbedeutung des Pascha* (Munich: Kösel, 1963), pp. 132– 38.

26. R. DeVaux, *Studies in Old Testament Sacrifices* (Cardiff: University of Wales Press, 1964), p. 24; D. Daube, "He That Cometh" (Lecture given in St. Paul's Cathedral, London, 1966; privately printed). Even the controverted question of the *berakah* ("blessing") assumes a more eschatological shape within the Passover context; cf. Ligier, "From the Last Supper to the Eucharist," pp. 122–24.

27. H. Haag, *Vom alten zum neuen Pascha: Geschichte und Theologie des Osterfestes* (Stuttgart: KBW, 1971), p. 110.

28. Füglister, *Die Heilsbedeutung des Pascha,* pp. 233–49.

29. *Pace* Patsch, *Abendmahl und historischer Jesus,* pp. 23–24; cf. B. Childs, *The Book of Exodus* (Philadelphia: Westminster, 1974), pp. 497–511.

30. J. Guhrt, "Covenant," in C. Brown, ed., *The New International Dictionary of New Testament Theology* (Exeter: Paternoster, 1975), vol. 1, pp. 365–72, esp. p. 369. My position in no way denies the expiatory dimensions in the Old Testament concept of sacrifice. Even if B. Levine's arguments against the exclusive connection between meal-sacrifice and covenant sacrifice are valid, they would not affect the theological symbolization of covenant-meal as described in the Last Supper accounts; see *In the Presence of the Lord* (Leiden: Brill, 1974), pp. 35–52; esp. pp. 38–39; 48–50.

31. S. Terrien, *The Elusive Presence* (New York: Harper & Row, 1978), p. 396.

32. Füglister, *Die Heilsbedeutung des Pascha,* p. 143; for a different view, cf. Patsch, *Abendmahl und historischer Jesus,* pp. 34–36.

33. Guhrt, "Covenant," p. 369, and as distinguished from blood rites of holocaust (DeVaux, *Old Testament Sacrifices,* p. 38). For the complex origins of this rite with the covenantal meal, cf. D. McCarthy, "The Symbolism of Blood and Sacrifice," *Journal of Biblical Literature* 88 (1969): 166–76; ibid, 92 (1973): 205–10. The Mark/Matthew tradition of "covenant blood" is usually traced to Exod. 24:8, while Paul/Luke's "new covenant" is referred to Jer. 31:31–34. W. L. Holladay's work on the "new covenant" concept retrieves the radical character of the Old Testament idea (Holladay, "New Covenant," *Interpreter's Dictionary of the Bible,* suppl. vol., pp. 623–25 [bibliography]).

34. Holladay, "New Covenant," p. 625. Holladay points out that even the Mark/Matthew tradition of "blood covenant" might well include the Jer. 31 theology.

35. H. Schürmann has made a good case for understanding Jesus' double action of offering bread and wine to his disciples as eschatological gifts; see "Das Weiterleben der Sache Jesu im nachösterlichen Herrenmahl," *Biblische Zeitschrift* 16 (1972): 1–23. P. Lebeau has traced wine as an eschatological symbol in the Old Testament and its meaning for the New Testament accounts; see *Le Vin Noveau du Royaume: Etude exégétique et patristique sûr la Parole eschatologique de Jésus à la Cène* (Paris: Desclée de Brouwer, 1966).

36. Whether one agrees with Patsch that Jesus did not abstain from the cup (*Abendmahl und historischer Jesus,* p. 131–39) or with Jeremias' contrary position (Jeremias, *Eucharistic Words,* pp. 207–18), it is difficult to remove the eschatological thrust of this tradition.

37. E. Schweizer, *The Good News According to Mark* (Atlanta, Ga.: J. Knox, 1970), pp. 304–05; cf. also, H. Conzelmann, *The Theology of St. Luke* (New York: Harper & Row, 1960), pp. 80 (n.2), 115, 117 (n.3); *pace* Patsch, *Abendmahl und historischer Jesus,* pp. 116–50, esp. pp. 141–42.

38. B. Sandvik, *Das Kommen des Herrn beim Abendmahl im Neuen Testament* (Zürich: Zwingli, 1970), pp. 13–40; Merklein, "Erwägungen zur Überlieferungsgeschichte der neutestamentlichen Abendmahlstraditionen," 239.

39. Cf. Roloff, "Anfänge der soteriologischen Deutung des Todes Jesu," 44–45; cf. Hahn's discussion, *Titles of Jesus,* pp. 54–67.

40. Bornkamm, *Early Christian Experience,* p. 144.

41. Conzelmann, *First Corinthians,* p. 172; S. Aalen, "Das Abendmahl als Opfermahl im Neuen Testament," *Novum Testamentim* 6 (1963):128–52. This, in my opinion, represents a more satisfying and complete explanation

than that of J. A. T. Robinson, *The Body: A Study in Pauline Theology* (London: SCM, 1952), pp. 57–58; R. Jewett, *Paul's Anthropological Terms* (Leiden: Brill, 1971), pp. 263–65; or R. Gundry, *SOMA in Biblical Theology* (London: Cambridge University, 1976), pp. 237–38.

42. W. Orr and J. Walther, *1 Corinthians* (Garden City, N.Y.: Doubleday, 1976), p. 269.
43. Bornkamm, *Early Christian Experience,* p. 139; Neuenzeit, *Das Herrenmahl,* pp. 60–62.
44. Bornkamm, *Early Christian Experience,* p. 149; cf. C. D. F. Moule, "The Judgment Theme in the Sacraments," *The Background of the New Testament and Its Eschatology* (Cambridge: University Press, 1964), pp. 472–73; C. Roetzel, *Judgment in the Community: A Study of the Relationship between Eschatology and Ecclesiology in Paul* (Leiden: Brill, 1972), pp. 137–42.
45. *Constitution on the Sacred Liturgy, The Documents of Vatican II,* ed. W. Abbott (New York: Guild Press, 1966), par. 11, p. 143. Italics mine.
46. Conzelmann, *Theology of St. Luke,* p. 80.
47. P. Ricoeur, "Biblical Hermeneutics," *Semeia* 4 (1975): 105.
48. Augustine, *In Joan. 26, 11: Et tamen accepit, et cum accepit, in eum inimicus intravit; non quia malum accepit, sed quia bonum male malus accepit.*
49. Bornkamm, *Early Christian Experience,* pp. 146–48; P. Pringent, "Une trace de liturgie judéochrétienne dans le chapitre XXI de l'Apocalypse de Jean," *Judéo-Christianisme,* ed. J. Moingt (Paris: Recherches de Sciences Religieuses, 1972), pp. 165–72.
50. Cf. G. Theissen, "Soziale Integration und Sakramentales Handeln. Eine Analyse von I Cor. XI. 17–34," *Novum Testamentum* 16 (1974): 179–206.

CHAPTER 7

Fragmented Stories

The stories of Judas and Peter fascinated the early Christian communities. Both men were similar in their early commitment to Jesus. They accompanied him throughout his public ministry and betrayed him in the last week of his life. But there the similarities end. Peter repented, while Judas committed suicide. Peter assumed a leadership role in the early Church, while Judas' example became a warning for later generations of disciples.

Both Judas and Peter were no doubt certain of their commitment to the Master at one stage of their discipleship. But they had not foreseen the crises of those last months of Jesus' life when he would be rejected by the religious leaders of Israel. Even then, in response to Jesus' prediction of his sufferings, Peter, somewhat naively, renewed his commitment: "Even though all are shaken in faith, it will not be that way with me. . . . Even if I have to die with you, I will not deny you" (Mark 14:29, 31). No one was perhaps more surprised by his denial of Jesus than Peter himself.

We, too, find it difficult to conceive of Mother Teresa or Dorothy Day becoming "uncommitted." Though perhaps less confident of the quality of our own commitment when we take on significant responsibilities such as marriage, parenting, or religious vows, we regard these decisions as permanent. Yet, one of the continuing surprises of our lives is finding ourselves once again uncommitted (or so it may seem). We learn again that the only "permanent" commitment is a continuing and renewed one.

We have already pointed out some of the reasons for this. Each stage of our lives involves conflict and change. New commitments should result from the painful awareness of our current life-stage and a new conscience in that stage. A few years of shared experience can make a great deal of difference in our lives, as it did in the lives of Peter and Judas. As we struggle to sort out our old commitments in our new situations, we begin to redefine our needs and service. Though we have been through similar transition periods, the experience is never the same. The forty-five-year-old person who is reconsidering an original commitment to a marriage, a profession, or a religious practice made twenty years earlier may well find the second decision more complex and painful than the first.

Our presence always accurately reflects how we deal with (or evade) the decisions and commitments of our current situation. As we decide to become more aware of our own and others' needs, to take on new roles and relinquish others, to deal with the limitations of advancing age, we are defining our presence. If, for the Christian, sacrament is a symbol of mutual presence, then the honesty and integrity of our intentions and decisions are important. Christian men and women who do not struggle with change in their lives will not be willing to answer God's call for further presence and service because they will feel they have nothing more to give. If Mother Teresa, in her late thirties, had felt that she was doing all she could for the poor, she would still be teaching in a school and the poor of the world would have been deprived of much service and hope.

This explains, in part, why Penance and reconciliation in the Church has always been problematic. The Christian who entered the rigorous penitential system of Rome or Carthage in the third century, the Irish monk who fulfilled the stringent demands of the new "tax" Penance of the sixth century, and the contemporary Christian in New York or Paris who participates in the post–Vatican II rituals of Penance all share one temptation: to divorce the question of sin and conversion, Penance and reconciliation from the contexts and purpose of their lives. In other words, people still tend to reduce Penance to a discussion of private sins. Even there, to specify that one has been "impure twice, drunk too much once, and missed Mass several times" is not necessarily to confront the possible underlying issues of fear, selfishness, and lack of direction in life that can permeate the story of a twenty-five-year-old teacher or a forty-year-old house-wife. Conversion is not a theological formula but God's realistic demand for change at a certain point in our lives, a demand he repeats many times in the course of one lifetime.

Sin, on the other hand, always involves a lack of continuing conversion and commitment, whether we are speaking of an in-dividual's selfish sexual life, the unjust distribution of wealth in a particular country, or the morality of an arms race between nations. The message of God is again being denied: sin brings about disunity. It is the antithesis of the Kingdom of God and its unity. Salvation is recognized by its results: "But now in Christ Jesus you who once were far off have been brought near through the blood of Christ. It is he who is our peace, and who made the two of us one by breaking down the barrier of hostility that kept us apart" (Eph. 2:13–14).

The purpose of this chapter is to uncover the connection be-tween sin and a lack of Christian commitment, between recon-ciliation and renewed commitment. New rituals of Penance, a result of Vatican II, seem to have had little effect on Christians' privatized notions of sin and conversion. As a result, Penance and reconciliation can still be reduced to a spiritual self-improvement program, devoid of any New Testament concern about the shared commitment of disciples, going "two by two" to proclaim the Good News.

THE GOSPEL WAY

God's compassion for and forgiveness of the repentant sinner is a recurring theme of the Old and New Testaments. The Gos-pels recount in detail the teachings and actions of Jesus about the forgiveness of sin.[1] Parables, such as the Prodigal Son (Luke 15:11–32), dramatize this teaching of forgiveness: "This brother of yours was dead, and has come to life. He was lost, and is found" (Luke 15:32). Jesus' message is clear: God's forgiveness is the beginning of salvation.

Yet, both the Pauline and Johannine writings speak of the continuing problem of sin among Christians. Paul sums up the perdurable temptation to radical sin in our lives: "My inner self agrees with the law of God, but I see in my body's members another law at war with the law of my mind" (Rom. 7:22–23).[2]

Further, the Christian community has a certain responsibility toward sinful Christians in their midst: "What I really wrote about was your not associating with anyone who bears the title 'brother' if he is immoral, covetous, an idolater, an abusive person, a drunkard, or a thief. It is clear that you must not eat with such a man" (1 Cor. 5:11) Conzelmann comments on the theology behind this list of vices: "The community practices not an ascetic ideal, but that freedom which includes freedom to separate itself from vice. It is of the very essence of the community to manifest its freedom from sin in the world, not alongside it. We do not have to depart from the world in order to be able to believe."[3]

The Christian community's concern with sin among its members in no way precludes God as the source of all salvation and forgiveness. Much useless polemic over denying or defending the sacrament of Penance has clouded the important issue: *the natural link the early Church made between God's gratuitous and forgiving love and the consequent responsibility of the disciple-group of Christians.* (In fact, any group of believers, conscious of their eschatological role to witness to the nearness of God's Kingdom and the call for conversion, will usually stress the need for continuing forgiveness in the community, as the Qumran documents show.[4])

Certainly, Matthew's teaching on "binding and loosing" in the community (Matt. 16:19; 18:18) preserves the connection between the saving work of the Risen Lord and the responsibility of the community to heal and forgive its members in his name.[5] In the Johannine community, the ability of the disciples to forgive sins was a proof that the Spirit of the Risen Jesus had been poured out on his community: "Then he breathed on them and said: 'Receive the Holy Spirit. If you forgive men's sins, they are forgiven them; if you hold them bound, they are held bound" (John 20:22–23).[6]

Throughout this book we have argued that the consequence of God's saving us is our ability to respond to him in a covenant community. The covenant communities of the Old and New Testaments did not exist for their private purposes but to proclaim God's present salvation and future Kingdom. A covenantal unity is the result of God's presence among us, assisting us in overcoming the divisiveness of sin and, thus, challenging a world fragmented by sin.[7] "I have given them the glory you gave me that they may be one, as we are one . . . that their unity may be complete. So shall the world know that you sent me and that you loved them as you loved me" (John 17:22–23). Johannine unity is always the result of conversion and remains the primary witness and service that the community gives to the people of its time.

These summary comments are not meant to replace available scriptural studies on the nature of sin and conversion, but to argue for the implicit biblical connections between conversion, covenant community, and commitment. Neither communal nor personal sin can be correctly understood apart from these connections. Just as we respond to God's salvation with commitment to the Gospel life of his son, so we sin, communally and personally, in turning away from that commitment.

Under this broad rubric, we distinguish radical sin (a continuing "No" to God, seen in our attitudes, values, and lifestyles) and sins (serious or less serious thoughts and actions that result from our less-than-perfect Gospel commitment). In analyzing a particular action (such as abortion or war) as serious or an individual's intention as directly or indirectly willed (for example, murder as opposed to self-defense), we have not exhausted the discussion of sin, by any means. In fact, we may be forgetting the purpose of struggling against sin in our lives: "Now, therefore, *through the church, God's manifest wisdom is made known* to the principalities and powers of heaven, in accord with his age-old purpose, carried out in Christ Jesus our Lord" (Eph. 3:10–11). In becoming Christian, Christ's work becomes ours.

In the letter to the Ephesians, we find a metaphor that sums up these dimensions of conversion and reconciliation. As J. Paul Sampley points out: "For Jews and gentiles in Jesus' time, 'walk' was a widespread metaphor for the way one lived. To 'walk' a certain way was to live in that manner. When one's situation changed, one 'walked' differently."[8] Although English versions often employ the word *live* to translate this idea, the original metaphor is a powerful image of both commitment and conversion: "to walk worthy of the calling" (Eph. 4:1) and to "no longer walk as the gentiles do" (Eph. 4:17). The metaphor also indicates what sin is: to walk according to our own plans rather than those of God.

To live out Christian commitment, then, is to "walk" with others in a certain direction—that of God's Kingdom. Christian morality and honesty in worship and sacrament are delineated by the Gospel criterion: do our lives bespeak God's unifying presence and his coming reign? Our intentions and actions, our value systems and life-styles as Christians, are not evaluated by Stoic ideals or humanistic goals, but by the radical vision of the Gospel: our happiness is tied to the realization of God's plan for his creation.[9]

The biblical test of commitment and conversion is the growing unity of God and his people. This is more than group consensus or political solidarity. It means that the divisive selfishness that permeates our world at every level of human living is gradually being replaced by a God-centered oneness: "Make every effort to preserve the unity which has the Spirit as its origin and peace as its binding force. There is but one body and one Spirit, just as there is but one hope given all of you by your call. There is one Lord, one faith, one baptism, one God and Father of all, who is over all, and works through all, and is in all" (Eph. 4:3-5).

RITUALS OR REALITY OF PENANCE?

Penance is the continuing process of conversion that helps us "walk" in the Gospel way of life, as credible disciples of a Risen Lord. Penance, therefore, is an ongoing act of commitment that continually affects our overall vision of life as well as the practical details of everyday living. Such Penance begins with a renewed willingness to be "on account of the others." Just as every sin, in one way or another, is another refusal to serve, so Christian Penance is demonstrated by taking up the old and new forms of Gospel ministry.

If this understanding of Penance is accepted, then it is easier to explain why a change in rituals of Penance does not necessarily bring about the reality of Penance. The post–Vatican II rituals of Penance, for example, with their options of face-to-face confession and communal penitential celebration, are a technical improvement over the Tridentine rituals of the dark confessional and the almost exclusive attention to lists of sins. More relevant rituals, however, do not necessarily assure a more penitential spirit. The current disaffection with the sacrament of Penance may not ultimately be with its ritual forms but with an incomplete theology of Penance that provides some consolation but does not evoke enough commitment. Before examining this thesis in more detail, we will briefly look at two earlier historical periods to see how the Church tried to evoke renewed commitment and conversion in its celebration of Penance.

Penance, as it was practised in the first six centuries of the Christian era, is usually described as "canonical" (the "norm" or "rule"). To illustrate the problem of Penance in this period, let us return to the example of the young Roman soldier in the second century, introduced in Chapter 5. This young man, having spent a fairly lengthy probation period preparing for his Initiation as a Christian, might have assumed that he had turned away from serious sin in his life. After all, his commitment had been tested in a number of ways. Even though he still lived in a Roman barracks, he had begun to make new decisions about his sexual life, his attitudes and manner of dealing with others, what military orders he could morally fulfill. He had made sacrifices to attend the gatherings and liturgies of the community. Therefore, on the day this soldier passed from the catechumenal stage into that of the initiated, he could honestly say that he had already "walked" in the Gospel way a long time. His Initiation and Eucharist, with their "forgiveness of sins," were a turning point in his life.

What a shock it must have been to this young soldier when he seriously sinned for the first time after his Baptism. Old habits of sin that he thought he had laid aside still exercised a powerful attraction. Or perhaps his sin was more public: denying, under pressure, his newfound faith in some way. What could the Christian community do for such a person?

The letter to the Hebrews gives us a typical reaction of early Christian communities:

For when people have once been enlightened and have tasted the heavenly gift and become sharers in the Holy Spirit, when they have tasted the good word of God and the powers of the age to come, and then have fallen away, it is impossible to make them repent again, since they are crucifying the Son of God for themselves and holding him up to contempt. [Heb. 6:4–6]

The text refers to those already initiated and presumably committed to the Gospel.[10] The particular sin in question seems to be apostasy. The lack of forgiveness for such sinners is not God's doing but their own. They have freely made certain irrevocable decisions.[11] Though once forgiven their sins in Baptism (*aphesis*), conversion (*metanoia*) had not become a part of their lives.[12] This text does not deny the possibility of renewed Penance so much as underline the eschatological character of Christian commitment. Apostasy and other such sins can hinder the building of the peaceable Kingdom.[13]

One way of reading such texts is to recognize the context: the demand for committed witness to Christ as a corollary of Christian Initiation. The early Church communities that preserved and responded to the teaching of Christ understood the Christian's role as disciple and witness. Every sin, in addition to the personal weakness or selfishness it re-enforces, interferes with the work of the disciple, which is to proclaim the "newness" of God's salvation and its power to renew those who were once "dead" in their sins.

The writer of the letter to the Colossians saw the logical connection between the Christian's renewed life and commitment: "You yourselves were once alienated from him. . . . But now Christ has achieved reconciliation for you in his mortal body by dying, so as to present you to God, holy, free of reproach and blame. But you must hold fast to the faith, be firmly grounded and steadfast in it, unshaken in the hope promised you by the Gospel you have heard" (Col. 1:21–23).

This demand for ongoing commitment and conversion explains the Church's hesitation in giving Christians a "second chance" after Baptism. Hermas provides a second century witness to this attitude: "I have heard it said by certain teachers that there is no other penitence than that which we received the day when we descended into the water [of Baptism] and when we received the pardon of our past sins. He [the Lord] said to me: 'You have heard correctly; it is so. . . . But since you ask me for some clarifications, I will reveal to you still another thing, without giving a pretext for sinning to recent or future converts . . . if, after the important and solemn call, *someone, tempted by the devil, falls into sin, he may do penance once.*"[14]

This was the beginning of canonical Penance. Until the sixth century, a Christian might receive this forgiveness only once in a lifetime for sins that required the public intervention of the Church. In other words, the distinction of mortal and venial sins (or serious and less serious sins) did not result from an analysis of sinful acts but from the way in which the sin was expiated: "Mortal sin is that which requires, for its reparation, the official penance and intervention of the Church in the reconciliation; venial sin . . . is that which is taken care of by private works of mortification without recourse to ecclesial penance."[15]

Because of the severity and lifetime effects of the penitential state (public acts of mortification, giving up certain professional work, sexual abstinence in marriage, etc.), the praxis of canonical penance had, by the sixth century, all but disappeared from the pastoral praxis of the Church. There are, however, some important lessons to be drawn from canonical Penance.

First, there is always compassion for the repentant sinner, but it is coupled with a Pauline concern that scandal and lack of commitment can tear apart the fabric of unity in a Christian community.[16] In a real sense, then, canonical Penance is a continuation of catechumenal formation with its emphasis on the ecclesial nature of both sacrament and mission. Canonical Penance is a second reminder of that teaching.

Secondly, canonical Penance is actually a form of the "com-

mitment mechanism" discussed in Chapter 5. The community
attempts to call out new commitment from its members. Since
sin blocks Christian commitment, the Church community ad-
dresses the individual's weakness in a practical way, asking for
service and a life-style that bespeaks the Christian vision. Cae-
sar of Arles, a plainspoken but effective bishop of the sixth century, said, for example, to his people: "Here are the works by
which less serious faults are expiated: visit the sick and prisoners, make peace among enemies . . . wash the feet of guests . . .
give alms to the poor. . . . For more serious sin, these remedies
do not suffice. Tears . . . severe and uninterrupted fasts and
alms which cost us something are necessary. . . . *It is just, in
effect, that the sinner who caused others to be lost with himself,
should expiate by the good example given to the whole community.*"[17] Just as the candidate in the catechumenate was asked
for practical signs of conversion, so too the baptized sinner was
challenged to "walk" the Gospel way of life again by renewed
self-gift and service. Even those in private Penance were challenged by those in public Penance to examine their priorities
and assess their commitment as Christians.

What questions does this outline of the ancient discipline of
Penance suggest to the contemporary Church? First, does our
current penitential system renew ecclesial commitment to the
work of Christ as well as facilitate private repentance? In other
words, does the Saturday afternoon confession or the Lenten
communal penitential celebration effectively demand changes in
the professional lives of penitents or motivate others to help the
sick, the elderly, and the poor of the community?

This certainly seems to be the *theological theory* of the new
ritual of Penance; "Thus the people of God becomes in the
world a sign of conversion to God. All this the Church expresses
in its life and celebrates in the liturgy when the faithful confess
that they are sinners and ask pardon of God and of their brothers and sisters."[18] In other words, the sacrament of Penance
should be an occasion for both the community and individual
penitents to recommit themselves to their Christian task of being
a light in this world. I would suggest, however, that this is not
the experience of many Christian confessors or penitents.

Secondly, is personal reformation being equated with Christian commitment in our current penitential praxis? Certainly, dealing with the sins and virtues of our lives is part of the penitential process and is, in fact, one important aspect of commitment. But to "walk" the Christian way also involves an active witness and mission to our own age and society as the new ritual stresses. If this were being more consistently accomplished, would not parish life be much different than it actually is in many places?

We do not need the type of public Penance that Nathaniel Hawthorne so vividly described in *The Scarlet Letter,* in which a woman's adultery permitted her community to indulge in the worst kind of self-righteous scorn and hyprocrisy. But we do need some shared challenge to conversion that permits us to "walk" through the seasons of our lives together with a renewed conscience and purpose. We turn now to a second historical praxis of Penance from which we can learn how the Christian community once again tried to evoke commitment and conversion from its members in a very different sociological climate.

THE BOOKS OF WRATH?

While Europe was trying to maintain the remnants of a Christian civilization in the aftermath of barbarian invasions, a unique sort of monasticism flourished in Ireland. It reflected some characteristics of Eastern monasticism as well as those of the Irish temperament and society. The Irish church very quickly seems to have become a monastic rather than an episcopal church (that is, abbots rather than bishops led Christian communities).[19] Canonical Penance, as discussed above, does not seem to have been known in these communities.

It is not surprising that this unique setting gave rise to a radically new approach to Penance among Christians. Without trying to specify the probable origins of the so-called Irish "tax" (or tariff) Penance, the monastic practice of a monk having an "anmchara" (soul-friend) with whom he could discuss the commitments and weaknesses of daily Christian living was the key to this new expression of Penance.[20]

In a way similar to the monastic Chapter of Faults, Irish

Christians gave detailed lists of their sins, including their number and special circumstances. The confessor assigned a Penance appropriate to the frequency and gravity of the sins recounted.[21] After the Penance was performed, the penitent returned for absolution. (Later, this praxis was reversed: after promising to do the Penance, the penitent revealed absolution immediately.[22])

In assigning Penance, the confessor had at his disposal so-called "penitential books" that proposed Penances for every conceivable (and some inconceivable) sins. These Irish penitentials, forming one of the most curious and revealing bodies of Christian literature, might be called the "books of wrath" at first sight.[23] The severity of the Penance imposed is shocking to modern ears: lustful desires, for example, could earn forty days on bread and water (the Penitential of Finnian).[24]

But, as with canonical Penance, the pastoral sensitivity of this form of Penance must be evaluated in terms of its time and the people it addressed. This new approach attempted to deal with a people who, although converted to Christianity, still retained some of the wilder components of the Celtic character. The Irish penitentials, with all their severity, were not so much books of wrath as an attempt to evoke Gospel commitment in a very different social and ethnic situation than that of third-century Rome or fourth-century Carthage.

As in the case of all rituals that deal with the complexity of human life, there were both strengths and weaknesses in this new approach. Christians were asked to be accountable for specific areas of their lives (even though sexual sin tends to predominate in some of the penitentials). The penances seem to have fitted into the Irish social mentality and its handling of irresponsible actions. Unfortunately, a certain legalism also accompanied this "number and species" approach to sin.

The most significant change, however, centered around absolution. In canonical Penance, there was a ritualized moment of reconciliation with the Church.[25] But, as noted above, Penance and conversion were seen as a lifetime process: once in Penance, one remained there. (There was no conception of a Christian being at one moment "in the state of sin" and, at the next, "in the state of grace.") In the newer approach, however, one performed the Penance to receive the absolution which could, in contrast to the earlier Penance, be repeated. Inevitably, a short-range definition of conversion, on a praxis level, begins to emerge.[26] Forgiveness becomes a chain of absolutions that may not necessarily be accompanied by conversion and commitment.

Accompanying this new praxis is the danger of a more privatized notion of Christian commitment and sin. The idea of ecclesial witness and service begins to recede into the background. An emphasis on personal holiness and correct conduct is not balanced by the larger purpose of all Christian commitment: that God's Kingdom come. The works of Penance can subtly be equated with the attitudes of conversion.

In noting all this, I do not wish to denigrate the penitential spirit of so many Christians who used these forms of Penance to turn to God with more commitment. It was, after all, a spirit of Gospel service that impelled the Irish monks to rekindle the Gospel message on the European continent and to bring with them this new form of Penance. Nor do I wish to detract from the pastoral sensitivity that prompted a different generation of Christians to once more shape the commitment demands of the Gospel in new and more relevant ways.

Irish "tax" Penance was innovative and probably quite suited to the Celtic situation of the early medieval period. Once again, the Church asked for a new commitment from penitents. Although this approach encouraged a Pelagian tendency to "earn one's salvation," there were also Gospel demands to live uprightly in a rough society and to show compassion in practical ways to the poor.

Irish Penance eventually developed into a form of auricular confession, familiar to Roman Catholics in particular. T. Tentler has recently suggested that this later praxis is actually a continuation of the "social control" exercised in canonical Penance in "the preserved order in a highly restricted local community, which expected strict obedience to its rules."[27] This suggestion has some merit but is an oversimplification. Over the centuries, the Church has tried, with varying effectiveness, to urge Christians to "help each other in doing penance . . . [and] work with all men of good will for justice and peace in the world."[28] But to return to our earlier question, does our current praxis of Penance actually evoke enough commitment to ensure the ongoing vision of the Gospel in our lives? For neither "social order" nor private consolation represent the ultimate purpose of Penance in our lives.

We can learn much from canonical as well as Irish "tax" Penance. In both approaches, an innovative praxis was shaped to the needs of a particular socio-historical situation. (Even in a canonical Penance, for example, there were significant differences in Eastern and Western praxis.) Although there were negative features in both penitential disciplines, each attempted to help the Christian deal with the complexities of conversion in practical ways. The lists of sins and their penalties, for example, focused on specific areas of living where commitment must be formed and then renewed time and again.

An effective contemporary Penance, for example, must assist married people not in "maintaining" their vows, but in developing a generativity that knows how to care for what has been created in the marriage (Erikson). An effective Penance must do more than prevent the young from being "impure": it must foster responsible intimacy and an integrated sexuality so that young Christians may be a prophetic sign to their peer group. An effective Penance must challenge the professional and working person to a new conscience in his or her familiar job situation. Canonical Penance and "tax" Penance, at their best, succeeded in making conversion and commitment possible in their times. An effective contemporary Penance must do no less for us.

FRAGMENTED STORIES

When we have experienced another crisis and begin to reorient our lives, we speak of "picking up the pieces." The immediate problem may be a loss of confidence, a difficult professional situation, a divorce, an unexpected serious illness, or a growing disaffection with the institutional Church. If we are to "pick up the pieces" in these or similar life-situations, we must re-evaluate our stories so that we can draw the necessary vision and strength for a new phase of our lives. Augustine summed up the results of his own autobiographical review: "You were right before me. But I had moved away from myself. *I could not find myself; how much less, then, could I find you*" (*Confessions*, 5, ii, 2).

Augustine was describing the kind of people who are "out of touch" with themselves and others. Instead of gaining an increasingly integrated experience, such people can only cope with certain areas of their stories. The result is a series of partial commitments and uncertain priorities in life. There is little repentance for the selfishness and irresponsibility in their stories because so much of their experience has been blocked out. In fact, such people may not break any specific commandments, but they consistently refuse deeper self-gift in important relationships. God seems absent in their lives, but, as Augustine insightfully noted, it is these people themselves, deprived of their own experience, who are really absent.

Penance and conversion must begin with the stories of our lives. It is only there that we see both our sin and our gifts. It is only there that we find the meanings that lead to commitment. But as Augustine discovered, it is difficult to tell our stories with honesty and insight. Any counselor or therapist knows how devious and self-serving a client's account of his or her experience can be, as if to verify the paraphrase of Polanyi (Introduction): we know more than we care to tell. If the outcome of Penance is to be new commitment to the Gospel way of life, then we must understand why we tell our stories so inaccurately, why we "move away from ourselves" and, thus, from God.

An important part of every story is the expectations that others invariably entertain about us. Often enough, these expectations are not objectively bad, but they may completely bypass our real experience. Some of the conditional love we receive is premised on the ideal person others think we should be. For example, the statement, "Mommy doesn't love you when you do that," usually expresses a parent's loving concern about her child's conduct. Yet the child may hear it as an expression of conditional love: "Mommy will only love you if you measure up to her expectations."

Because we need the love of the significant people in our lives and yet cannot always (or ever) be the ideal self they may wish we were, collusion can shape our relationships.[29] The word *col-lusion* derives from Latin roots that mean "to play together." As used here, collusion refers to the masking of whatever experiences in our lives would make us unacceptable to ourselves and others. Thus, whole areas of experience can be labelled "unacceptable" and filed away. As we quietly suppress important parts of our story, we limit the meaning we can draw from that story. If, for example, we cannot admit feelings of hate for a parent (because "good children don't hate their parents"), then we cannot begin to deal with all the connected strands of our experience that have galvanized that feeling.

Virginia Axline gives an excellent example of this incongruence in *Dibs: In Search of Self.*[30] She describes the true case of a disturbed young boy who, supported by Axline's acceptance, gradually begins to symbolize his pain and need in play therapy. In a crucial moment of this therapy, Dibs acts out a dramatic scene in which his home is on fire. His parents are locked inside the house. At that moment, Dibs symbolically possesses the power to save or destroy the people who have hurt him. But he has to decide, and thus, to recommit himself.

In the midst of his decision he begins to cry. Axline asks him: "Do you weep because the mother and father are locked in the house and can't get out and the house is burning?" Dibs replies: "Oh no! . . . I weep because I feel again the hurt of doors closed and locked against me."[31] The locked door represented for Dibs an extended experience of what he perceived as conditional love on the part of his parents. Until Axline enabled the boy to symbolize this "unacceptable" feeling in play therapy, he had suppressed it and much more.

The ideal expectations of his parents and his own collusion contributed to an impasse in which real expectations and commitments had become impossible. Once Dibs had the needed support and courage to symbolize all this, he was free to make new commitments. "I'll save them. . . . I'll unlock the doors and let them out" was the decision that Dibs ultimately made.

The sequel to Dibs' story is instructive. He became a well-adjusted boy, a brilliant student, and a natural leader at school. Some years later, Axline had occasion to read a letter of protest Dibs wrote to his high school authorities on behalf of a fellow student who had been dismissed. In the course of the letter, he noted: "I think you fail to understand the reasons why we sometimes do the things we do." The final words of Dibs' letter were: "With sincerity and intent to act."[32] Axline concluded her book with those words. Her point is obvious: Dibs had learned to understand the meanings behind his story, and, as a result, he had indeed both the "sincerity and intent to act."

Penance is tested by commitment. But such Penance must spring from the ground of our own experience. As we saw in Chapter 2, God goes before us in our experience. It is there that he redeems us. God knows our story, but Augustine reminds us that we, too, must know it. To remain ignorant of what God has continually done in our lives and to flee from commitments that seem to demand what we do not possess is the result of refusing the pain and joy of telling our story.

Those who begin to take responsibility for all the chapters of their stories with their "acceptable and unacceptable" experiences can, paradoxically, repent of their sins and, at the same time, rejoice in their new commitments. This is the common teaching of traditional theology and contemporary therapy. Such penitents symbolize more honestly because they are more aware of their experience. They assume new roles in their communities because they now see their gifts as well as their guilt. They responsibly participate in a new covenant community and its sacraments because they are really present in response to God's presence.

Walter Brueggemann has distinguised five characteristics of a covenant person: hoping, listening, answering, raging (as, for example, Leonard Bernstein's narrator in the *Kaddish* symphony rages against God because he trusts him), and grieving.[33] Even in the brief account of Dib's therapy, we discern these characteristics. The young boy could only begin to rage and grieve when he became willing to trust his experience. As Carl Rogers points out:

To the extent that this person is open to all his experience, he has access to all of the available data in the situation, on which to base his behavior. He has knowledge of his own feelings and impulses, which are often complex and contradictory... When a client is open to his experience, he comes to find his organism most trustworthy. He has less fear of the emotional reactions which he has. . . . Consciousness, instead of being the watchman over a dangerous and unpredictable lot of impulses . . . becomes the comfortable inhabitant of a society of impulses and feelings and thoughts, which are discovered to be very satisfactorily self-governing when not fearfully guarded.[34]

Dibs' listening and answering, as well as his newfound hope, were the result of honest response to his experience. His bewilderment, anger, and sorrow were the corollary of his willingness to deal with the illogical, the unexpected, and the undeserved in his story and were a prelude to his renewed commitment ("with sincerity and intent to act").

Again the letter to the Hebrews offers a strikingly complementary image of Jesus, one already cited: "In the days when he was in the flesh, he offered prayers and supplications with loud cries and tears to God, who was able to save him from death, and he was heard because of his reverence. Son though he was, he learned obedience from what he suffered; and when perfected, he became the source of eternal salvation for all who obey him" (Heb. 5:7–9). Here is the model of commitment for the contemporary Christian who would wish to be honest in worship and sacrament. "Loud cries and tears to God" can only come from stories honestly retold. Both penance and commitment begin there.

THE SERVICE OF RECONCILIATION

We have argued that conversion is always characterized by commitment. This is the very nature of justification, which is experienced as reconciliation (*katallage*).[35] From this gratuitous gift, Paul drew the consequence: "The love of God has been poured in our hearts through the Holy Spirit who has been given to us" (Rom. 5:5). This gift of reconciliation calls us to an active ministry of that same healing.[36]

Paul had just employed the metaphor of "new creation" to describe the Christian. He then spelled out the consequences of this unearned gift:

All this has been done by God, who has reconciled us to himself through Christ and has given us *the ministry of reconciliation* . . . he has entrusted *the message of reconciliation* to us. This makes us ambas-

sadors for Christ, God as it were appealing through us. We implore
you in Christ's name: be reconciled to God. [2 Cor. 5:18–20]

This ministry of reconciliation was not finished and indeed
continued to form the heart of Paul's own work.[37] It was a central point of his message. (Appropriately enough, this teaching
is found in a second letter to the Corinthians, who had not yet
understood the ongoing process of conversion or the demands of
commitment.) The service of reconciliation is the responsibility
of the whole Christian community. God reconciles, but we must
proclaim it. Reconciliation must address what is happening in
the shared experience of people, if they are to believe what will
happen in the Kingdom.

The minister of reconciliation, in this sense, is any Christian
who has been reconciled and ministered to. This does not denigrate the role of ordained ministers in reconciliation. Rather, it
underlines the shared responsibility of that ministry. For every
teenager that a priest may see, for example, in his role as reconciler, there are ten others who will not be seen until adulthood.
Who will reconcile and call these young people to the responsible living of the Gospel if not the one teenager who does worship and receive sacraments? Here is one realistic example of
clarifying and calling out commitment in sacrament. To "wor-
thily receive" reconciliation, should not this teenager be made
more conscious of the need to be a "soul friend" to others and,
thus, take up the service of which Paul spoke?

But the reconciler must have certain healing qualities to facilitate this process. In discussing the question of presence in
Chapter 4, we summarized these qualities under the term *affiliation process:* unconditional acceptance, creative communication,
and prophetic confrontation. One result of this process is a certain transparency that not only permits the healer to share with
another, but allows him or her to be fallible and flawed. The
healer does not have to hide behind a professional facade of
psychological technique or theological expertise. In other words,
imperfect Christians have no excuse for not being healers.

We do not preserve the objective character of Penance (what
God alone does) by ignoring the subjective reality of its ministry.
To ask whether the healer's own growth and experience of
God's redemptive presence support or contradict the very signs

of reconciliation he or she is privileged to offer is a fair question. On the other hand, a true healer, like Peter, serves as a role model in being willing to be seen in his or her own weakness and struggles. The healer is then healed, and fragmented people begin to accept ministries.

A second quality in the ministry of Penance is empathy. Note that the root meaning of the word *empathy* is "to suffer in." As characteristic of a therapeutic relationship, empathy refers to one's ability to perceive another human being as one knows oneself. Origen, a third-century theologian, gave these guidelines: "But search out diligently the one to whom you ought to confess your sin. First approve the physician to whom you should manifest the cause of your ailment, *one who knows how to be weak with the weak, to weep with one who weeps, who has learned the art of sympathy and compassion.*" [38]

SUMMARY

In the beginning of this book, we asked why there is so much Christian worship and, apparently, so little Christian commitment. The question was not meant to be flippant but Pauline. In Paul's experience, the Corinthian church's continuing need for Penance was a learning situation for both him and the community.

On the one hand, Paul had to remind the community of its responsibility not only to judge (1 Cor. 5:12) [39] but to evoke commitment: "As your fellow workers we beg you not to receive the grace of God in vain" (2 Cor. 6:1). Paul knew that with reconciliation come decisions, based on the Cross and its implications for our present and future. [40] This is why, as Käsemann insightfully remarks, Paul did not use the term *forgiveness*. For him, reconciliation and salvation primarily meant the positive force of God's freedom and new life in this passing world. [41]

The Christian Church has always used rituals of Penance so that we might hear the Word of God and celebrate sacraments more honestly. But rituals are not yet symbols. The latter demand both God's and our own presence to be efficacious. As the unreflected experience of our successive life-stages begin to pile up, the need for Penance deepens. Like the Corinthians, we begin to receive sacraments to avoid decisions and commitments to the Gospel and its mission.

Obviously, an occasional "face-to-face" confession or communal penitential celebration, no matter how well celebrated, is not sufficient for a constant renewal of Christian commitment. There is a need for daily reflection on our experience and its meaning (the monastic examination of conscience was such an attempt). At the beginning of every Eucharist, members of the community are called to serious accountability and recommitment when, after some reflection, they pray, "I confess to almighty God," in one form or another.[42] Above all, we must learn again to ask forgiveness of one another in nonritual situations of home life, at work, and in school, and the community must learn to ask forgiveness when it has failed an individual member.

The penitential solution is "musical chairs" once more. Christians must begin to call out the gift of others as they themselves move again in their lives. Augustine, addressing his catechumens, asked for their assistance in his own first days of ordained ministry by calling them "my fellow beginners."[43] Penance teaches us to say that to one another regularly.

NOTES

1. For scriptural and systematic approaches to the different dimensions of sin, see P. Delhaye et al., *Pastoral Treatment of Sin* (New York: Desclée, 1968); *The Mystery of Sin and Forgiveness*, ed. M. Taylor (Staten Island, N.Y.: Alba, 1970); *Dienst der Versöhnung* (Trier: Paulinus, 1974), pp. 9–44.

2. Eicholz, *Die Theologie des Paulus im Umriss* (Neukirchen: Neukirchener Verlag, 1977), pp. 258–60.

3. H. Conzelmann, *First Corinthians* (Philadelphia: Fortress, 1975), p. 100.

4. R. E. Brown, *The Gospel According to John* (New York: Doubleday, 1966), vol. 2, pp. 1043–44.

5. H. Thyen, *Studien zur Sündenvergebung im neuen Testament und seinen alttestamentlichen und jüdischen Voraussetzungen* (Göttingen: Vandenhoeck & Ruprecht, 1970), pp. 236–43; 251–59; E. Schweizer, *The Good News According to Matthew* (Atlanta: John Knox Press, 1975), pp. 371–74. For a connection with 1 Corinthians 5:4–5 (the "incestuous man"), see Thyen, *Studien zur Sündenvergebung*, p. 241; C. K. Barrett, *A Commen-*

tary on *The First Epistle to the Corinthians* (New York: Harper & Row, 1968), p. 136; Conzelmann, *First Corinthians*, pp. 97–98.

6. Brown, *Gospel According to John*, vol. 2, pp. 1036–45. For a somewhat different (and more polemic) view, cf. Thyen, *Studien zur Sündenvergebung*, pp. 243–51. This is not to harmonize the Matthaean and Johannine texts, but to insist on their common eschatological and ecclesial underpinnings.

7. Brown, *Gospel According to John*, vol. 2, pp. 774–79.

8. J. Paul Sampley, *Ephesians, Colossians, 2 Thessalonians, The Pastoral Epistles* (Philadelphia: Fortress, 1978), p. 14.

9. For a well-argued statement of this viewpoint from the biblical and moral disciplines, see P. Hoffmann and V. Eid, *Jesus von Nazareth und eine christliche Moral: Sittliche Perspektiven der Verkündigung Jesu.* Quaestiones Disputate 66 (Freiburg: Herder, 1975), pp. 27–72.

10. One need not agree with F. Bruce, *The Epistle to the Hebrews* (Grand Rapids, Mich.: Eerdmans, 1964), pp. 120–22, in seeing specific sacraments in the text.

11. See ibid, pp. 118–19; C. Spicq, *L'Epître aux Hébreux* (Paris: Gabalda, 1952), vol. 1, pp. 57ff.

12. For the difference between the two terms, see the appropriate articles in *Theological Dictionary of the New Testament,* vol. 1, pp. 510–12 (Bultmann), and vol. 4, pp. 1000–04 (Behm). It is best summed up in the latter's statement: "To convert is not just to give one's life a new direction but in practice to reorientate oneself continually to the goal by the radical setting aside of evil" vol. 4, p. 1004).

13. Similar exhortations to acknowledge Christ before the world and warnings against "being ashamed" of the Son of Man are found in the Gospels (Mark 8:38; Luke 12:8ff.); see I. H. Marshall, *Commentary on Luke* (Grand Rapids, Mich.: Eerdman's, 1978), pp. 509–12.

14. This famous text is found in Hermas' *Precepts* IV, 1–3. I have translated from the French text in C. Vogel, *Le Pêcheur et la Pénitence dans l'Eglise Ancienne* (Paris: Cerf, 1966), pp. 65–66. For similar texts in Clement of Alexandria, cf. ibid, pp. 66–72.

15. Ibid, p. 11. It is not my purpose to deal with the complicated history of canonical Penance in the Eastern and Western churches; see B. Poschmann, *Paenitentia Secunda: Die kirchliche Busse im ältesten Christentum bis Cyprian und Origenes* (Bonn: P. Hanstein, reprint, 1964 [1940]); J. Grotz, *Die Entwicklung des Bussstufenwesens in der vornicänischen Kirche* (Freiburg: Herder, 1955); K. Rahner, *Theological Investigations* (New York: Crossroads, 1981), vol. 15.

16. The earlier form of this communal concern is seen in the relation between Eucharist and excommunication; cf. K. Hein, *Eucharist and Excommunication: A Study in Early Christian Doctrine and Discipline* (Bern: Lang, 1975).

17. In Vogel, *Pénitence dans l'Englise Ancienne*, p. 165; cf. also P. Christophe, *Cassien et Césare. Prédicateurs de la morale monastique* (Paris: Lethielleux, 1969), pp. 48–77.

18. *The Roman Ritual: Rite of Penance* (Washington, D.C.: USCC, 1974), par. 4 (p. 9).

19. For a succinct treatment, see J. McNeill, *The Celtic Churches* (Chicago: University of Chicago Press, 1974), pp. 69–86.

20. For more extended discussion, see J. McNeill and H. Gamer, *Medieval Handbooks of Penance* (New York: Octagon, reprint, 1965 [1938]), pp. 24–26. For a detailed description of Irish tax Penance, see J. McNeill, *A History of the Cure of Souls* (New York: Harper & Row, 1977), pp. 112–35.

21. The whole discussion of "lay-confessors" connected to the ideas of spiritual counselling and to the value ascribed to shame as a penitential act would exceed the purpose of this chapter. The classic reference in this area remains A. Teetaert's *La Confession aux laiques dans l'église latine depuis le VIII^{e}jusqu'au XIVe siècle* (Paris: Wetteren, 1926).

22. Cf. C. Vogel, *Le Pêcheur et la Pénitence au Moyen Âge* (Paris: Cerf, 1969), p. 21.

23. In addition to McNeill and Gamer's *Medieval Handbooks,* already cited, and Vogel's *Pénitence au Moyen Âge,* some of this documentation is also given in a critical edition of L. Bieler, *The Irish Penitentials* (Dublin: Dublin Institute for Advanced Studies, 1963).

24. As given in McNeill and Gamer, *Medieval Handbooks,* p. 90.

25. See, for example, W. Lentzen-Deis, *Busse als Bekenntnisvollzug* (Freiburg: Herder, 1969), and D. Chapelle, "L'absolution sacerdotale chez S. Cyprien," *Recherches de Théologie Ancienne et Médiévale* 7 (1935): 221–34.

26. The element of shame and guilt, often emphasized in penitential literature, is a complex factor which I do not have the space to go into here. For a typical statement, see Vogel, *Pénitence au Moyen Âge,* pp. 168–69.

27. T. Tentler, *Sin and Confession on the Eve of the Reformation* (Princeton: Princeton University Press, 1977), pp. 12–13.

28. *The Roman Ritual,* par. 5 (p. 10).

29. This brief discussion does not pretend to explain the origin of all psychological incongruence. Its limited purpose is to identify a major flaw in the narration of experience and the problem this presents for true Penance.

30. Virginia Axline, *Dibs: In Search of Self* (New York: Ballantine, 1964).

31. Ibid, p. 154.

32. Ibid, pp. 217–18.

33. Walter Brueggemann, "Covenanting as Human Interpretation," *Interpretation* 33 (1979): 115–29.

34. Carl Rogers, *On Becoming a Person* (Boston: Houghton Mifflin, 1961), pp. 118–19.

35. Cf. Romans 5:10, and E. Käsemann's remarks in *Commentary on Romans* trans. G. W. Bromley (Grand Rapids, Mich.: W. B. Eerdmans, 1980), pp. 138–39.

36. In the patristic writings, Gospel accounts of the curing of the lepers and the raising of Lazarus were favorite occasions for commenting on the forgiveness of sins. From this tradition the image of the confessor as "doctor" derives. For a typical statement at the Council of Trent by Melchior Cano and others, see *Concilium Tridentinum,* Pars Tertiae, volumen prius (Freiburg: Herder, 1950), vol. 6, pp. 262, 403, no. 2.

37. See F. Büchsel, *"allasso/katallasso,"* *Theological Dictionary of the New Testament,* ed. G. Kittel, vol. 1, pp. 255–58; here, p. 256.

38. On Psalm 37, hom. 2, in P. Palmer, *Sacraments and Forgiveness* (Westminster, Md.: Newman, 1959), p. 38. I wish to thank C. Dunn for reminding me of this citation.

39. See, for example, Conzelmann, *First Corinthians,* p. 102; Barrett, *First Epistle to the Corinthians,* pp. 132-33.
40. Thus also, C. K. Barrett, *A Commentary on the Second Epistle to the Corinthians* (New York: Harper & Row, 1973), p. 184.
41. E. Käsemann, *Perspectives on Paul* (Philadelphia: Fortress, 1971), p. 44.
42. In the Roman liturgy, the *confiteor* ("I confess") of the Mass has its origin in a private prayer for forgiveness; so, J. Jungmann, *The Mass of the Roman Rite: Its Origins and Development,* 2 vols. (New York: Benzinger, 1950), vol. 1, pp. 298-311. On the other hand, Luther and Calvin had more nuanced positions on the question of Penance than is sometimes supposed; cf., for example, J. Calvin's *Institution de la Religion Chrétienne* in J. D. Benoit's critical edition (Paris: Vrin, 1960-61), esp. Bk. III, iv, 12-13 (Benoit ed., vol. 3, pp. 110-13) and Bk. IV, xiv, 14 (Benoit ed., vol. 4, pp. 480-82).
43. Sermon 216, 2, in *St. Augustine: Sermons on the Liturgical Year,* trans. M. S. Muldowney (New York: Church Fathers, 1959), p. 151.

CHAPTER 8

The Future Community Now

When Leonard Bernstein was commissioned to compose a large work for the opening of the Kennedy Center in Washington, D.C., he followed the time-honored tradition of Mozart and Beethoven. He set the text of the Latin Mass to music with one important difference. Each Latin text is followed by songs in English, explaining why we will have difficulty doing what the Mass text proclaimed we could do. In other words, the Latin text suggests the objective possibility of worship (*ex opere operato*), while the related English texts reveal the subjective problem of response (*ex opere operantis*). Thus, *Confiteor* ("I confess") is followed by a song: "What I say I don't feel, what I feel I don't show. . . ." The function of the English text is to expose our blithe "confiteors" and to enable more honest confession.

But Bernstein did not stop there. He knew that the text and rituals of the Eucharist belong to a community, not simply to individuals. The context of such celebration is the honesty of the community, proclaiming what God has done in their midst. As Bernstein's *Mass* begins, a young man in blue jeans gathers people around him and dons the vestments of celebration. These people have all the appearances of a Christian community. But Bernstein aptly paraphrases the Pauline axiom (1 Cor. 10:17): "Because we eat the one bread, we are not necessarily one at all!"

Pauline unity and community are not the result of hymns

sung in unison or rituals performed together. Bernard Lonergan reminds us that community is "the achievement of common meaning . . . [which] is realized by decisions and choices, especially by permanent dedication, in the love that makes families, in the loyalty that makes states, in the faith that makes religions."[1] As *Mass* proceeds, we see that there are only private meanings in this group of worshipers. They prefer ceremonies to the challenging mystery of God's presence, ritual songs and dances to the commitments of the Cross.

Bernstein then goes on to illustrate this point. The climax occurs when the celebrant stands above the congregation (like Moses on the mountain), holding the symbols of Christ's presence and self-gift, the bread and the cup. Below, the people are carousing much as the Israelites did in the Golden Calf episode (Exod. 32:1–35). The celebrant hurls down the symbols of Christ's presence among people who are not really present, among ritualizing groups that are not yet sacramentalizing communities. In the monologue called "Things get broken so easily," he comments on the fragility of ritual and the weakness of people if left to their own devices.

Bernstein's insight is vital: relevant rituals alone do not form a New Covenant community. Rituals are the traditional way in which groups and societies cope with the feared and unknown in their shared existence, as the opening passage from *Grendel* indicates. Sacramental symbols and true worship always call out and enable renewed meaning and shared commitment. Bernstein's English texts in *Mass* are so many reflections on the problem of such shared and individual meaning and commitments. As already noted, it is the presence of God which, if honestly welcomed and proclaimed, prevents us from becoming content with our limited self-gift. It is that same committing presence which is the ground of any worshipping community and its Gospel unity.

In this final chapter, we will deal with the problem of honest ritual as the door to saving symbols. The letter to the Hebrews is a particularly important guide in this discussion. We will then ask if the current proclamation of the Word of God in our assemblies helps us to appropriate the attitudes of someone who worships "in spirit and truth." Finally, some theoretical and practical corollaries of our study of commitment will be proposed.

MEANINGS AND RITUALS

Christians can easily forget that rituals are of human origin. Their efficaciousness depends on God's presence and our honest participation. Creators of good religious ritual know how to shape seasonal rituals, fertility rites, and rites of passage into a rich source of creative religious response to God.[2] This is what Lonergan might call a "potential common meaning," that is, a common field of experience from which the community and individuals can make choices and commitments.[3] Although there are anthropological, sociological, and psychological components to any ritual action, we will confine our remarks to the question of honest and clarifying use of sacramental rituals by Christians.[4]

Luigi Pirandello in his play *Henry IV* (1923) insightfully dramatized the potential dangers of ritual. As the curtain rises, he leads the audience to believe that the action of the play takes place in the time of the Holy Roman Emperor, Henry IV. But as the play progresses, we discover that it is actually the twentieth century. The protagonist, after a fall from his horse, announces that he is the emperor, Henry IV. His family is wealthy enough to humor his apparent amnesia.

But Henry is not the dupe of his illusion. His life had been falling apart because of a crisis. What better way to maintain a facade than to imagine himself the Holy Roman Emperor whose court is governed by ritual. The function of court ritual, after all, is to reduce ambiguity and to control all situations in favor of the ruler. In imagining himself the emperor, Henry surrounds himself with a buffer zone against reality. Ritual becomes Henry's escape from crisis and commitment.

Ritual has always been used to reduce conflict and to deal with the fear of the unknown. The simple rituals of saying the rosary or lighting a candle, for example, can exercise a calming influence on some people at the moment of fear or crisis. Ritual, however, only becomes dishonest and neurotic when its other tasks are excluded, as in Henry's case. As Julian Huxley has pointed out, successful ritual is also communicative of meaning and it bonds people together in deeper ways.[5] The liturgist may bemoan the fact, but even the secularized French society, for example, still insists on "solemn first communions" of its young because, aside from any religious meaning, such a ritual possesses certain shared meanings for the community. Erikson sums up the anthropological meaning of ritual as "a deepening communality, a proven ceremonial form, and a timeless quality from which all participants emerge with a sense of awe and purification."[6] Anyone who recalls the funeral of President John Kennedy would probably attest to the accuracy of Erikson's observation.

The difference between a purely secular notion of ritual and the Christian understanding of sacrament was pinpointed early in this book: *lex orandi lex credendi* ("the law of worship is the law of belief"). From the experience of God's initiative in our stories (justification), the Christian prays and participates in sacramental actions (*lex orandi*). Ideally, this sacramental use of ritual should lead not only to clearer doctrinal understanding of the Christian faith but to a commitment to and appropriation of its meaning (*lex credendi*). This, I believe, is Fowler's concern when he tries to clarify the interplay between structure and content in faith as a way of looking "more radically and inclusively at faith as a particular person's way of constituting self, others and world in relation to particular values, powers and stories of reality he or she takes as ultimate."[7]

In elaborating on this interplay, Fowler offers as one major element of the contents of faith, *centers of value,* that is, "the causes, concerns or persons that consciously or unconsciously have the greatest worth to us."[8] He then notes that the words *worship* and *worth* have the same etymological background. In other words, we worship that which calls out our loyalty and commitment because it is worthy. Returning to an earlier interview, Fowler comments: "In Mary's story . . . it was only when she experienced the reality of God and of a divine lawfulness that she began to bring to consciousness the centers of a value around which her life had recently been spinning and to face how chaotic it had been."[9] In brief, honest worship and life commitments are inextricably bound together.

In contrast to Henry IV's ritualism, which effectively blocked out his experience and therefore the possibility of honest commitments, Christian worship can be the source of shared meanings and renewed commitments that "reshape one's life in a new community of interpretation and action."[10] To achieve this integration, however, we must make better use of the ritualization of our life cycles. Expressed differently, the interplay of God's presence and our own takes place in our daily rituals as well as in our more formal and periodic sacramental rituals. If deeper commitments are to emerge from our worship and sacrament, then we must deal more authentically with our experience in its daily expressions.

Erikson points out that "ritualization . . . depends on that blending of surprise and recognition which is the soul of creative interplay, reborn out of instinctual chaos, confusion of identity and social anomie."[11] Eventually, good ritual must include the complexity of our shared experience, in sharp contrast to pseudo-rituals that allow us to factor out much of this same experience and remain in a make-believe world.

The conflicts of a particular stage of life can be imaged and perhaps reconciled by means of rituals, for we "recognize in a given playful construction the basic way in which the experiences of a stage of life and of a state of conflict are translated into and reconciled in a specific space-time arrangement."[12] In the previous chapter, we saw how Dibs, by means of play therapy, recognized and reconciled such conflict in his own story.

In Chapter 2, we discussed limit-experiences of our lives (such as academic and professional "burn-out," failing health, an environmental problem that affects a whole community, etc.). In former times, the Church ritualized similar limit-experiences (producing, for example, specific blessings for personal sickness or tragedy, prefaces for widows, processions for crop failure and plague, etc.) so that Christians might learn "the will of God," that is, discern new meaning in the conflicts and crises of their lives. The parables, we noted, are also a model for recognizing and reconciling the meaning and commitment demands in our past and current experience.

Sunday morning rituals, proclaiming the death and Resurrection of Jesus, have their reality-testing in the weekday rituals of rush-hour traffic, hurried or unhurried meals, our daily schedule of work and play, our sexual lives, and so on. We know when there is an honest interplay between sacramental rituals and our experience because we discover once again our need and God's abundance. Unlike Eastern practices of chanting and yoga, which may effectively produce a sense of peace and "being centered" without any complementary sense of community and service, true Christian ritual is always a bridge to God and the needs of others, a hope that exceeds our limits.

THE NEW PELAGIANS

The new Pelagians, unlike their predecessors of the fifth century, are not those who deny their need for God's gratuitous and continuing help, but rather, *Christians who have forgotten the purpose of that help.* Jesus is the model of God's redeeming purpose for this creation: someone obedient to the Father and "on account of others." Salvation, therefore, involves more than our private spiritual well-being. Those who forget this are the new Pelagians whose rituals of worship have become a refuge from the needs of a world that is not yet transformed into a peaceable Kingdom. The image of the people in Bernstein's *Mass* is all too often being played out in such uncommitted rituals that will not save. But the Word of God does not allow us to rest easy in this heresy.

In Chapters 9 through 12 of Romans, Paul reminds us of the purposes of God's saving presence in time. Paul Minear notes, moreover, that Paul was dealing with a specific pastoral problem in giving this teaching to the Roman Christians: the narrow, prejudiced attitudes of Gentiles in the community. If their worship was to be "spiritual" or appropriate (*logikēn*), then their praxis had to change.[13]

"And now I beg you through the mercy of God to offer *your bodies as a living sacrifice,* holy and acceptable to God, *your spiritual worship.* Do not conform yourselves to this age but *be transformed by the renewal of your mind* so that you may judge what is God's will . . ." (Rom. 12:1–2). He rounds out this teaching with his Corinthian theme of "many members in one body" and the service we should render one another (Rom. 12:4–21). Paul's sequence of thought is a traditional one that weaves together the concerns of salvific need, honest worship, and the practical corollaries of a covenant and serving community.

Paul, using liturgical language, argued for worship's purpose and goal. "Living sacrifice" is a biblical phrase that epitomizes the attitudes of those who listen and respond to God's presence within the changing shapes of their lives.[14] Paul viewed the Christian as someone who integrates life and worship. As Käsemann remarks, "Either the whole of Christian life is worship, and the gatherings and sacramental acts of the community provide equipment and instruction for this or these gatherings and acts lead to absurdity."[15]

The result of transformed attitudes ("the renewal of your mind") is summed up in a remarkable line: "so that you may judge what is God's will" (Rom. 12:2). C. K. Barrett sees the emphasis on praxis in this verse: "The Christian finds out the will of God not to contemplate it but to do it."[16] Paul regarded the true Christian as capable of moral decisions bespeaking mature and evolving commitment.[17] The spelling out of this Gospel decision-making is found later in Chapter 12 of Romans: "Your love must be sincere . . . be generous in offering hospitality . . . weep with those who weep . . . conquer evil with good" (Rom. 12:9–21).

"Spiritual worship" is the prophetic antidote, of course, to the new Pelagianism. It is marked by the attitudes of self-gift and conversion, described in the prophets (such as Isaiah 66), and shows itself in the decisions of daily life. In the New Testament, spiritual worship is the bridge that spans the Old Testament view of honest worship and the unique model of Jesus as "presence" and perfect sacrifice because he does the will of the Father.

Nowhere, perhaps, in the New Testament is this better developed than in Hebrews. In the Old Testament, Isaiah had recounted God's poignant lament in a worship context: "When I called, no one answered, when I spoke, no one listened" (Isa. 66:4). But in Hebrews, Jesus is the one who listens and responds. Against a carefully constructed background of ineffectual sacrifice of the Old Testament, Jesus stands out as the perfect sacrifice because he is obedient: "I have come to do your will" (Heb. 10:9).[18]

The blood of Christ is an evocative image of his commitment: "He entered [the holy of holies], not with the blood of goats and calves but with his own blood . . ." (Heb. 9:12).[19] His listening and responding, his obedience have cost him. Hebrews announces what this means for us: "Since the blood of Jesus assures our entrance into the sanctuary by the new and living path he opened up for us . . . let us draw near in utter sincerity and absolute confidence. . . . *Let us hold unswervingly to our profession which gives us hope*" (Heb. 10:19–23). "Drawing near" is descriptive of a covenant people and the presence of God among them.[20] The result of Christ's self-gift is that the New Covenant community may live up to its baptismal "profession" of commitment: to live realistically in hope in God's present time.[21]

But the writer, with all of his theological insights, had not forgotten the praxis-situation of the community he was addressing. He reminded them of earlier commitment-demands ("You endured a great contest of suffering"; Heb. 10:32) because he was concerned about a current crisis demanding new witness and self-gift from this community of Christians. In a ringing challenge to their Gospel commitment, Hebrews says: "We are not among those who draw back and perish, but among those who have faith and live" (Heb. 10:39).[22]

Anyone who has tried to grow in a typical Christian parish community and to experience its worship and sacrament as evocative of deeper commitment might find all this attractive but unrealistic nonsense. But the writer of Hebrews had a realistic approach to the limitations of Christians. To develop his argument, outlined above, he proceeded to illustrate the meaning of Christian faith ("confident assurance concerning what we hope for, and conviction about things we do not see"; Heb. 11:1) by recounting the faith of a spectrum of biblical figures. In this way he prepared his audience for Chapter 12's eloquent call to renewed commitment, with Christ as paradigm: *"Let us keep*

our eyes fixed on Jesus, who inspires and perfects our faith. For
the sake of the joy which lay before him he endured the Cross .
. ." (Heb. 12:2). Once more he described a festal worship context with Jesus as the New Covenant mediator and sacrifice
(Heb. 12:18–24) to encourage wavering Christians to become
more deeply committed.[23]

Centuries later, Augustine would make similar connections
between faith and sacrament: "From whence does the water
which touches the body and purifies the heart have such power
except *from the act of the word, not because it is said but because
it is believed*" (Tract. in Joan. 80, 3).[24] Here is the underlying
reason for pastoral optimism in how worship and sacrament can
enliven the meaning of the commitment of the Christian community and its individual members. God's Word has not lost its
power to arouse faltering Christians, caught once more unaware
in the conflicts of their lives.

If this were not so, the final bold commitment metaphor of
Hebrews would be naive: "Therefore Jesus died outside the
gate, to sanctify the people by his own blood. *Let us go to him
outside the camp, bearing the insult which he bore. . . . Through
him let us continually offer God a sacrifice of praise*" (Heb.
13:12–13, 15).[25]

We have commented extensively on Hebrews because its concerns are more relevant than ever. Perhaps in no other New
Testament writing do we find such a developed connection between worship and commitment, with Christ as the challenging
model. Whatever events may have provoked this crisis in the
faith-commitment of the members of the community,[26] the writer was determined to evoke renewed dedication to their baptismal commitments. In a final prayer for the community, the
writer of Hebrews condensed his whole teaching on commitment into one magnificent metaphor: "May the God of peace,
who brought up from the dead the great Shepherd of the sheep
by the blood of the eternal covenant, Jesus our Lord, furnish
you with all that is good *that you may do his will. Through
Jesus Christ may he carry out in you all that is pleasing to him.*
To Christ be glory forever! Amen" (Heb. 13:20–21).[27]

In Hebrews, then, we find a normative teaching on honest
worship and sacrament. Translated into twentieth-century lan-

guage, the question of Hebrews is this: are you worshipping God, receiving the sacraments of his Son, and yet missing the point? Jesus, the great Shepherd, is raised up because of his commitment, proved by his serving life and saving death.[28] This is not a picture of salvation to be stared at, but an event to be participated in.

There is a type of ritualism, or rubricism, concerned only with the external forms of reverence. Hebrews can serve as a trenchant reminder that in being accountable to God, we can only plead a worship that has resulted in renewed faith and service. Celebrations of our faith are authentic when "we mean the words and want to do what is done. . . . Faith grows when it is well expressed in celebration. Good celebrations foster and nourish faith. Poor celebrations weaken and destroy faith."[29]

THE DEAFENING QUESTION

Vatican II, after specifying how Christ is sacramentally present in the Church, said: "He is present in His word, since it is He Himself who speaks when the holy Scriptures are read in the church."[30] Without the Word of God, the honesty of our celebrations would be in jeopardy. But covenant communities have always had the temptation of selectively hearing that Word. The lament of Jeremiah has not disappeared with the new covenant: "The prophets prophesy falsely, and the priests teach what they wish; yet my people will have it so. What will you do when the end comes?" (Jer. 5:31).

Proclaiming the Word of God seems to have always been a part of Christian worship. The average Sunday liturgy, for example, has readings of the Scriptures and preaching. The recitation and repetition of the Word of God, however, should not be confused with its proclamation. The Greek biblical terms *to exhort* and *to announce the good news* imply that the proclaimers have experience of what they preach.[31] It is the Spirit that constantly discloses our need: we are the blind, the deaf, and the lame. In the face of such need, we hunger and thirst for God's Word. The Spirit enables effective proclamation of the Word and honest response on our part.[32]

That is the theory, at least. In praxis, however, such preaching seems rare these days. Whether it is the slickly packaged television preaching or simply the dull, irrelevant Sunday morning homily, few Christians seem challenged to alter their business or sexual ethics, to re-examine their current life-stage priorities in view of Gospel values, or to witness prophetically against the arms race or their consumer society. Can Gospel proclamation leave us so comfortably uncommitted?

God's presence in his Word enables but does not coerce our response. (These are, again, the objective and subjective dimensions of worship and sacrament.) If our response is committed, we will be participants in the action-words and praise of God. But the very nature of such response involves our experience. The ministry of God's Word should facilitate that involvement. This is not to be mistaken for interesting preaching or satisfying lecturing that may comfort and stir us, but not move us to re-commit ourselves.

Much preaching presumes knowledge of the congregation's experience in a general way ("We are all sinners, generous at times, angry occasionally," etc.). Rhetorical questions may be directed to the listeners' experience, but no answer is expected or required ("Are we not all sinners?"). A preacher may speak as if already knowing the redemptive problem of and solution for the community. This preaching may inform us without questioning us. It may fascinate us, but not challenge the versions of our stories. The fundamental theological fallacy of such preaching is its implicit definition of redemption as generalized healing and conversion, as a once-for-all experience that admits no development. Sacramental celebrations, preceded by such preaching, will more easily slip into ritualism because our responsibility for God's time and space has not been further questioned.

In contrast to this, there is a type of preaching, punctuated by what I would call the "deafening questions." These questions invite participation on the deepest level of the listeners' experience. Just as the prophet's action-word interrogated the lived history and praxis of his listeners, so these questions allow the listeners to re-see their experience and, thus, be "deafened" with God's presence and action in their lives. In charismatic circles, "Praise the Lord" is a frequent acclamation. After liturgical reading, the congregation says, "Thanks be to God" or some similar words of praise. But these acclamations remain ritual formulas until the moment they are wrung from the fibers of our lives, provoked by the living Word of God.

Deafening questions nourish honesty in ritual and reflect the shape of our lives. With the help of such questions, we can again "bless God" (*berakhah*) because we have seen anew, with gratitude, our familiar experience. Above all, new commitments begin to emerge from apparently old questions. To "serve" (in Latin, *ministrare*) such a provocative Word, those who preach and teach must be willing to submit to the same questions they pose to others. They must be willing to be disturbed from their complacency by the radical demands of the Gospel as they announce those same demands to others.

Such ministry of God's Word requires more of a proclaimer than insightful exegetical understanding, relevant questions and examples, and more time spent in preparation, as important as these elements are. We cannot proclaim and preach the Word of God despite our own experience. Like Paul, Ambrose, Augustine, and other authentic Christian proclaimers, our own flawed experience is a source of prayer, praise, and proclamation of God's action. We need not use autobiographical anecdotes to make our homilectic points, but we must allow God's questions about our stories to "deafen us." Otherwise, our own questions to others will ring hollow.

SPIRITED SYMBOLS AND THEIR USERS

In speaking of how we participate in Word and sacrament, the long-range commitments of our life-praxis have been a major concern. Within this context, several propositions about the honest use of worship and sacrament can now be offered. In these propositions, we gratefully recognize the gratuitous, objective presence of God in all Word, worship, and sacramental expressions of faith, but attempt to spell out the Gospel demands of commitment that such a gift elicits.

Honest participation in Word, worship, and sacrament is aided or hindered by the way in which we deal with our experience. This thesis summarizes a major direction of this book. Such ex-

perience, shaped by the crises and commitment-demands of each
stage, is as varied as the typical Sunday morning community of
symbolizing Christians. Rituals of worship and sacrament
should play a functional role in helping us clarify our experience. Naive ritualism results, in part, from ignoring this basic
principle.

A simple example is the penitential rite that forms part of the
introductory rite of the Eucharist. The celebrant invites the
community to reflect briefly on another week of living and see
what they have done with God's time. If this rite is to become
something more than negative breast-beating, the positive dimensions of our experience must be included in such an examination. . . . Our current stage of life, with its special priorities
and needs, tasks and conflicts, is an important source of this
honest self-scrutiny. The question, "What was I like this
week?" will probably admit of many answers. "What (and
who) really mattered to me this week?" is a complicated question that should affect the way in which we hear the Word of
God. Such questions and their answers are an attempt to rejoice
once again, like Mary, in what God has done for us and to cry
out to him in our need.

We discussed another aspect of experience in Chapter 4 when
we considered how much connection there must be between our
stories and our intentions before our rituals are honest. Intentionality sums up the way we look at our experience and our
world. The shape of our stories is inseparable from our intentions. To ask what we intend (*ex opere operantis*) in a sacrament is to confront the decisions and values of our lived experience. As I stretch out my hand for the Eucharist, for example,
what do I intend? I cannot follow Augustine's advice about this
ritual ("Be what you see, receive what you are") unless I invest
more of myself in this action. Augustine's "I could not find myself. How much less could I find you" applies to Word and
sacrament as much as it does to the question of conversion.

In Augustine's time, the Donatists managed to distort the
whole sacramental question of personal intention and commitment and objective validity by insisting that unworthy ministers
of sacraments rendered these symbols invalid. In response, Augustine emphasized the distinction between objective validity

and subjective fruitfulness in ministering and receiving sacrament, as well as a certain perduring possibility of accepting God's free gift (*character*) when we withdraw from a sinful situation.[33] Augustine quite correctly denied that there is an infallible connection between sacrament and grace, between personal holiness and real sacrament, because every sacrament has a wider ecclesial concern.[34] But this great theologian would have been shocked, I suspect, if he had thought that the Christian Church would accept this brilliant insight, countering a contemporary heresy, as the definitive and perennial answer to the question of honest participation in faith and sacrament.

Augustine, as cited earlier, attributed the efficaciousness of sacrament to the act of the Word, "not because it is said but because it is believed." But this act of belief includes not only a rational assent but a commitment to what is proclaimed in that Word. Our true intentions, rooted in our experience, are the door to such commitment.

Moreover, the Christian community has an important responsibility in facilitating honest participation. Providing rituals that can set the stage for such participation is only the first step. Ministries that do more than ritualize are also needed. In teaching, preaching, and celebrating the Word of God and sacrament, true "ministers" serve the community both by opening themselves to the symbols they propose to others and by cultivating a keen sensitivity to God's continuing action in others' lives.

Parents and teachers of religious education are a model of praxis for children and adolescents by the way in which they involve themselves in the "deafening questions" of their own lives and their authentic participation in worship and sacrament. This is the practical test of Erikson's insight that only mature people invite the young to symbol-making: "Without old people in possession of such integrity, young people in need of an identity can neither rebel nor obey."[35] No Christian leader or teacher can afford to ignore that insight.

EVOKED SERVICE

Honest worship and sacrament must continue to call out of us the commitment and service we are uniquely capable of at each stage of life. It is ironic that the Christian community sometimes expects less of its members in terms of Gospel service than it would of a friend, employer, or philanthropic fund-raising group. Even more ironic is the ignorance of a celebrating community that does not know experientially the dynamic and evocative character and purpose of worship and sacrament. The prophets taught the same lesson to such congregations many times: praise of God that is not coupled with service is an abomination. Such ritual deceives no one except the participants.

The Church has always had an important and privileged task in this area, as we have pointed out more than once.[36] *To "administer" or "serve"* (in Latin, *administrare,* meaning "to serve") *a sacrament is to help ritualizers become symbolizers.*[37] The bridge between ritual and sacrament is commitment to God's peaceable reign in his current creation. But the universal and local Church must spell out, in positive terms, what that commitment concretely means in the praxis-situations of each historical epoch and social situation.

An example from current praxis might be instructive at this point. Although marriage is not regarded as a sacrament by all the Christian churches, the powerful teaching of the letter to the Ephesians, using marriage as a metaphor for the unity of Christ and the Church (Eph. 5:32), has always been recognized.[38] As J. P. Sampley notes: "Throughout 5:21–33 there is an eschatological tension between what has already been done for the church and what is to be expected in the future of the church."[39] Ephesians presents a strong Old Testament dimension with covenant overtones: "The marital relationship is shown to be grounded in Torah and patterned on YHWH's marriage to Israel as reflected in Christ's relation to the church."[40]

The very least one can say about marriage in the Christian tradition is that it is much more than a private contract between two (perhaps nominal) Christians. The tradition that has regarded marriage as a privileged symbol, in which the couple is the actual "minister" of a continuing prophetic action-word, reminds the larger Christian community of its present mission and future goal. A Christian couple, then, is called to become symbol-maker and covenant-gatherer. This will be a process usually involving several stages of the two individuals' lives and dependent on the honesty with which they work through the corresponding conflicts and commitments.

What faith-commitment should be present in a couple asking for not simply a contract or a church ritual, but a sacrament or the symbol of Ephesians? Can a baptismal certificate, the absence of close consanguinity, and some premarital instructions be considered even minimal criteria for such prospective symbol-carriers? Is every Christian couple capable at the beginning of their marriage to be such a symbol if even minimal Christian commitment-demands are not met?

Here again, both the specific life-stage of each partner (for example, the difference between a young adult and one in the subsequent "settling-down" stage) and the social context of the local church (such as the important differences between marriage in Appalachia, New York, or San Francisco) help to concretize what "commitment" means for the couple and the community in which they must be a Christian symbol. If we will not be responsible for these dimensions of sacrament before its celebration, why should we be so canonically rigorous after the failure of a marriage?

Rigoristic demands should not be confused with God's enabling presence in Word, worship, and sacrament to call out commitment from a couple over the years if there is honesty in their use of such symbols. Furthermore, the Christian community does not necessarily support that honesty by assuming faith-commitment because of canonical regularity.

SHARING MINISTRIES

Commitment to the Gospel begets ministries to proclaim and serve its message. If Pauline identification (Chapter 5) calls us to serve as Christ did, his symbols continue to question and challenge that ministry. *Honest Word, worship, and sacrament evoke committed and appropriate ministries at each point of our lives.* These ministries must be characterized by the early Church's criteria of ministry: continuity with the Risen Lord and flexibility in shaping those ministries.

All ministry in the apostolic and sub-apostolic periods had to be connected with the work of the Risen Lord. Each Gospel minister was a symbol of continuity with that healing and messianic presence. When the community called such a person out of its midst for service, it would gladly strengthen the weak Christian for service but not tolerate the dishonest or uncommitted one. (The Pastoral letters are an extended lesson in this regard.) Continuity of ministering Christians with the Risen Lord was tested and proved by their shared and continuing efforts to be "on account of the others."

But, as the Church moved into the seventies of the first Christian century, the needs of communities and their individuals continued to change.[41] The Church demonstrated a creative flexibility in evoking and structuring service that was tailored to diverse situations and peoples. She was helped in this by the rich variety of gifts to be found among committed Christians. Converted Roman soldiers quietly preached and ministered to their comrades. Christian widows found a new purpose in their lives. Christian intellectuals taught their newfound wisdom, motivated by the new commitments in their lives.

In mission countries, the Church has always had to call out the varied ministries (such as catechists) from its lay members. More recently, the "basic communities" of Christians in South America, the Cursillo, and Marriage Encounter movements in several countries have had some success in helping Christians to recommit themselves to practical Gospel living and service. But this is not the case in the average Christian parish community. On the contrary, there is a danger of a certain "liturgical consumerism" in which Christians pick up their spiritual commodities and leave without any deepened commitment to the mission of the Church. But as we increasingly face a situation of parishes without priests,[42] we must once again learn from the early Church how to encourage ministries geared to the needs of the young and the elderly, the married and the divorced, the worker and the professional, the heterosexual and the homosexual.

SUMMARY

Conditions for fruitful reception of a sacrament and honest worship arise from Christian commitment and the fused purpose of many people gifted for mission. The demands of such Christian commitment are not rigoristic or unrealistic. Rather, they are based on a keen appreciation for the flawed but gifted Christians and a hope that is more than the sum total of those same Christians.

But if there is to be a theology of commitment that deals realistically with the praxis of the Christian community, then it must begin with this question: is there anyone among us who is harboring the "unreasonable expectations" of the Gospel these days? In other words, in our sacramental praxis are we dealing with the rituals of the committed or the uncommitted? Are we willingly searching for God's new meanings, etched out in the stages of our lives, or are we comfortable with our old memories of him?

If we find much worship and too little commitment, then perhaps we should remember the suggestion Paul made to a community with a similar problem, the Corinthians: "We too are weak in him [Christ], but we live with him by God's power in us. Test yourselves to see whether you are living in faith; examine yourself. Perhaps you yourselves do not realize that Christ Jesus is in you—unless, of course, you have failed the challenge" (2 Cor. 13:4-5).

Real presence is measured by God's presence, which we continue to encounter in our lives. His presence bespeaks a faithful commitment and so is called "covenant presence." Our Christian presence—the sum of what we are and do—is real to the extent that we are a responding and covenant people whose flawed commitments give hope to others.

In brief, there is no real presence that does not demand commitment. But commitment tests the honest awareness we have of our life experience and, thus, the quality of our presence. Biblical symbols for the Kingdom of God attempt to describe the mutual presence of God and his people at the end of time. These people were strengthened by God in stages of time to

bear the pain and the liberation of disclosure symbols that invited them literally "to go with the others" (*committere*) once
more. Ultimately, Christian commitment is a test of any theological praxis or theory that claims to explain that which we, as
yet, have no full experience of: God's redemption in Christ and
our participation in it.

NOTES

1. B. Lonergan, *Method in Theology* (New York: Herder and Herder, 1972),
   p. 79. Italics mine.
2. It is not my purpose to review all the work done in the different areas of
   ritual. Some of the work of M. Douglas and V. Turner has already been
   cited. In addition, cf. R. Furth, *Symbols, Public and Private* (Ithaca, N.Y.:
   Cornell University Press, 1973); W. Jetter, *Symbol und Ritual* (Göttingen:
   Vandenhoeck und Ruprecht, 1978); K. Grainger, *The Language of the
   Rite* (London: Darton, Longman and Todd, 1974); A. Hahn, "Anthropologie des Kults," *Anthropologie des Kults* (Freiburg: Herder, 1977), pp.
   51–81.
3. Lonergan, *Method,* p. 79.
4. I generally agree with the critical analysis of F. Isambert in *Rite et Effica-
   cité Symbolique* (Paris: Cerf, 1979), though I am not at all sure that efficaciousness can be fully discussed without the question of commitment.
5. J. Huxley, "Ritual in Human Societies," *The Religious Situation: 1968,*
   ed. D. Cutler (Boston: Beacon, 1968), pp. 696–711.
6. E. Erikson, *Toys and Reasons: Stages in the Ritualization of Experience*
   (New York: W. W. Norton, 1977), p. 78.
7. J. Fowler, *Stages of Faith: The Psychology of Human Development and
   the Question of Meaning* (San Francisco: Harper & Row, 1981), p. 273;
   cf. also Jetter, *Symbol and Ritual,* pp. 108–21.
8. Fowler, *Stages of Faith,* p. 276.
9. Ibid.
10. Ibid, p. 282, for part of Fowler's definition on conversion, which we dis-
    cussed in Chapter 3. I have not tried to use Fowler's symbolic functions
    (ibid, pp. 244–45) because they seem to have a more general and, as yet,
    undeveloped place in his work.
11. Erikson, *Toys and Reasons,* p. 113.
12. Ibid, p. 34.
13. P. Minear, *The Obedience of Faith,* Studies in Biblical Theology, 2nd se-
    ries (Naperville, Ill.: Allenson, 1971), vol. 19, pp. 83–84.
14. For comments on the sacrificial language used throughout this passage, see
    C. K. Barrett, *A Commentary on the Epistle to the Romans* (New York:
    Harper & Row, 1957), p. 231.
15. E. Käsemann, *Commentary on Romans,* trans. G. W. Bromley (Grand
    Rapids, Mich.: W. B. Eerdmans, 1980), p. 327. See also, J. Koenig, "Vi-

sion, Self-Offering and Transformation for Ministry," *Sin, Salvation and the Spirit,* ed. D. Durken (Collegeville, Minn.: Liturgical Press, 1979), pp. 307–23; here, pp. 312–13, although I do not read Käsemann as "mounting a heavy attack on cultic worship," as Koenig does (p. 313). In fact, Käsemann has specifically refuted this charge (*Commentary on Romans,* p. 327).

16. Barrett, *Epistle to the Romans,* p. 233. Also, Käsemann is particularly forceful here (*Commentary on Romans,* pp. 329–31); and see Koenig, "Vision, Self-Offering and Transformation," pp. 313–15.

17. Compare these commitment demands with F. C. Power and L. Kohlberg, "Religion, Morality and Ego Development," pp. 343–72, and J. Fowler, "Faith and the Structure of Meanings," pp. 51–85, in *Toward Moral and Religious Maturity* (Morristown, N.J.: Silver Burdett, 1980).

18. B. F. Wescott's classic work is still helpful here; cf. *The Epistle to the Hebrews* (Grand Rapids, Mich.: W. B. Eerdmans, reprint, 1974), pp. 242–66.

19. For the current exegetical discussion and literature, see C. Spicq, *L'Épitre aux Hébreux* (Paris: Gabalda, 1977), pp. 153–62.

20. See C. Spicq, *L'Épitre aux Hébreux* (Paris: Gabalda, 1952), vol. 1, pp. 280–83; vol. 2, pp. 314–17.

21. Westcott, *Epistle to the Hebrews,* p. 323; Spicq, *L'Épitre aux Hébreux* (1977), pp. 172–74.

22. Spicq, *L'Épitre aux Hébreux* (1977), pp. 180–81.

23. Ibid, pp. 208–11.

24. For a discussion of this text in Augustine's thought, see L. Villette, *Foi et Sacrement,* 2 vols. (Paris: Bloud et Gay, 1959–64), vol. 1, pp. 231–39. For the subsequent misunderstanding of the text, see vol. 2, pp. 258–62; B. Leeming, *Principles of Sacramental Theology* (Westminster, MD.: Newman, 1960), pp. 36–37.

25. Cf. J. Thompson, "Outside the Camp: A Study of Hebrews 13:9–14," *Catholic Biblical Quarterly* 40 (1978): 53–63.

26. Spicq, *L'Épitre aux Hébreux* (1977), p. 12.

27. Westcott *Epistle to the Hebrews,* pp. 559–60), in commenting on these verses, makes some pertinent remarks on the interaction between God's action and our own.

28. Cf., for example, Spicq, *L'Épitre aux Hébreux* (1977), pp. 227–28.

29. Bishops' Committee on the Liturgy, *Music in Catholic Worship* (Washington, D.C.: USCC, 1972), no. 3, p. 1.

30. *Constitution on the Sacred Liturgy,* Par. 7 (ed. Abbott), p. 141. See also, E. Kilmartin, "A Modern Approach to the Word of God and Sacraments of Christ: Perspectives and Principles," *The Sacraments: God's Love and Mercy Actualized,* ed. F. Eigo (Villanova, Penn.: Villanova University Press, 1979), pp. 59–109; and the articles of R. Schreiter, pp. 57–65, and C. Molari, pp. 93–105, in E. Schillebeeckx and B. van Iersel, eds., *Revelation and Experience,* Concilium 113 (New York: Seabury, 1979).

31. This is seen in the technical usage of two key Greek terms: *euaggelizomai,* meaning "to announce the good news" (see G. Friedrich's article on the term in *The Theological Dictionary of the New Testament,* ed. G. Kittel, vol. 2, pp. 717–21, esp. 720) and *parakaleo,* meaning "to exhort" (see O. Schmitz's article on the term in ibid, vol. 5, pp. 793–99, esp. pp. 794–95). About this latter term, Käsemann says: "Christian exhortation makes

claims because it can bear witness to enacted mercy and seeks to extend it" (*Commentary on Romans,* p. 326).

32. See, for example, the magnificent Nestorian description of the relation between the Spirit and fallible ministry in J. Robinson, ed., *The Liturgical Homilies of Narsai* (Cambridge: Cambridge University Press, 1909; reprint, 1967), pp. 20–23. For the ecclesial dimension of the Word of God, K. Rahner, "What Is a Sacrament?" *Theological Investigations* (New York: Seabury, 1976), vol. 14, pp. 135–48.

33. For a background discussion, see P. Brown, *Augustine of Hippo* (Berkeley: University of California Press, 1969), pp. 216–25; Villette, *Foi et Sacrement,* vol. 1, pp. 219ff; Leeming, *Sacramental Theology,* pp. 143–52.

34. Leeming, *Sacramental Theology* p. 150.

35. Erikson, *Insight and Responsibility* (New York: W. W. Norton, 1964), p. 95.

36. In classical scholastic theology, validity of administration of sacraments involved "intending what the Church does." For a traditional statement of this position, see Leeming, *Sacramental Theology,* pp. 435–96. For a more perceptive view of the problematic, see J. M. Tillard, "The Intentions of the Minister and Recipient," in E. Schillebeeckx and B. Willems, eds., *The Sacraments in General,* Concilium 31 (New York: Paulist, 1967), pp. 117–33.

37. This view accepts the ecclesial context of such intentions, that is, the redemptive need of the worshipping community overrides the inadequacies of the minister of a sacrament (as witnessed in the axiom, *Sacramentum propter hominem* ("A sacrament is for the sake of people"); see Tillard, "Intentions of the Minister and Recipient," pp. 120–26.

38. For three approaches, see K. Rahner, "Marriage as a Sacrament," *Theological Investigations* (New York: Herder and Herder, 1973), vol. 10, pp. 199–221; E. Kilmartin, "When Is Marriage a Sacrament?" *Theological Studies* 34 (1973): 275–86; T. Horvath, "Marriage: Contract? Covenant? Community . . . " *The Sacraments: God's Love and Mercy Actualized* (Villanova, Penn.: Villanova University Press, 1979), pp. 143–81.

39. J. P. Sampley, *"And the Two Shall Become One Flesh": A Study of Traditions in Ephesians 5:21–33* (Cambridge, Mass.: Cambridge University Press, 1971), p. 154.

40. Ibid, p. 162.

41. For an instructive example, see J. Meir, "*Presbyteros* in the Pastoral Epistles," *Catholic Biblical Quarterly* 35(1973): 323–45.

42. Cf. J. Kerkhofs, "Priests and 'Parishes'—A Statistical Survey," in E. Schillebeeckx and J. B. Metz, eds., *Right of the Community to a Priest,* Concilium 133 (New York: Seabury, 1980), pp. 3–11.

Index